SPACES OF PEACE, SECURITY AND DEVELOPMENT

Series Editors
John Heathershaw, Shahar Hameiri,
Jana Hönke and Sara Koopman

Volumes in this cutting-edge series move away from purely abstract debates about concepts and focus instead on fieldwork-based studies of specific places and peoples to demonstrate how particular spatial histories and geographic configurations can foster or hinder peace, security and development.

Available now

Doing Fieldwork in Areas of International Intervention
A Guide to Research in Violent and Closed Contexts
Edited by **Berit Bliesemann de Guevara and Morten Bøås**
HB £75.00 | US $115.00 ISBN 9781529206883
288 pages June 2020

Surviving Everyday Life
The Securityscapes of Threatened People in Kyrgyzstan
Edited by **Marc von Boemcken, Nina Bagdasarova, Aksana Ismailbekova and Conrad Schetter**
HB £75.00 | US $115.00 ISBN 9781529211955
208 pages July 2020

Forthcoming

Development as Entanglement
An Ethnographic History of Ethiopia's Agrarian Paradox
By **Teferi Abate Adem**
HB £75.00 | US $115.00 ISBN 9781529210873

Shaping Peacebuilding in Colombia
International Frames and Local Contestations
By **Catalina Montoya Londono**
HB £75.00 | US $115.00 ISBN 9781529211702

For more information about the series and to find out how to submit a proposal visit

**bristoluniversitypress.co.uk/
spaces-of-peace-security-and-development**

 SPACES OF PEACE, SECURITY AND DEVELOPMENT

Series Editors
John Heathershaw, Shahar Hameiri,
Jana Hönke and Sara Koopman

International Advisory Board

Rita Abrahamsen, University of Ottawa, Canada
John Agnew, University of California, Los Angeles, US
Alima Bissenova, Nazabaev University, Kazakhstan
Annika Björkdahl, Lund University, Sweden
Berit Bliesemann de Guevara, Aberystwyth University, UK
Susanne Buckley-Zistel, Philipps University Marburg, Germany
Toby Carroll, City University, Hong Kong
Mick Dumper, University of Exeter, UK
Azra Hromadžić, Syracuse University, US
Lee Jones, Queen Mary University of London, UK
Louisa Lombard, Yale University, US
Virginie Mamadouh, University of Amsterdam, Netherlands
Nick Megoran, Newcastle University, UK
Markus-Michael Müller, Free University Berlin, Germany
Daniel Neep, Georgetown University, US
Diana Ojeda, Xavierian University, Colombia
Jenny Peterson, The University of British Columbia, Canada
Madeleine Reeves, The University of Manchester, UK
Conrad Schetter, Bonn International Center for Conversion (BICC), Germany
Ricardo Soares de Olivera, University of Oxford, UK
Diana Suhardiman, International Water Management Institute (IWMI), Laos
Arlene Tickner, Del Rosario University, Colombia
Jacqui True, Monash University, Australia
Sofía Zaragocín, Universidad San Francisco, Quito, Ecuador

DOING FIELDWORK IN AREAS OF INTERNATIONAL INTERVENTION

A Guide to Research in Violent and Closed Contexts

Edited by
Berit Bliesemann de Guevara
and Morten Bøås

First published in Great Britain in 2020 by

Bristol University Press
1-9 Old Park Hill
Bristol
BS2 8BB
UK
t: +44 (0)117 954 5940
www.bristoluniversitypress.co.uk

© Bristol University Press 2020

British Library Cataloguing in Publication Data
A catalogue record for this book is available from the British Library

ISBN 978-1-5292-0688-3 hardcover
ISBN 978-1-5292-0692-0 ePub
ISBN 978-1-5292-0691-3 ePdf

The right of Berit Bliesemann de Guevara and Morten Bøås to be identified as editors of this work has been asserted by them in accordance with the Copyright, Designs and Patents Act 1988.

All rights reserved: no part of this publication may be reproduced, stored in a retrieval system, or transmitted in any form or by any means, electronic, mechanical, photocopying, recording, or otherwise without the prior permission of Bristol University Press.

Every reasonable effort has been made to obtain permission to reproduce copyrighted material. If, however, anyone knows of an oversight, please contact the publisher.

The statements and opinions contained within this publication are solely those of the editors and contributors and not of The University of Bristol or Bristol University Press. The University of Bristol and Bristol University Press disclaim responsibility for any injury to persons or property resulting from any material published in this publication.

Bristol University Press works to counter discrimination on grounds of gender, race, disability, age and sexuality.

Cover design by blu inc, Bristol
Front cover: Mile 91/C & A Foundation / Alamy Stock Photo
Printed and bound in Great Britain by CPI Group (UK) Ltd, Croydon, CR0 4YY
Bristol University Press uses environmentally responsible print partners.

Contents

List of Figures ix
List of Abbreviations x
Notes on Contributors xiii
Acknowledgements xviii

1   Doing Fieldwork in Areas of International Intervention   1
into Violent and Closed Contexts
Berit Bliesemann de Guevara and Morten Bøås

Part I: Control and Confusion

2   Shifting Identities, Policy Networks, and the Practical   23
and Ethical Challenges of Gaining Access to the Field
in Interventions
Roland Kostić

3   Interpretivist Methods and Military Intervention   37
Research: Using Interview Research to De-centre the
'Intervener'
Casey McNeill

4   The Interview as a Cultural Performance and the Value   49
of Surrendering Control
Markus Göransson

5   Unequal Research Relationships in Highly Insecure   61
Places: Of Fear, Funds and Friendship
Morten Bøås

Part II: Security and Risk

6   The Politics of Safe Research in Violent and Illiberal   75
Contexts
Alessandra Russo and Francesco Strazzari

7	The Politics and Ethics of Fieldwork in Post-conflict Environments: The Dilemmas of a Vocational Approach *John Heathershaw and Parviz Mullojonov*	93
8	Challenges of Research in an Active Conflict Environment *Boukary Sangaré and Jaimie Bleck*	113
9	On Assessing Risk Assessments and Situating Security Advice: The Unsettling Quest for 'Security Expertise' *Judith Verweijen*	127
10	Being Watched and Being Handled *Jesse Driscoll*	143

Part III: Distance and Closeness

11	Positioning in an Insecure Field: Reflections on Negotiating Identity *Maria-Louise Clausen*	159
12	A Different Form of Intervention? Revisiting the Role of Researchers in Post-war Contexts *Daniela Lai*	171
13	The Road to Darfur: Ethical and Practical Challenges of Embedded Research in Areas of Open Conflict *Mateja Peter*	185
14	Interpretation by Proxy? Interpretive Fieldwork with Local Associates in Areas of Restricted Research Access *Katarina Kušić*	199

Part IV: Sex and Sensitivity

15	Sex Workers and Sugar Babies: Empathetic Engagement with Vulnerable Sources *Kathleen M. Jennings*	215
16	Lifting the Burden? The Ethical Implications of Studying Exemplary, Not Pathological, Wartime Sexual Conduct *Angela Muvumba Sellström*	229
17	Unexpected Grey Areas, Innuendo and Webs of Complicity: Experiences of Researching Sexual Exploitation in UN Peacekeeping Missions *Henri Myrttinen*	243

CONTENTS

18	Sexual Exploitation, Rape and Abuse as a Narrative and a Strategy *Ingunn Bjørkhaug*	257
19	Ten Things to Consider Before, During and After Fieldwork in a Violent or Closed Context *Berit Bliesemann de Guevara and Morten Bøås*	271
Index		283

List of Figures

10.1　　Game Payoffs (Hawk–Dove)　　　　　　　　　　　　149

Abbreviations

AFRICOM	US Africa Command
AMIS	African Union Mission in Sudan
ANC	African National Congress
ANC-MK	African National Congress uMkhonto weSizwe (South Africa)
AQIM	al-Qaeda in the Islamic Maghreb (Mali)
AU	African Union
BiH	Bosnia and Herzegovina
CAR	Central African Republic
CMA	Coordination of Movements for Azawad (Mali)
CRSV	Conflict-Related Sexual Violence
CSO	Civil Society Organization
DDR	Demobilization, Disarmament and Reintegration
DfID	Department for International Development (UK)
DRC	Democratic Republic of the Congo
ESRC	Economic and Social Research Council (UK)
EUFOR-RCA	European Union Force in the Central African Republic
EUSEC-DRC	European Union Security Assistance Mission to the Democratic Republic of the Congo
FARDC	Forces Armées de la République Démocratique du Congo
FCO	Foreign and Commonwealth Office (UK)
FDLR	Forces Démocratiques de Libération du Rwanda
FNL	Forces Nationales de Libération (Burundi)
GBAO	Gorno-Badakhshan Autonomous Region (Tajikistan)
GCC	Gulf Cooperation Council
GDPR	General Data Protection Regulation
ICC	International Criminal Court
ICG	International Crisis Group

ICITAP	International Criminal Investigative Training Assistance Programme
ICTY	International Criminal Tribunal for the former Yugoslavia
IDP	Internally Displaced Population
IMF	International Monetary Fund
INGO	International Non-Governmental Organization
IR	International Relations
IRB	Internal Review Board
MILOBS	United Nations Military Observers
MINUSCA	Mission Multidimensionnelle Intégrée des Nations Unies pour la Stabilisation en Centrafrique
MISCA	Mission Internationale de Soutien à la Centrafrique sous Conduite Africaine
MK	uMkhonto weSizwe (South Africa)
MNLA	Movement for the National Liberation of Azawad (Mali)
MONUSCO	Mission de l'Organisation des Nations Unies pour la Stabilisation en République démocratique du Congo
NGO	Non-Governmental Organization
NP	Nonviolent Peaceforce
NRA/M	National Resistance Army/Movement (Uganda)
NSAG	Non-State Armed Groups
OHCHR	Office of the High Commissioner for Human Rights (United Nations)
OHR	Office of the High Representative (Bosnia and Herzegovina)
OPM	Office of the Prime Minister (Uganda)
OSCE	Organization for Security and Cooperation in Europe
PCE	Post-Conflict Environment
PEP	Post-Exposure Preventive Treatment
PI	Principal Investigator
PKF	Peacekeeping Force(s)
PKO	Peacekeeping Operation(s)
REC	Research Ethics Committee
REF	Research Evaluation Framework
REF	Research Excellence Framework (UK)
SCNS	State Committee on National Security (Tajikistan)

SEA	Sexual Exploitation and Abuse
SGBV	Sexual and Gender-Based Violence
Sida	Swedish International Development Cooperation Agency
SIPA	State Investigation and Protection Agency (Bosnia and Herzegovina)
TRC	Truth and Reconciliation Commission (South Africa)
UCDP	Uppsala Conflict Data Programme
UNAMID	United Nations–African Union Hybrid Operation in Darfur
UNDP	United Nations Development Programme
UNHCR	United Nations Refugee Agency
UNPOL	United Nations Police
UPDF	Ugandan People's Defence Forces
ZTP	Zero-Tolerance Policy

Contributors

Ingunn Bjørkhaug is a researcher at Fafo (Oslo, Norway) and PhD fellow at Noragric, NMBU (Ås, Norway). She has worked in the African context for 14 years and conducted numerous studies on displacement, gender-based violence, children and youth, and ex-combatants in conflict and post-conflict settings, including Uganda, Liberia and the Democratic Republic of the Congo. Her PhD focuses on displacement economies in northern Uganda, Nakivale, Uganda and the Liberian side of the Liberian–Ivorian borderland. Her articles on refugees have been published in *Forum for Development Studies* and *African Studies Review* (2017).

Jaimie Bleck is an associate professor of Political Science at the University of Notre Dame. She has published articles on society and governance in Mali and is the author of *Education and Empowered Citizenship in Mali* (Johns Hopkins University Press, 2015). She co-authored *Electoral Politics in Africa Since 1990: Continuity in Change* with Nicolas van de Walle (Cambridge University Press, 2018).

Berit Bliesemann de Guevara is a reader at the Department of International Politics and the director of the Centre for the International Politics of Knowledge at Aberystwyth University. Her research focuses on international peacebuilding and statebuilding interventions, and the role of knowledge in/about peace, conflict and intervention. She is currently principal investigator of a project exploring the subjectivities of former guerrilla fighters in Colombia and co-investigator of the 'Raising Silent Voices' project on local conflict knowledge in two states of Myanmar, which is discussed in Kušić's contribution to this volume.

Morten Bøås is research professor at the Norwegian Institute of International Affairs (NUPI). His research focuses on conflict, politics and statebuilding in Africa and the Middle East. His most recently published book is *Africa's Insurgents: Navigating an Evolving Landscape* (Lynne Rienner, 2017, with Kevin Dunn).

Maria-Louise Clausen holds a PhD in Political Science from the University of Aarhus, Denmark, and is currently a postdoctoral researcher in International Security at the Danish Institute for International Studies (DIIS). She specializes in theories of the state and approaches to statebuilding including the interaction between state and non-state actors in governance as well as the role of external actors in statebuilding interventions. Her geographical focus is on the Middle East, particularly Yemen and Iraq, where she has carried out fieldwork.

Jesse Driscoll is an associate professor of Political Science at the School of Global Policy and Strategy at the University of California at San Diego. His first book, *Warlords and Coalition Politics in Post-Soviet States* (Cambridge University Press, 2015) was honoured with the Best Book Award by the Central Eurasian Studies Society and the Furniss Award. He has conducted fieldwork in Tajikistan, Georgia and Ukraine. In 2012 he oversaw the first representative survey of Mogadishu in 25 years. He has a book forthcoming on fieldwork from Columbia University Press tentatively titled *Doing Global Fieldwork: A Social Scientist's Guide to Mixed-Methods Research in Difficult Places*.

Markus Göransson is an assistant professor in War Studies at the Swedish Defence University in Stockholm. He has previously been a postdoctoral researcher at the Stockholm School of Economics and holds a PhD in International Politics from Aberystwyth University. In 2013 and 2014, he conducted research in Tajikistan as an affiliate with the University of Central Asia and the Academy of Sciences of the Republic of Tajikistan for his PhD thesis about Tajik Soviet Afghan war veterans. He also holds an MA in Conflict Studies and Human Rights from Utrecht University and a BA in Modern History from the University of Oxford.

John Heathershaw is a professor of International Relations at the University of Exeter. His research addresses international aspects of conflict, security and development in authoritarian political environments, especially in post-Soviet Central Asia. His most recent monograph, co-authored with Alexander Cooley, is *Dictators without Borders* (Yale, 2017).

Kathleen M. Jennings is Head of Section for Research and Development at the Faculty of Social Sciences, Oslo Metropolitan University. Previously she was a senior researcher at Fafo Research Foundation, Oslo. Jennings's work focuses on gender, peacekeeping, political economy ('peacekeeping economies') and qualitative methods, primarily in west and central African contexts. Her work has been published in (among others) *International Studies Quarterly*, *Security Dialogue*, *International Peacekeeping*, *Global Governance* and *Journal of Intervention and Statebuilding*. She has degrees from the University of Oslo, Oxford University and Stanford University. Jennings tweets at @kmjennings.

Roland Kostić is a senior lecturer in Holocaust and Genocide Studies and an associate professor at the Department of Peace and Conflict Research at Uppsala University's Hugo Valentin Centre. His research focuses on knowledge production in conflict and peacebuilding, diversification and privatization of knowledge production by think tanks, experts, policymakers and diplomats, and the transfer and shaping of intervention knowledge through formal and informal networks. He also works on transitional justice, reconciliation and social memory after mass violence. Roland is co-editor of *Knowledge and Expertise in International Interventions* (with Berit Bliesemann de Guevara, Routledge, 2018) and author of articles on the strategic use of knowledge by intimate networks of interveners and experts in Bosnia and Herzegovina.

Katarina Kušić is an Economic and Social Research Council postdoctoral fellow at the Department of International Politics at Aberystwyth University. Her work uses multi-sited ethnography to investigate processes of statebuilding, development and social transformation in southeast Europe. She is particularly interested in methodological and analytical approaches that centre on experiential knowledge, and in intersections of studies of post-socialism with postcolonial and decolonial perspectives.

Daniela Lai is a lecturer in International Relations at London South Bank University. She obtained her PhD in 2017 from Royal Holloway, University of London, and taught at University College London and the London School of Economics before joining London South Bank University. Daniela's research deals with the socio-economic dimension of transitional justice processes and the connections between post-war justice and political economy. She also has an interest in critical methodologies and research ethics.

Casey McNeill holds a PhD from Johns Hopkins University and is an assistant professor in the Political Science Department at Fordham University. Her current research examines the theory and practice of US military interventions in Africa and their relationship to security conditions on the continent.

Parviz Mullojonov is an independent researcher from Tajikistan who conducts research as a practitioner and academic. He holds a PhD from the University of Basel and has held fellowships in France, Germany, the UK and the US. His research concerns various aspects of conflict, security and development in Central Asia.

Angela Muvumba Sellström is an assistant professor at Uppsala University's Department of Peace and Conflict Research. She leads the Project on Preventing Sexual Violence, funded by the Swedish Research Council (2015-03094) and contributes to research on international interventions and civil wars. She has over 17 years of policy and research experience and has worked at the Nordic Africa Institute, the African Union Commission and think tanks in New York, Cape Town and Durban. Her doctoral dissertation (Uppsala University, 2015) examined the causes of armed group impunity for sexual violence. She is a co-editor of *The African Union and its Institutions* (Jacana Media, 2008) and *HIV/AIDS and Society in South Africa* (University of KwaZulu-Natal, 2008).

Henri Myrttinen is a researcher with the Mauerpark Institute in Berlin. He has around 15 years of experience of working on gender, peace and security, including on sexual and gender-based violence prevention. He holds a PhD from the University of KwaZulu-Natal, South Africa, where his thesis focused on masculinities and violence in Timor-Leste, and he has published widely on issues of gender, peace and security.

Mateja Peter is a lecturer in International Relations at the University of St Andrews, where she co-directs the Centre for Global Constitutionalism. She is the co-editor of *United Nations Peace Operations in a Changing Global Order* (Palgrave Macmillan, 2019) and her articles have appeared in journals such as *Third World Quarterly*, *Global Governance* and *European Security*. She is is currently working on a book on international authority in statebuilding.

Alessandra Russo is a research fellow at the Université Libre de Bruxelles. She specializes in the study of regional organizations with a focus on the post-Soviet region, critical theories of Security Studies, transnational organized crime and terrorism. Since 2016 she has been reflecting on the safety and security of researchers travelling to zones that are considered dangerous and at risk, and has been part of a task force called on to design a fieldwork research policy for her then home institution.

Boukary Sangaré joined the Institute for Security Studies (ISS) in March 2019 as a research consultant based in Bamako. Before joining ISS, he was a programme officer for the Peaceful Coexistence, Peacebuilding, and Reconciliation Program at the Danish Embassy in Bamako. Boukary has worked in the Sahel for the past decade on conflict, violent extremism, radicalization, governance, social mobility and social media. He also teaches at the University of Bamako, in the Letters, Languages, and Human Sciences Department. Boukary is finishing his PhD on radicalization and intercommunal conflicts in central Mali at Leiden University.

Francesco Strazzari is an associate professor of International Relations at Scuola Superiore Sant'Anna, Pisa and an adjunct research professor at the Norwegian Institute of International Affairs, Oslo. He specializes in conflict and security studies, focusing on extra-legal governance, transnational organized crime, terrorism and armed groups.

Judith Verweijen is a lecturer in International Relations at the University of Sheffield. Having earned her PhD in Conflict Studies, Judith's research examines the interplay between violence, conflict and armed mobilization; the inner workings of state and non-state armed forces; the militarization of conflicts around natural resources; and violence against civilians. Her main geographical focus is eastern Democratic Republic of the Congo (DRC), where she has regularly conducted field research since 2010. Prior to her PhD, she worked in the DRC for various NGOs, including as election observer and on forest and mining governance.

Acknowledgements

This book would not have been possible without the extensive fieldwork we have carried out over soon to be three decades. In addition to praising the authors in this volume, who have generously and with honesty shared their experiences of confusion, frustrations and mistakes in the field, and the book series editor, reviewers and editorial team at Bristol University Press, who immediately saw the value of a book of this type for our academic community, we would also like to offer sincere thanks to all those who in various ways have helped us in our often clumsy ways of trying to understand their societies. We would also like to thank our colleagues and research partners in a number of countries in the Global South for advice, travels, warmth and joint projects and publications.

This book is the outcome of a conversation between the two editors that has spanned several years and that, over time, has also involved many of this volume's authors and other colleagues in locations such as Sicily (EISA conference 2015), Barcelona (EISA conference 2017), Florence (EUI workshop 2018), Prague (EISA conference 2018) and Toronto (ISA annual convention 2019). As much as we are pleased with the outcome, this is not the end of this conversation. The conversation about fieldwork practices must be a continuous process, and particularly researchers like us, who are fairly established in our respective fields of study, have an obligation to keep the dialogue alive and contribute to making it as honest and practice-oriented as possible.

Berit Bliesemann de Guevara and Morten Bøås
Aberystwyth and Oslo, December 2019

1

Doing Fieldwork in Areas of International Intervention into Violent and Closed Contexts

Berit Bliesemann de Guevara and Morten Bøås

This is a book about fieldwork. It is not yet another volume about research methods, the pros and cons of qualitative versus quantitative research, or the virtues of mixed-methods approaches. There are plenty of these guidebooks and all of them contain useful information, but they generally also turn a blind eye to the messy *practice* of fieldwork, which is different from reading about field-based methods and research designs. This book is about *experiences of doing fieldwork*. A gender-balanced group of authors at different stages of their careers, working in central and southeast Asia, the Middle East, central, west, and south Africa, the Caucasus and southeast Europe—some of them nationals of the countries under study—raise questions about and reflect on how they did fieldwork in areas of international intervention into violent conflict and/or illiberal states. These experiences are neither the sanitized versions of the messy reality of fieldwork, which we find in the majority of methods sections of research monographs and articles;[1] nor are they the hero or adventurer stories some of us tell each other at conferences over a drink (we both plead guilty to have done this on occasion). Rather, this book assembles the frank, (self-)critical accounts of field researchers who have taken the courage to publicly reflect upon some of their mistakes and to name the dilemmas of fieldwork in violent and closed contexts—dilemmas that we can prepare to face, but that we cannot resolve (for a similar approach, see Kušić and Zahora, 2020; Rivas and Browne, 2019).

The authors in this book write from a first-person perspective focusing on personal reflections of their practices, performances and positionalities in the field. Their contributions address questions currently discussed in related literatures—such as the question of how positionality and intersectionality affect the research process (for example, Caretta and Jokinen, 2017; Dempsey, 2017; Kappler and Lemay-Hébert, 2019; Thapar-Björkert and Henry, 2004)—however, they do so not from the comfort of (meta-)theoretical positions but from their own hard-earned experiences in the field. Authors also touch upon the research approaches they have taken (for example, positivist or interpretivist research; cf. Schwartz-Shea and Yanow, 2012) and the methods used—which cover a wide range from interviews with intervention elites, focus groups with sex workers, and surveys among refugees to participatory observation among political activist, and drawing workshops with violence-affected communities—and highlight the advantages and difficulties of these methods in the violent or illiberal contexts discussed. Their main focus, however, is on the more generable difficulties and dilemmas that any fieldwork in violent or closed contexts presents to the researcher and that seem to cut across the very different epistemological and methodological stances represented by the authors.[2]

Why do we see the need for such a book? The main reason is that this is the type of book we would have loved to read when we embarked on our first attempts at doing fieldwork in areas of armed conflict, military deployment and peacebuilding interventions, and it is the type of book we would like to discuss with our students and the PhD researchers supervised by us before they do so. While every field and fieldwork are certainly unique, many of the dilemmas, ethical pitfalls and mismatches between pre-fieldwork plans and fieldwork reality are remarkably similar. The only book available to us when we embarked on our careers as fieldwork-based researchers in violence-affected contexts was Nordstrom and Robben's (1996) *Fieldwork under Fire*. While this book is still a great read, which we recommend without hesitation, much has changed since it was written—changes that affect not only how we understand the world we live in, but also how we do fieldwork. Most importantly, while there is a higher number of researchers conducting fieldwork now than there was perhaps ever before, fieldwork today tends to be much shorter, is conducted by researchers from other disciplines than those classically involved in fieldwork, and the choice of the field and time spent in the field are more impacted upon by an increase in risk aversion at most universities of the Global North. We return to these issues in more detail later.

To be sure, we do not think that any text can replace the hard lessons, let alone the rollercoaster of emotions (Hedström, 2018; Rivas and Browne, 2019), all researchers will have to endure in the field, yet we also think that not every academic in this line of research needs to repeat the same mistakes. Letting students and colleagues know that others have struggled with the same issues and learning about how other researchers have tried to deal with them, will, we hope, be helpful to our professional community. As the authors of *Designing Social Inquiry* in qualitative research have cautioned us, '[Researchers] mistakenly believe that other social scientists find close, immediate fits between data and research. This perception is due to the fact that investigators often take down the scaffolding after putting up their intellectual buildings, leaving little trace of the agony and uncertainty of construction' (King, Keohane and Verba, 1994, pp 12–13). This book puts the 'scaffolding', 'agony' and 'uncertainty of construction' of fieldwork-based research centre-stage.

Many of the experiences discussed speak to a broader community of researchers or are similar to questions discussed in other publications, yet authors in this book also highlight the particular challenges and dilemmas arising from research in a specific area of study: *fieldwork in areas of international intervention*, broadly conceived, *characterized by past or present violent conflict and/or illiberal stateness* (for example, Bekmurzaev, Lottholz and Meyer, 2018; Glasius et al, 2018; Sriram et al, 2009). Intervention research in war and post-war societies, including in authoritarian states, emerged as an important interdisciplinary field of study in the 1990s, accompanying liberal interventionism's rise and its critique. It has since not only grown but also attracted researchers from a wide range of social-scientific and arts-and-humanities disciplines. Fieldwork has become a central modus of conducting research in this field and is no longer the prerogative of social anthropology, the discipline most actively training its scholars for field-based research in countries of the Global South. And while certainly a lot has improved over the last 15 years or so, fieldwork-based methods training in theory-loaded disciplines such as International Relations is only slowly catching up with the fact that more and more of its researchers are conducting fieldwork-based empirical research on interventions. Fieldwork practice therefore often remains a 'muddling through' rather than a conscious engagement with the field, and much of what is being called fieldwork tends towards shorter (if not fleeting) visits, most of which would not qualify in any way as 'ethnography', despite an inflationary use of this term (see further, Millar, 2017; Schatz, 2009; Vrasti, 2008). Yet, even the classical anthropological fieldwork with its emphasis on long-term immersion in one location has clearly become 'red-listed' for some time.

There are several reasons for this. One has to do with the increased risk aversion of many universities to fieldwork (Strazzari and Peter, 2016), which we discuss in more detail in this chapter and in Part II of this book. Yet, the old ways of doing fieldwork are also changing because the world has changed. As global social anthropology has long acknowledged, researchers on fieldwork are no longer disappearing into off-the-beaten-track villages with little or no connectivity to the rest of the world (for example, Gupta and Ferguson, 1997). Rather, most of the research subjects are just as connected as the researchers. This, together with the fact that the sources of intervention politics are based in different locations, implemented by a range of different actors, and originating and taking effect at different scales of politics at the same time, makes the question of where 'the field' is actually located particularly pertinent.

Is 'the field' of intervention studies in Northern capitals and headquarters of international organizations, or their Southern areas of deployment (cf. Bliesemann de Guevara, 2012)? What characterizes these locations of intervention, that are supposedly 'peacekept' or 'post-conflict' but where peacekeepers and civilian staff live in highly guarded compounds that effectively separate them from most meaningful interactions with the populations they have come to serve (Duffield, 2010; Fisher, 2017; Heathershaw and Lambach, 2008; Smirl, 2015)? How does this 'field' look different when it is not liberal interveners, but illiberal states managing the conflict (Heathershaw and Owen, 2019)? Is the field located among the local communities in conflict zones, among specific socio-professional groups such as political activists, soldiers, humanitarian aid workers, sex workers or, indeed, academics-as-interveners, or at the interplay between 'natives' and 'outsiders' (for example, Autesserre, 2014; Goetze, 2017; Lai, in this volume)? Is it on the Internet or in the media as virtual ideological battlefields (Bliesemann de Guevara and Kostić, 2017)? Or perhaps all of the above simultaneously?

The answer to the question of where the field in intervention studies is will partially depend on the specific focus or puzzle a researcher chooses to address, but it is also clear that locating 'the field' only in certain locations of the Global South or among the most obvious participant groups is not enough to understand the interventionist part of international politics (for example, McNeill, in this volume; Richmond, Kappler and Björkdahl, 2015), and this realization also shapes, or ought to shape, fieldwork on international interventions in violent or closed contexts. This said, it seems that the most pressing challenges still arise from fieldwork located in the actual geographical locations in which interventions politics is implemented, as it is here where researchers are most directly subjected to the effects of violent or repressive politics on their research. It should not come as a surprise then that most authors in this book concentrate on this type of field.

Dilemmas of fieldwork-based intervention research in violent and closed contexts

In the following we carve out those areas of questions, challenges and dilemmas arising from fieldwork-based research in areas of international intervention, which we think are particularly pertinent and which are developed further in the contributions to this book. There are four broad types of challenges and dilemmas that we consider particularly pertinent and universal beyond the context-specificity of each individual research: control and confusion, security and risk, distance and closeness, and sex and sensitivity. While they are not exclusive to the field of intervention research, we argue that the dilemmas discussed, and the research ethics interwoven with them (cf. Brewer, 2016; Cronin-Furman and Lake, 2018, Fujii, 2012; Helbardt et al, 2010), take on specific forms in the particular contexts of interventions into violent conflicts and/or illiberal states.

Control, confusion and failure in the research process

The first set of dilemmas arises from the tension between the ideal of control in and over fieldwork and the actual confusion in the research process, a tension that most fieldwork-based researchers will have grappled with at one point or another. 'Control' is the normal portrayal of the research process by the apt field researcher. With a few noticeable exceptions, we find (meta-)narratives of control in most guidebooks on field research and fieldwork-based methods and in the grant proposals researchers write to convince funders to finance their research. No wonder then that many first-time researchers experience confusion, if not outright feelings of personal failure, when the expectations and (self-)narratives of control over the research process meet the messy reality of fieldwork-based research (Kušić and Zahora, 2020; Perera, 2017a). While this reality check does not only concern research in violent and closed contexts, it is in these contexts with their tense social dynamics that the perception and reality of loss of control over the research process can be particularly profound—and potentially dangerous for the researcher and those they interact with in different roles as assistants, informants, participants or wider communities in which research takes place.

Interviews are an illustrative example of the effects that a violent or illiberal context can have on how we access informants or interviewees and secure their consent or how we determine the form the interview will take. Also what is shared in an interview is influenced in particular ways by such contexts (paradigmatic: Fujii, 2010, on meta-data in interviews about war and mass violence). The most common form of intervention research interview is certainly the elite or expert interview, which is usually seen as fairly unproblematic as it does not involve vulnerable participants and is mostly done in a 'safe location' such as the intervened country's capital (although power relations at play in elite interviews are also recognised: see Boucher, 2017). Yet, as Roland Kostić shows (Chapter 2), interviewing intervention elites brings about its own series of challenges and dilemmas. Through his discussion of interview-based research with international intervention elites in Bosnia and Herzegovina, Kostić shows how long-term engagement with this field, shared family and career backgrounds with his interlocutors, and his shifting roles as researcher and policy expert have been crucial for opening the door to these elite networks in a way that has allowed for behind-the-scenes insights and information far beyond a formal expert interview situation. However, he also reflects on how this privileged access posed central dilemmas: in order to keep the access, he had to decide how to deal with invitations to contribute to the policy process as expert and to constantly balance which information to include in his writings and which to ignore. Long-term research access to elites is thus not a one-way street, and the researcher can quickly find him- or herself in a position where the line between being a critical scholar and a member of a policy network becomes increasingly blurred.

Often, elite interviews go to plan but—perhaps due to a lack of privileged back-stage access as the one described earlier—they may not generate anywhere near the kind of insights that the researcher had expected based on a previous analysis of available documents. This rather common experience may put the whole research design into question and, consequently, the researcher into momentary crisis, as in the case of Casey McNeill's research on the US Africa Command (AFRICOM) (Chapter 3). Her chapter reminds us of the mismatches that often exist between the intervention's official narrative of its purpose and the actual priorities and practices encountered in interviews at the headquarters, and cautions us that intervention research based on published material such as the intervening organization's self-descriptions, documents and evaluations can be utterly misguiding in understanding how staff do their day-to-day work and make sense of it. McNeill's chapter offers useful strategies of how to overcome such challenges with the help of interpretivist methodologies.

Among non-elite research participants in violent and/or illiberal contexts, already the mere use of the word 'interview' may scare cautious research participants away, as Markus Göransson reports from Tajikistan (Chapter 4). He recounts how he went into the field, equipped with literature-based knowledge on how to conduct oral history interviews and secure the informed consent of interlocutors, only to find that doing formal interviews would make his research among Tajik veterans of the Afghan–Soviet war largely impossible. Rather, Göransson's data gathering took place ad hoc, in informal, private and often group settings, requiring flexibility and creativity on his behalf and a willingness to relinquish control of the process to some extent. While the author does not delve deeper into the history of interviewing and how it is culturally and politically charged in some contexts, critical security studies scholars have pointed out the deep affinities between states' disciplining techniques and scientific research method (for example, Aradau and Huysmans, 2014; Borneman and Masco, 2015). That researcher behaviour may have different, potentially damaging, consequences in illiberal/repressive contexts than it does in liberal states, is also argued by Jesse Driscoll (Chapter 10), whose contribution we discuss in more detail later.

Violent contexts equally represent specific challenges and threats to researchers and their collaborators and brokers, as highlighted by Morten Bøås (Chapter 5). Bøås offers a self-critical reflection on his research with local associates in the highly insecure context of the Sahel. Specifically, he unpacks how researchers from the Global North may wittingly or unwittingly incentivize associates to adopt risky strategies. At the centre of his reflections are questions of friendship and respect in research with assistants from the intervened country, and how both are shaped by the unequal power relationships involved in such North–South collaborations due to the money and career opportunities the Northern researcher brings to the table (cf. also the contributions in Eriksson Baaz and Utas, 2019). Bøås's reflections are insightful not least because he describes the mixed bag of emotions experienced during fieldwork in this highly dangerous setting where researchers have more recently become the explicit target of some armed groups. It is only in hindsight that Bøås is able to make sense of the wider political and security situations at play and of his own passive and active roles in shaping the unpleasant fieldwork encounters described.

All these are just examples of the issues discussed in Part I of the book, but what they illustrate is how even the most prepared or experienced researchers have struggled with the idea of control over the fieldwork-based research process in a closed or violent context, and how this has affected the fieldwork plans, the data generated and the people involved. The examples also show that there is no way to prevent researchers in areas of intervention from having to take decisions on the go, no matter how prepared they enter 'the field', and the authors discuss how they have dealt with these challenges, for better or (in some cases) for worse.

The debate of control and confusion in fieldwork-based research discussed in Part I of this book also links to a broader emergent debate on researcher failure (see specifically, Kušić and Zahora, 2020). As experiences reported throughout this book suggest, perceptions of 'failure' in research are not the exception but the rule. In general, however, failure—once the basis of positivist research in the form of Popper's falsification that leads to progress in science—seems to have been pushed into the shadows of private conversations among friends or close colleagues. The propensity to acknowledge (or not) failures in the research process has less to do with the general approach a researcher is taking, although qualitative-interpretivist approaches may be more prone to embrace 'failures' as those moments of surprise or 'creative ruptures' that spark research in the first place (Kurowska and Bliesemann de Guevara, 2020). Rather, the silencing of failures and dilemmas in research is a bigger problem that has to do with research as a career and academia as a competitive marketplace, in which individuals compete for positions, promotions and research funding. Normalizing supposed 'failure' in academia would go a long way in addressing some of the dilemmas around control and confusion in fieldwork—as it would reveal that what is deemed failure is actually the effect of a sanitized and formalized understanding of what social-scientific research entails.

Dilemmas of security and risk

The tense social dynamics of violent or repressive contexts do not only affect the access to or course of interviews, but also what observations and findings can be written about and how. Indeed, in both contexts there may be very good reasons for a researcher to relinquish control and not publish specific information, as this may put at risk not only the researcher's future access (a bearable cost), but more importantly the safety of local collaborators and their families, who cannot leave the country when things go from bad to worse (Bekmurzaev,

Lottholz and Meyer, 2018; see also, Vanderstaay, 2005; on the general necessity to decolonize research relationships, see Adedi Dunia et al, 2019). As Bøås's contribution suggests, when it comes to research with local brokers or collaborators, the financial and career opportunities represented by the Northern researcher may indeed cause things to spin out of control, if they incentivize a collaborator to take more risks in a violent or highly state-monitored situation than they would normally do.

The second set of challenges and dilemmas of fieldwork-based research in violent and closed contexts unpacked in this book revolves around such questions of security and risk. Much of the research discussed in this book takes place in areas that are classified as posing a heightened risk to researchers, their collaborators and research participants, either because of active armed violence in the area of fieldwork, or because the research may put them at risk of repressive measures by the security agencies of the state in which the research takes place. Sometimes it is both at the same time. There is a certain tendency among conflict and intervention researchers to downplay these risks, based on experiences of successful—in the sense of uneventful—research (again, we probably have to plead guilty of having done so on occasion), and it may well be that most research taking place in the contexts discussed in this book remains untainted by violence or state repression. We would like to caution against too sweepingly brushing security concerns away, however: researchers may be specifically targeted by some armed groups (through kidnappings or killings), and researchers' very presence in the field may represent grave dangers to those they work or simply interact with. The chapters in Part II of this book contribute to discussions of the dilemmas of balancing restrictive ethics and risk assessments of ever more cautious universities with real risks and meaningful research in areas of international intervention (cf. also Bøås et al, 2006; Kovats-Bernat, 2006).

Francesco Strazzari and Alessandra Russo lay the groundwork for this discussion by reflecting on more recent developments in the research ethics and risk assessment procedures of universities, research institutions and funding bodies in the Global North (Chapter 6). Drawing on their own research experiences as well as their involvement in projects addressing these institutional developments, the authors argue that there are two main tendencies negatively affecting research in violent and closed contexts: the securitization of ethics and risks and their bureaucratization and judiciarization. Their argument is that these two combined processes do not necessarily make research safer, as they are too rigid and uniform to be context-specifically meaningful, but that they do restrict or prevent forms of much needed independent knowledge production on intervention politics in violent and/or illiberal settings (cf. also Bhattacharya, 2014).

Following directly on from this, John Heathershaw and Parviz Mullojonov illustrate the slippery slope that research in violent and closed contexts can be despite complying with the tight institutional ethics and risk assessment procedures of a UK university (Chapter 7). Employing the case of the detention of a Tajik researcher by Tajik security agencies, they discuss the limits of the procedural approach to research ethics and security currently employed by many universities in the Global North. Unpacking dilemmas such as researcher and research participant safety, on the one hand, and the questions of whether research should be conducted at all, on the other, or the dilemma of trade-offs between access and impartiality, they argue that conscious vocational engagement with the field can help make better choices, but that ultimately no approach—neither procedural nor vocational—can fully overcome the interlinked dilemmas explored.

What context-specific safety protocols and procedures of research in a highly violent context could look like is discussed by Boukary Sangaré and Jaimie Bleck (Chapter 8). The authors draw on their experience of conducting research in Central and Northern Mali across the lines of North–South collaboration (see also Bleck, Dendere and Sangaré, 2018), to discuss strategies of fieldwork in areas of armed conflict where the state has almost disappeared. They recommend close collaboration between foreign and local researchers and show that safety in high-risk contexts is dependent on up-to-date information from local networks that is continuously fed into the security assessment. They also caution that risk assessments will always have to consider the long-term effects of research, as violent situations can be highly volatile, making what was safe yesterday potentially dangerous tomorrow, for example if the power balance between armed factions in the research area changes.

Judith Verwejien (Chapter 9) further tackles the challenges of security in violent research contexts by offering in-depth insights into how she assessed security risks when she researched micro-dynamics of conflict in the eastern part of the Democratic Republic of the Congo (DRC). The chapter goes into detail regarding practical forms of preparing for potential harm and how to avoid it, such as analyzing patterns of kidnappings or imaging an ambush and practising how to behave in such a situation. While acknowledging that security risks can never be eliminated, Verweijen's chapter also shows that the combination of good security analysis and realistic preparations can help to minimize risk even in a highly violent context such as eastern DRC.

While many risk assessments at universities in the Global North revolve around the Northern researcher and their associates and participants, the wider and longer-term consequences of researcher behaviour in the field are less well considered or understood. Jesse Driscoll (Chapter 10) illuminates this question in the context of research in illiberal states. Employing a game-theoretical model drawing on extensive fieldwork experiences in Central Asia and the south Caucasus, he shows the stakes involved in the game for two types of players: a bureaucrat in the security sector of the state where the research is taking place and a researcher who wants to publish critical aspects of the politics of the state in question. By taking the reader through a set of situations in which the two players take different options of either escalating or ignoring the engagement with sensitive political issues, the chapter highlights the potential dangers of academic work that interprets the role of the researcher in an oppressive context also as that of a social and political activist.

The contributions to Part II of the book show that security and risk issues are real, and that in worst-case scenarios they can get researchers killed, like in the case of the Cambridge PhD student Giulio Regeni briefly discussed by Russo and Strazzari (Chapter 6) or detained by authoritarian states, as in the case of Alexander Sodiqov, discussed in detail by John Heathershaw and Parviz Mullojonov (Chapter 7). Questions of security and risk in intervention research should thus not be taken lightly, and 'non-events' not mistaken for general safety and lack of risk. However, what the authors also suggest is that the securitized, bureaucratized and judicialized measures to minimize risk and maximize ethical research are not fully suited to meet the challenges and dilemmas of fieldwork-based research in violent and closed contexts. Importantly, functioning security assessments are not based on static pre-fieldwork assessments, but on ongoing relationship-building and information-gathering on the ground, that is, among local communities and with the help of trusted local partners. Travel advice by European or US ministries of foreign affairs, on which much of universities' risk assessment is based, by contrast, appears to be less useful when it comes to tailored security assessments. The answer to security and detention risks cannot be to refrain from any research in 'difficult' geographical areas or on 'sensitive' political topics, as this would leave blank spaces on our social-scientific research maps. Rather, security and risk assessments are crucial, but need to be contextualized, embedded and constantly updated to be meaningful.

Dilemmas around distance and closeness

The presence of international organizations and actors, both military and civilian, affects the extent to which the dilemmas of fieldwork-based intervention research play out in the research process or can be addressed by the researcher. This dynamic is an integral element of what we call the challenges and dilemmas of distance and closeness, which arise in different forms that are discussed in the contribution to Part III of this book.

These challenges refer, first, to the negotiations of identity and positionality that take place during fieldwork. Gender, culture, educational and professional backgrounds, and so on, can be factors contributing to closeness as well as distance between researcher and researched, and the boundaries can shift not only from one field to another, but also from one situation to another in the same field. Maria-Louise Clausen reflects on questions of distance and closeness during fieldwork in Yemen's capital Sana'a (Chapter 11). Drawing on Schwedler's (2006) idea of a 'third gender', she discusses the balancing of security concerns with being a white female researcher in a highly conservative Islamic context. Clausen's experience is that what appear to be binary categories, such as the male–female gender bias expected to shape conservative society, may be more nuanced at the interplay of gender and nationality. Where different elements of the researcher's and her interlocutor's identity intersect, her positionality as 'insider' or 'outsider' may be less clear-cut than assumed, with similar educational careers and other markers of cosmopolitanism sometimes creating more commonalities across national borders than within them. Performances of identity are important in these negotiations of positionality, but their possibility space is also to some extent shaped by the context of the international intervention: no matter how independent outside researchers actually are from international organizations and agencies operating in the country, they will to some extent always be seen as somehow part of the intervention—shaping research relationships beyond their control.

Some forms of distance between researcher and researched are created by academic research itself, which can be seen as a form of intervention, as Daniela Lai argues for the case of Bosnia and Herzegovina (Chapter 12). Research-as-intervention has consequences for what can be researched and how since, just like political and military intervention, the intervention by academia shapes the very field it sets out to research. Lai discusses on the one hand how the over-research certain areas of Bosnian society are experiencing due to academic biases leads to distancing. A second form of distancing concerns those communities, groups and topics that are sidelined by intervention research, either because they are not the focus of the military and political interventions—a consequence of many scholars' unfortunate propensity to adopt the agendas of their field of study—or because they do not align with academic trends and conjunctures. Thus, even in the seemingly most over-researched post-/conflict societies there are people, places and problems that are curiously absent and distant from fieldwork-based research.

Distances between researcher and research participants are also created through physical access restrictions to the field, which may arise either from the dangers of an active conflict—which shaped Mateja Peter's research in Darfur, Sudan (Chapter 13)—or from travel restrictions for foreigners put in place by the host country of the research—as in the case of a project on conflict-affected communities in Myanmar discussed by Katarina Kušić (Chapter 14). The physical distance from the field is overcome in these examples in two different ways: in the first case through embedded research with the UN mission in Darfur, in the second case through working with Burmese research associates to implement the fieldwork-based components in foreign travel-restricted areas. In the case of Darfur discussed by Peter, embedded research as a strategy to overcome the physical distance to the field paradoxically creates such a close relationship with one particular actor (here: an armed actor) that this restricts what can be researched at the same time as it enables the research in the first place. The result is often 'good enough' research, which is better than no research at all, but far from the ideal of independent fieldwork. In the second case, the research 'by proxy' in Myanmar discussed by Kušić, the help of local associates is able to overcome the physical distance created by a controlling state and has advantages in terms of cultural closeness between researchers and researched; yet at the same time the fact that the commissioning researchers are not present during the fieldwork severely curbs their ability to follow up on interesting observations in the process and limits what they can safely infer from the generated data—in addition to the potential danger of putting local associates at risk.

With the tendency towards more restrictive ethics and risk assessment procedures at universities and research institutions in the Global North, and a general reluctance among Northern funders to directly support researchers in the Global South, it is to be feared that these 'good-enough', 'remote' and 'proxy' forms of research will only become more prevalent in future, raising questions about our academic knowledge and the expert advice to intervening agencies based on it (cf. Duffield, 2014; Perera, 2017b). The only antidote to this is at least that we are aware of the pitfalls that such strategies contain.

Sensitivities of research with vulnerable or marginalized participants

The last type of practical challenges and ethical dilemmas in intervention research discussed in this book revolves around fieldwork with marginalized or vulnerable participants. There are several groups in intervened societies that qualify as marginalized or vulnerable, due to violence, poverty or other risky and precarious circumstances shaping their daily lives. Of the many types of research with vulnerable participants in areas of intervention, Part IV of this book concentrates on two issues in particular: research on sexual and gender-based violence and on violently displaced persons and refugees. Research with marginalized or vulnerable participants warrants a specific sensitivity that accounts for human suffering, while refraining from infantilizing 'victims' by ignoring their agency, or drawing generalizing conclusions about 'perpetrators' by missing out on nuances and counterexamples (for example, Boeston and Henry, 2018; Eriksson Baaz, Gray and Stern, 2018).

Research on wartime and intervention-related sexual violence has become an important subfield of conflict and intervention studies. In this book, it is addressed from three perspectives. Kathleen Jennings discusses the practicalities and ethics of research among sex workers as part of wider peacekeeping economies (Chapter 15). Reflecting on her research among sex workers in Liberia and the DRC, she observes a worrying proliferation of research with 'victim-survivors' of wartime sexual violence, and calls on researchers' ethical obligation to interrogate themselves and their motives when deciding to interview members of vulnerable groups. Jennings also critically examines the ways and limits of empathic research among vulnerable subjects and addresses practical questions of access to and compensation for research participants.

Angela Muvumba Sellström (Chapter 16) reflects on three ethical dilemmas of conducting research on 'non-cases' of wartime sexual violence, that is, among armed groups that have regulated sex in wartime conduct. First, a focus on the non-use of sex as a weapon of war may exculpate these groups also from other human rights violations they may have committed. Second, while these groups have regulated sexual conduct, there may still be some sexual violence survivors who are unwittingly silenced by such a research focus. Third, as the regulation of sexual conduct may be based on male leadership of the armed group rather than female sexual autonomy, such regulations may foster entrenched gender inequalities in society.

Henri Myrttinen (Chapter 17) discusses the problems of conducting research on the perpetrators of sexual exploitation and abuse in peacekeeping missions, arising from regulatory and definitional grey areas and the difficulties of triangulating data on these sensitive topics. He relates that while stories abound, much of the information is shared in the form of innuendo, rumours and stereotyping urban legends, which are hard to verify and follow their own logic. The chapter discusses how this research situation can be navigated and what can be known and written. In the last contribution to this part, Ingunn Bjørkhaug also reflects on a research that raised problems of rumours and unverifiable stories, albeit in a different context. Her fieldwork took place among refugees in a camp in Uganda, where studying sexual violence and exploitation was not the aim of the study, but where these topics surged continuously without solicitation in interviews and focus groups in what she later understood to be a competition for resettlement prospects (Chapter 18). Bjørkhaug reflects on how research participants' agency to engage in strategic storytelling influenced the collection of data, what it revealed about the larger context of life in the refugee camp, and how she dealt with the permanent exposure to stories of human suffering.

There are several themes that arise from these different chapters that researchers need to think through in fieldwork with marginalized or vulnerable groups. One is the power of bureaucratic processes and categories. In Myrttinen's contribution, rigid definitions and theorizations of sexual exploitation and abuse in peacekeeping missions leave many areas of transactional body politics unaccounted for and create unequal regulations for different types of interveners. For example, while soldiers' sexual conduct may be sanctioned, civilian interveners' conduct may not, and it is seldom the most severe cases of sexual violence that are actually investigated and prosecuted. The power of administrative categories and procedures is also clear in Bjørkhaug's chapter, where the criteria and interview process for refugee resettlement into third countries shaped to large extents the narratives of the research participants in view of a rumour that her research may be part of this process. In both cases, the power of categorizations does not just impact on research subjects' lives; it impacts directly on the research itself, on how the researcher is perceived, which data can be generated, and what possible conclusions can be drawn from the fieldwork material.

As Bjørkhaug elaborates in detail, the dilemma is that this context is largely beyond the researchers influence, while shaping the fieldwork to a large extent.

Categories' power often stems from the privileges they allow or deny access to—there is something at stake in struggles over categories, and this affects research. Money can have similar effects, as Jennings discusses (in Chapter 15; see also Bøås, Chapter 5; Molony and Hammett, 2007; Vanderstaay, 2015). While paying participants in cash or kind for their time is a common practice and can be handled in ethical ways, the availability of research money can nonetheless create a research economy for gatekeepers, brokers and research participants. Jennings also discusses how the researcher can find out about and act upon such participation for money in the process of interviewing, but without putting the vulnerable research participants on the spot, thereby acknowledging the socioeconomic opportunity structures the very research creates.

This links with a third area of challenges in research with marginal or vulnerable groups and on topics of sexual and gender-based violence, namely how to maintain a critical and nuanced view on topics that may be highly distressing and how to avoid marginalizing some groups or individuals further. Muvumba Sellström's research explicitly brings such nuance into the study of wartime sexual violence through a research focus on armed groups that have regulated sexual conduct. Her chapter also discusses how such counterexamples bear a similar danger of missing out on nuances as the mainstream literature does, for example by marginalizing some cases of rape or condoning paternalistic attitudes. Myrttinen's chapter similarly reminds us how difficult it may be to remain open and maintain nuance in research when faced with the perpetrators of acts (short of criminal ones) that the researcher normatively rejects—how to show empathy with research participants who are openly misogynist, racist or sexist? Another major challenge of research among marginalized and vulnerable participants is to balance empathy with all research subjects and ethical fieldwork practice with the researcher's critical and normative research aims (see all chapters in this part).

In the conclusions to this book, we—the editors—return to some additional themes that arise from the chapters and that we think constitute ten points all academics planning fieldwork-based research on international intervention in violent or closed contexts should consider before they leave for whatever field they deem central to their research. We have consciously refrained from formulating 'lessons learned'. If there is one central lesson to this book, it is that there are no easy or universal answers to the questions raised by the authors. Rather, what we need is a flexible practice around central areas of concern, which avoids the mistakes made by others, while paying attention to the volatility, context-specificity and long-term and wider effects of research in violent or illiberal contexts. This discussion has to be continuous, and it has only just started.

Notes

[1] Feminist scholarship is certainly a welcome exception here, as it recognizes and centrally writes into its texts the partly understood and unfamiliar, rather than glossing it over; however, embracing messiness as productive opportunity is not easy while actually doing the fieldwork. For a useful overview of feminist methodologies for the study of war, see Wibben (2016).

[2] For first-person accounts of experiences with specific methods in peace and conflict research, see MacGinty, Vogel and Brett (2020).

References

Adedi Dunia, O., et al (2019) 'Moving out of the backstage: How can we decolonize research?', *The Disorder of Things*, 22 October, https://thedisorderofthings.com/2019/10/22/moving-out-of-the-backstage-how-can-we-decolonize-research/.

Aradau, C. and Huysmans, J. (2014) 'Critical methods in International Relations: the politics of techniques, devices and acts', *European Journal of International Relations*, 20(3): 596–619.

Autesserre, S. (2014) *Peaceland: Conflict Resolution and the Everyday Politics of International Intervention*, New York: Cambridge University Press.

Bekmurzaev, N. Lottholz, P. and Meyer, J. (2018) 'Navigating the safety implications of doing research and being researched in Kyrgyzstan: cooperation, networks and framing', *Central Asian Survey*, 37(1): 100–18.

Bhattacharya, S. (2014) 'Institutional review board and international field research in conflict zones', *PS: Political Science and Politics*, 47(4): 840–4.

Bleck, J., Dendere, C. and Sangaré, B. (2018) 'Making North–South research collaborations work', *PS: Political Science and Politics*, 51(3): 554–8.

Bliesemann de Guevara, B. (ed.) (2012) *Statebuilding and state-formation: the political sociology of intervention*, London: Routledge.

Bliesemann de Guevara, B., and Kostić, R. (2017) 'Knowledge production in/about conflict and intervention: finding "facts", telling "truth"', *Journal of Intervention and Statebuilding*, 11(1): 1–20.

Boesten, J. and Henry, M. (2018) 'Between fatigue and silence: the challenges of conducting research on sexual violence in conflict', *Social Politics*, 25(4): 568–88.

Borneman, J. and Masco, J. (2015) 'Anthropology and the security state', *American Anthropologist*, 117(4): 781–5.

Boucher, A. (2017) 'Power in elite interviewing: Lessons from feminist studies for political science', *Women's Studies International Forum*, 62: 99–106.

Bøås, M., Jennings, K.M. and Shaw, T.M. (2006) 'Dealing with conflicts and emergency situations', in V. Desai and R.B. Potter (eds), *Doing Development Research*, London: Sage, pp 70–8.

Brewer, J.D. (2016) 'The ethics of ethical debates in peace and conflict research: notes towards the development of a research covenant', *Methodological Innovations*, 9: 1–11.

Caretta, M.A. and Jokinen, J.C. (2017) 'Conflating privilege and vulnerability: a reflexive analysis of emotions and positionality in postgraduate fieldwork', *The Professional Geographer*, 69(2): 275–83.

Cronin-Furman, K. and Lake, M. (2018) 'Ethics abroad: fieldwork in fragile and violent contexts', *PS: Political Science and Politics*, 51(3): 607–14.

Dempsey, K.E. (2017) 'Negotiated positionalities and ethical considerations of fieldwork on migration: interviewing the interviewer', *ACME—An International Journal for Critical Geographies*, 17(1): 88–108.

Duffield, M. (2010) 'Risk-management and the fortified aid compound: everyday life in post-interventionary society', *Journal of Intervention and Statebuilding*, 4(4): 453–74.

Duffield, M. (2014) 'From immersion to simulation: remote methodologies and the decline of area studies', *Review of African Political Economy*, 41(1): 75–94.

Eriksson Baaz, M. and Utas, M. (eds) (2019) 'Research brokers in conflict zones' (special issue), *Civil Wars*, 21(2): 157–295.

Eriksson Baaz, M., Gray, H. and Stern, M. (2018) 'What can we/do we want to know? Reflections from researching SGBV in military settings', *Social Politics*, 25(4): 521–44.

Fisher J. (2017) 'Reproducing remoteness? States, internationals and the co-constitution of aid 'bunkerization' in the East African periphery', *Journal of Intervention and Statebuilding*, 11(1): 98–119.

Fujii, L.A. (2010) 'Shades of truth and lies: interpreting testimonies of war and violence', *Journal of Peace Research*, 47(2): 231–41.

Fujii, L.A. (2012) 'Research ethics 101: dilemmas and responsibilities', *PS: Political Science and Politics*, 45(4): 717–23.

Glasius, M., de Lange, M., Bartman, J., Dalmasso, E., Lv, A., Del Sordi, A., Michaelsen, M. and Ruijgrok, K. (eds) (2018) *Research, Ethics and Risk in the Authoritarian Field*, Cham: Palgrave Macmillan.

Goetze, C. (2017) *The Distinction of Peace: A Social Analysis of Peacebuilding*, Ann Arbor: University of Michigan Press.

Gupta, A. and Ferguson, J. (eds) (1997) *Anthropological Locations: Boundaries and Grounds of a Field Science*, Berkeley/Los Angeles/London: University of California Press.

Heathershaw, J. and Lambach, D. (2008) 'Introduction: post-conflict spaces and approaches to statebuilding', *Journal of Intervention and Statebuilding*, 2(3): 269–89.

Heathershaw, J. and Owen, C. (2019) 'Authoritarian conflict management in post-colonial Eurasia', *Conflict, Security & Development*, 19(3): 269–73.

Hedström, J. (2018) 'Confusion, seduction, failure: emotions as reflexive knowledge in conflict settings', *International Studies Review*, online first, https://doi.org/10.1093/isr/viy063.

Helbardt, S., Hellmann-Rajanayagam, D. and Korff, R. (2010) 'War's dark glamour: ethics of research in war and conflict zones', *Cambridge Review of International Affairs*, 23(2): 349–69.

Kappler, S. and Lemay-Hébert, N. (2019) 'From power-blind binaries to the intersectionality of peace: connecting feminism and critical peace and conflict studies', *Peacebuilding*, 7(2): 160–77.

King, G., Keohane, R.O. and Verba, S. (1994) *Designing Social Inquiry: Scientific Inference in Qualitative Research*, Princeton, NJ: Princeton University Press.

Kovats-Bernat, J.C. (2002) 'Negotiating dangerous fields: pragmatic strategies for fieldwork amid violence and terror', *American Anthropologist*, 104(1): 208–20.

Kurowska, X. and Bliesemann de Guevara, B. (2020) 'Interpretive approaches in political science and international relations', in L. Curini and R.J. Franzese (eds), *The SAGE Handbook of Research Methods in Political Science & IR*, London: Sage.

Kušić, K. and Zahora, J. (eds) (2020) *Fieldwork as Failure: Living and Knowing in the Field (of IR)*, Bristol: E-International Relations Publishing.

Mac Ginty, R., Vogel, B. and Brett, R. (eds) (2020) *Companion to Conducting Field Research in Peace and Conflict Studies*, London: Palgrave.

Millar, G. (ed.) (2017) *Ethnographic Peace Research. Approaches and Tensions*, Cham: Palgrave Macmillan.

Molony, T. and Hammett, D. (2007) 'The friendly financier: talking money with the silenced assistant', *Human Organization*, 66(3): 292–300.

Nordstrom, C. and Robben, A.C.G. (1996) *Fieldwork under Fire: Contemporary Studies of Violence and Culture*, Berkley: University of California Press.

Perera, S. (2017a) 'Bermuda triangulation: embracing the messiness of researching in conflict', *Journal of Intervention and Statebuilding*, 11(1): 42–57.

Perera, S. (2017b) 'To boldly know: knowledge, peacekeeping and remote data gathering in conflict-affected states', *International Peacekeeping*, 24(5): 803–22.

Richmond, O., Kappler, S. and Björkdahl, A. (2015) 'The "field" in the age of intervention: power, legitimacy, and authority versus the "local"', *Millennium: Journal of International Studies*, 44(1): 23–44.

Rivas, A.-M. and Browne, B.C. (2019) *Experiences in Researching Conflict and Violence: Fieldwork Interrupted*, Bristol: Policy Press.

Schatz, E. (ed.) (2009) *Political Ethnography: What Immersion Contributes to the Study of Power*, Chicago, IL: University of Chicago Press.

Schwartz-Shea, P. and Yanow, D. (2012) *Interpretive Research Design: Concepts and Processes*, New York and London: Routledge.

Schwedler, J. (2006) 'The third gender: western female researchers in the Middle East', *PS: Political Science and Politics*, 39(3): 425–8.

Smirl, L. (2015) *Spaces of Aid: How Cars, Compounds and Hotels Shape Humanitarianism*, London: Zed Books.

Strazzari, F. and Peter, M. (2016) 'Securitisation of research: fieldwork under new restrictions in Darfur and Mali', *Third World Quarterly*, 38(7): 1531–50.

Sriram, C.L., King, J.C., Mertus, J.A., Martin-Ortega, O. and Herman, J. (eds) (2009) *Surviving Field Research: Working in Violent and Difficult Situations*, New York: Routledge.

Thapar-Björkert, S. and Henry, M. (2004) 'Reassessing the research relationship: location, position and power in fieldwork accounts', *International Journal of Social Research Methodology*, 7(5): 363–81.

Vanderstaay, S.L. (2005) 'One hundred dollars and a dead man: ethical decisions in ethnographic fieldwork', *Journal of Contemporary Ethnography*, 34(4): 371–409.

Vrasti, W. (2008) 'The strange case of ethnography in International Relations', *Millennium: Journal of International Studies*, 37(2): 279–301.

Wibben, A.T.R. (ed.) (2016) *Researching War: Feminist Methods, Ethics and Politics*, Abingdon: Routledge.

PART I

Control and Confusion

There is an idea inherent in a lot of advice on and critique of fieldwork-based research in areas of violent conflict and international intervention that the (Northern/outside) researcher is generally in control of the research process. Contributions to this first part of the book raise serious questions about this idea. Four authors reflect on misunderstandings in the research process and the confusions that have arisen during their specific researches. They discuss the effects such confusions have had on them as researchers, including a range of emotions such as frustration, anger, bewilderment and self-doubt, which are seldom discussed in academic outputs. They also address what effects misunderstandings and confusions had on others, especially research assistants and research participants or informants, but also the wider communities in which they have carried out their research (most seriously, for example, putting them in danger). From a recognition that the researcher is not always in control of the research, the authors develop strategies of how to mitigate the risks for themselves and others emanating from questions of control and confusion. Examples in this part are taken from fieldwork interactions with international intervention elites in Bosnia and Herzegovina; interpretivist research on the US Africa Command (AFRICOM) in Germany, Mali and Niger; oral history research with Soviet–Afghan War veterans in Tajikistan; and reflections relating to research relationships between a Northern conflict researcher and his Malian research partners in areas of high insecurity in the African Sahel zone.

2

Shifting Identities, Policy Networks, and the Practical and Ethical Challenges of Gaining Access to the Field in Interventions

Roland Kostić

During the autumn of 2012, I conducted fieldwork in Bosnia and Herzegovina (BiH) with an aim to interview the international and local judges and prosecutors working within the War Crime Chamber of the Court of Bosnia and Herzegovina. The Dayton Peace Agreement was in its 17th year of implementation. The West was seemingly losing its influence over the implementation process as the international judges and prosecutors were forced to leave the Court BiH by the end of 2012 as a result of the pressures from Bosnian Serb leader Milorad Dodik. This was my fourth extensive field trip since 2001. In many ways, it was different from my previous work on local elites, as I was now increasingly focusing on studying the different aspects of intervention policy devised by the international policy elites in the country. In the initial stage of my fieldwork, I arranged to meet up with a senior member of the Office of the High Representative (OHR), whom I knew since the time of my dissertation fieldwork. Having worked in the western Balkans since the early 1990s, co-founding two prolific international NGOs, working for NATO afterwards, and now working for the OHR, this person—a perfect example of the type of 'shape-shifting' policy entrepreneur who has been called 'flexian' in the literature (Wedel, 2009)—seemingly knew almost everyone in international policy circles and among local elites in Bosnia and had been helpful in facilitating contact with specific local politicians during my previous fieldworks.

Unlike our prior meetings at the trendy patisserie owned by a spouse of a senior OHR policymakers, which was located in the proximity of the OHR building, this time we met at the OHR's headquarters. During our chat in his office, we exchanged views regarding the political and economic developments in BiH. My interlocutor praised my dissertation work for its data and analysis, and for pointing the finger at the 'real problems' of the Bosnian peacebuilding process. He also enquired about my ongoing research regarding the Court BiH and, when hearing about my meetings, expressed his pessimism about the state of the peace process and cautioned about imminent risks of new violence. In addition, he explained that the international community had lost the battle to defeat the Bosnian Serb leader Milorad Dodik in 2009–10 when the American and Slovene prosecutors in the State Court BiH were preparing to indict him for corruption. He elaborated that he had fought hard together with a group of people at the OHR and Court BiH, mentioning the specific names as he was narrating, to keep that process alive and have the EU impose sanctions against Dodik. However, the corruption case against Dodik was dropped and the international judges and prosecutors were departing the country as a result of the political compromise between the EU and Bosnian Serb leader, leaving the international community split and running the peacebuilding mission on autopilot. As I listened, I became aware of the significance of the events that played out behind the scenes between late 2009 and early 2011 in Sarajevo. When I enquired about the official position of his old organization, the International Crisis Group (ICG), my contact explained that in 2008 a new group of people with new ideas had taken over the work of ICG Europe, while everyone who had worked there previously had left unhappy with this development. He added that I should not bother reading their recent reports on Bosnia as they were groundless, biased and, by criticizing the OHR, actively undermined the policy path that was assumed by the international community since 1996.

This visit to the OHR questioned much of my method training during my PhD years. Trained as a peace and conflict researcher with a positivist background, during my PhD research I relied on generally endorsed positivist methods such as semi-structured interviews and surveys (for example Höglund and Öberg, 2011). In my case, interview guidelines stemmed from a set of theoretical assumptions that I wanted to explore. In addition, after indicating the specific representatives of the political parties I wanted to interview, I used my existing contacts in Bosnia, both local and international, to arrange the interviews and secure the sample of representative opinions, both left and right, representing various communities in BiH. However, I strived to maintain little personal contact with my respondents after the interviews in an endeavour to maintain my academic independence and neutrality. While I focused on using stringent methods of data analysis and available textual analysis tools to capture dominant trends testing my assumptions, I was not particularly encouraged to reflect upon how the respondents' perception of my national identity, gender or use of language influenced, or how my ways of getting in touch with these elites affected, the data that was collected.

During the fieldwork in 2012, however, I realized that although I was conducting interviews with the international prosecutors and judges, this did not give me a holistic insight into the process, agendas and policy linkages that affected peacebuilding and transitional justice policy in BiH. A more comprehensive knowledge about the essence of the policy processes and ensuing battles behind the scenes of intervention came through my private interaction with my contacts, who were members of the international elite circle in Bosnia working on formulating and implementing intervention in the country. In the process, issues such as my positioning in the field in terms of who I was and what I was doing in BiH as well as their perception of my nationality, knowledge of languages and educational and career background mattered in developing trust and access to some discussions among the inner policy circles in BiH. Yet, this very trust and the relationships I established also limited significantly my own knowledge production about the processes I was observing.

This chapter focuses on doing fieldwork with elite participants and their networks working on intervention. It is organized in two parts. First, I discuss positioning and gaining access to policymakers and the specific networks working on intervention policy. Here I reflect upon my strategies of gaining access and how this affected and transformed my own role as a researcher. The second part focuses on the consequences of access to elite participants working on intervention for academic knowledge production about intervention. I discuss dilemmas I encountered during my research and what it meant for my publications about peacebuilding intervention in BiH. I conclude by summarizing some of the key findings from working with policy elites in spaces of intervention.

Gaining access to policy elites working on intervention

Access to the field in the context of intervention and conflict is almost always negotiated. Both dynamics of neoliberal academia preferring specific methodological solutions and quick outputs with a measurable impact, and host countries' concerns with the production of specific framings of problems and images, place boundaries on academic knowledge production about interventions and conflict (Bliesemann de Guevara and Kostić, 2018).

When possible, gaining access to elites working on intervention can be one way to address some of the challenges, both in terms of long-term update and access to information about specific processes, but also to circumvent physical limitations to access that may be put in place by domestic actors or by the practicalities of academic life. However, as I have learned from my experience, while these strategies may solve some issues in terms of access, they also create others. The access to these elites is an ambiguous process. It requires long-term engagement within the space of intervention populated by policy elites (cf. Autesserre, 2014; Coles, 2007), and there are different pathways of getting access to a specific expert of relevance to the researcher. The umbrella concept of policy elite working on intervention includes a typology of actors that may require different access strategies and pathways. Gaining and retaining access to policy elites in the spaces of intervention also impacts on the images, identities and roles researchers may assume in the interaction with the members of networks promoting intervention. Finally, this may shift over time based on change in the course of intervention as well as change in relations between the actors within a specific policy network. These are the access-related issues that are discussed in this section of the chapter.

Policy elites working on intervention are actors who formally and informally engage in knowledge production regarding intervention, are privy to first-hand information that they package in narratives to fit their policy objectives, and who compete for the influence over the direction of intervention. They are often connected in informal networks that populate formal organizations, while their loyalty is based on some sense of shared understanding of the conflict and common interests stretching beyond the boundaries of these organizations. The trust and loyalty of individual actors rest instead within a broader informal network—a so-called flex-net—geared towards producing the desired policy outcomes (Wedel, 2009: 21), while navigating 'organized anarchy' (Stone, 2019). One consequence of this type of structuring is that these actors per definition are not inclined to share intrinsic details about dynamics of policy development to outsider academics, especially when knowledge is embattled (Leander, 2014) and academics do not subscribe to interveners' understanding of a specific event.

In my case, when writing about a controversial intervention by the OHR into Bosnian politics that took place in early 2011 (Kostić, 2017), I tried to get in touch with one of the organization's leading legal experts who was involved in the process. He had been in Bosnia since the mid-1990s, working on legal affairs at the Organization for Security and Cooperation in Europe (OSCE). Subsequently, he followed his boss and moved from the OSCE to the OHR. However, unlike some other senior policymakers at the OHR that I interacted with over a period of time, he did not use multiple professional identities, was not present in the media, nor did he do consultancies or work for think tanks. He only came to my attention due to a recommendation by my other OHR contacts, former and present employees, who among themselves held a divided opinion on his legal recommendations and policy actions that followed in early 2011. In an email to this expert, I named my OHR contact who recommended me to him, explained the issues that I wanted to know more about, and gave him alternative narratives of the event that were shared with me by other former OHR employees. I never received a response. In hindsight, my impression is that gaining access to these international expert circles was easier when I was doing research on attitudes of the domestic elites and population, that is, when I was producing 'useful' knowledge for those working on intervention policy without directly questioning the course of the intervention. By contrast, it seems that the intimate knowledge in terms of events and anecdotes that were shared with me from within the inner policy circles of experts had the main function of creating trust and proximity between us, rather than to be used for knowledge production purposes. In addressing the tensions within the OHR over the 2011 intervention upfront in my email, I had most likely overstepped the mark.

Some of the policy elites that I encountered belong to the category of 'flexians', who engage in knowledge production (related to their intervention policy field) by altering their roles within a common policy flex-network—as government advisers, PR advisers, academics or media commentators—and in the process successfully circulating within a network of organizations that employ them, always maintaining the posture of a successful career trajectory (Wedel, 2009). However, as shown in the case discussed earlier, not all my contacts were flexians. Many were long-term experts within their fields and used their professional identity to justify a specific narrative about the problem. Yet, they nonetheless played a role within a broader network engaging in the specific production of narratives about problems and necessary solutions to them and in the process challenging other available policy alternatives. One commonalty of most of the senior intervention experts I met in BiH was that they were middle-aged males with family and career background in the West (cf. Goetze, 2017).

How does one get access to policy elites in an intervention space such as BiH that is saturated with experts, NGOs and think tanks? I deployed different ways of getting access depending on the circumstance and available opportunities. One of my first contacts took place during my doctoral thesis fieldwork in BiH in 2005. It was through a personal contact: a former colleague who had worked at the OHR, the organization charged with overseeing the implementation of the Dayton Peace Accords and, by definition, the most influential institutional actor in BiH at the time. He had introduced me to his more senior colleague who was interested in my research findings, especially my survey data, and who offered to help during my fieldwork.

During our first meeting we spoke for about two hours on a wide range of topics including my research and my survey findings and the political situation in BiH, but also about our career and family backgrounds. He explained to me that he had worked as a British journalist in the former Yugoslavia since 1991, before co-founding two influential think tanks. At the same time, while discussing my family connections to Bosnia, Croatia and Slovenia, I emphasized my educational background in the UK and Sweden. He brought my attention to his internationally acclaimed book on the war in former Yugoslavia. While most of the discussion was in English, having established common Slovenian connections part of our discussion was in Slovenian but, on occasions, we also shifted to Bosnian/Croatian/Serbian. At the end of this engaging discussion, he took out his mobile phone and asked me who I would like to talk to in BiH, insinuating that he could open any door for me. More importantly, we struck a good rapport and our conversations would stretch for years after this initial talk, shifting between meetings in Sarajevo and exchanges via email and occasional Skype calls.

Another way to get access to respondents in the field is by utilizing digital media (Käihkö, 2018). In my case, I contacted a European diplomat and former senior OHR policymaker via LinkedIn. In the course of my research, I realized that LinkedIn was populated by many of the policy experts I met and heard about in BiH. I have maintained a generally well-updated profile, vouching for my very cosmopolitan educational and career background, and a broad network of international contacts from my college and university years, but also many with a background in working on intervention in former Yugoslavia. At the same time, by emphasizing my policy reports for the Swedish International Development Cooperation Agency (Sida) and the UN, I have projected the problem-solving aspect of my scholarly production.

Thus, when working on a story concerning another debated OHR intervention into Bosnian politics in 2000–01 (Kostić, 2014), I first reconstructed the gist of the story with intricate details based on initial expert interviews and available publications. All paths unearthed at this initial stage pointed towards this senior European diplomat, but his role in the intervention was not entirely clear. I wrote him a message via LinkedIn, informed him of my project and offered him what I had found out until then. He agreed to speak to me via Skype. Our first meeting was a general introduction, where we established our positions and professional identities. I emphasized that I was a peace and conflict researcher from Sweden with an academic background in the UK and family background in former Yugoslavia. He was at the time teaching at a prestigious American university while leading a small NGO back in Europe and doing consultancy on the side. Even though this time we mainly communicated in English, we established commonality in speaking Bosnian/Croatian/Serbian as well as Slovenian during the first Skype call. Interestingly enough, my interlocutor was aware that much blame for the botched intervention in 2000–01 was placed on him, and he was keen to give his version of the story. All together we had four extensive Skype calls. He answered my questions in great detail, gave me accounts of network constellations, key individuals involved—including the chief negotiator of the Dayton Peace Accords, Richard Holbrooke—and elaborated the essence of the policy battle that raged behind the scenes at the time.

A few years later, he got in touch and informed me about a behind-closed-doors conference about BiH in Berlin where he was one of the speakers. He was interested in hearing my suggestions on new innovative policy approaches to the country. On a personal note I felt flattered; however, as a critical studies scholar I felt uneasy about interfering in the political processes I was studying. At the same time, although I was not interested in producing any kind of 'innovative' policy solution, I felt that not coming up with some advice risked closing the door for future discussions. This incident emphasized to me the fact that the access to policy elites is never a one-way process in which the researcher is in total control, but a two-way interaction that also puts demands on the researcher to play a specific expert role as long as one wants to maintain a specific relation.

This said, gaining and retaining access to policy elites in the context of intervention also impacts on the positioning, image, identity and roles a researcher may assume or be placed in during these interactions (see also Clausen, in this volume). In my case, I started as a Swedish PhD candidate in peace and conflict research at Uppsala University with roots in former Yugoslavia working on attitudes of domestic population and elites. As I mentioned earlier, by the nature of my research I was producing knowledge that was useful to those actors framing problems and formulating intervention policy in the country. In addition, having lived and studied in the UK and Sweden for all my adult life strengthened my background credentials as someone who shared a specific 'Western' epistemology of intervention, while having a connection to the region. This part of my image was further strengthened by having produced policy analyses on Bosnia, and Serbia and Montenegro for Sida. During this early period of my research, interaction with contacts belonging to the community of intervener elites gave me, as an outsider, ample insights into internal dynamics, jargon and gossip used to forge trust and intimacy. However, I would only start paying proper attention to this information as I shifted my research interests towards the community of interveners in BiH.

The transition in my positionality as more of an insider with specific knowledge occurred during my postdoctoral research. By now, I had received a postdoctoral project grant and could develop my research interests more autonomously. Since I was doing part of my research on intervention elites and their networks, I tried to maintain old and forge new contacts with policy experts of relevance for my specific research topics. Although I was not interested in producing policy reports and expert opinion, I needed to navigate the expert networks by adopting different identities as an academic and policy expert. For example, I conducted additional surveys in 2010 and 2013, and my findings were on a couple of occasions published in newspapers in Bosnia, Croatia and Serbia. In addition, I was approached by and gave interviews for Bosnian broadsheet newspapers and on the BiH TV news. My contacts at the OHR heard and enquired about my new data.

Having this exposure within the field of intervention expertise at the time created additional demands. The ICG Balkans contacted me at some point and used some of my data in one of their reports (ICG, 2012: 3). Since the ICG was interested only in the specific trends regarding one specific question, I provided the written summary of those trends. On the other hand, when the NATO headquarters in Brussels requested my survey data for their project on Serbian nationalism in BiH and its connections to Serbian attitudes towards NATO, I declined since they wanted all my raw data of all my surveys. When I visited the OHR headquarters in 2012, the Deputy High Representative, Roderick Moore, wanted to hear my view on how to resolve the political stalemate in the city of Mostar. By this point, maintaining multiple identities meant that, to an extent, I became a small nodal point in the very flexible networks that I was studying, which enabled me to trace paths in which 'power creates webs and relations between actors within and across institutions, and discourses that are produced to legitimize these connections' (Shore and Wright, 1997: 11). At the same time, it limited the extent to which I could use the acquired knowledge in my academic outputs as long as I remained entangled (see also Myrttinen, and Peter, in this volume). This dilemma is what I discuss in the next section of the chapter.

The consequences of access to intervention elites for knowledge production

Maintaining multiple professional identities allowed me to study intervention expert networks and their evolution and fragmentation over time, but also to remain updated on the current policy processes. This access gave me insight into some of the 'behind-the-stage' discussions that were often part of brainstorming sessions in the 'informal hubs' at the OHR (cf. Leroux-Martin, 2013: 8). However, this produced dilemmas for me as a researcher. As shown in the previous section, wearing several hats meant that at some point I was formally and informally invited to give an opinion on the very policy processes that I was studying from a critical perspective. As I became increasingly entangled with experts on the inside of the process, it became harder to maintain a critical position towards the processes and actions of intervention experts without consequences for my relationship with them and my access to the information and knowledge-production processes about intervention in Bosnia. This dilemma I unpack in this section of the chapter.

Gaining access and working with elites in intervention spaces comes with limitations on knowledge production. Most of those involved, but the 'flexian' actors particularly, need to maintain a success story, both in terms of being on the right side of history in terms of intervention policy and in terms of their career success (Wedel, 2009). In that sense, doing research on expert networks also meant to an extent dealing with the personal histories of the intervention actors. Consequently, by revealing too much about the processes and experts involved, my writing risked endangering individual standings and careers, as well as having me ostracized by other relevant contacts populating the flex-net.

In one case, one of my contacts, a former employee at the OHR, informed me that one of my other OHR contacts was removed from his position by another senior OHR policymaker who we all knew. Reportedly, this was a dispute over the policy course in the field but also included personal competition over authority within the organization. My contact was at the time deployed in the city of Mostar, which experienced a political stalemate partly due to a previous decision of the OHR. While in Mostar, he produced weekly reports in English that he emailed to a select group of policy experts and diplomats on his list. I received them too, and generally they represented a thorough overview of the political situation in the city at the time. The problem was that his initiative in Mostar was not seconded by the High Representative and his advisors, which led to internal friction over his conduct and his eventual departure from the position at the OHR. In our subsequent conversations, my contact eventually confirmed that he was in the process of leaving the organization to do other things, but I decided not to ask for the reasons. Although this was an interesting case of privatization of knowledge production and a battle over a specific peacebuilding policy, I restrained from writing about it in order not to ruin his career prospects and our relationship.

An additional question that I encountered during my fieldwork is what access to policy elites in interventions means for our research and knowledge production. A researcher may be privy to insider information about interactions and dynamics between specific actors within networks as well as about their general behaviour. However, much of it is difficult to write and theorize about because it may be highly controversial and be used by other actors for their purposes of undermining the status of whole organizations in the battles for policy and influence. In my case, through my occasional but continued interaction with my former and present OHR contacts, I was informed that one of the longest-deployed senior members of the OHR was suspected of fixing consultancy contracts with foreign donors for his wife's consultancy firm in Sarajevo. This was common knowledge among the senior staff at the OHR and something most of them disapproved of but did not do much about, considering the seniority and informal standing of the person involved. A further complication was that the international OHR staff had diplomatic immunity from prosecution and those who left the organization would have to sign a non-disclosure agreement. This was important. Since the late 1990s, the OHR has spearheaded the institutional and public anti-corruption campaign in BiH (Chandler,

2006: 153–7) and has been bent on keeping a pristine public image, which in essence prevented open discussions on the issue of abuse of public office for private gains by individuals within the organization.

This type of practice of sweeping irregularities under the carpet among the intervention elites was confirmed to me by a local investigative journalist and by my other OHR contacts when describing another case of a similar kind. In this instance, the suspect was one of the most senior American diplomats in charge of the International Criminal Investigative Training Assistance Programme (ICITAP). The programme is set up in many countries by the US Department of Justice, whereby US diplomats would work with a foreign government to develop professional and transparent law-enforcement institutions that are supposed to protect human rights, combat corruption and reduce the threat of transnational crime (US Department of Justice, n.d.). In BiH, the programme was run by a diplomat who had been there since the beginning of its implementation, and was considered a 'grey eminence' and one of the most influential diplomats in BiH due to his influence over the commanders of the police forces of Bosnia's two political entities (the Federation BiH and the Republic Srpska) and the State Investigation and Protection Agency (SIPA). In late August 2013, a Bosnian weekly newspaper ran a story about this American high-ranking diplomat: upon his arrival back in BiH after some travel, he was apprehended by US federal agents and flown back to the US. The reason given was sexual misconduct at work. According to my respondents and the newspapers, this was an excuse as the real reason for his removal was the suspicion that he had fixed tenders for the procurement of police equipment among other things (cf. Fazlić, 2013: 4–5). The ultimate outcome of the disciplinary process (if any) remains unclear; all that is known is that the person is now officially retired and lives in the US.

Although being aware of the importance of a more comprehensive discussion on the abuse of office for private gains in peacebuilding and its implications for theorizing about the phenomena of corruption in both the spaces of ambiguity (Comaroff and Comaroff, 2006: 5) and in an age of ambiguity (Wedel, 2012), I decided not to focus on this incident in my scholarship on knowledge production in interventions. In one way, as a researcher interested in critical scholarship on interventions, I was tempted to write about it but refrained out of my broader concern for access to my contacts. In essence, I have been aware that my speaking out on this sensitive issue would shut me out from my access to the inner circles. Besides, speaking out risked fuelling those politicians in BiH, such as Milorad Dodik, who wanted the internationals to leave the country by arguing, among others, that all of them were corrupt. At the same time, my decision not to write and theorize about this aspect of intervention in my research meant that I was helping to uphold the established binary scholarly and policy image of corruption in peacebuilding processes, whereby the source of corruption is generally localized among domestic elites, while the international elites are there to implement programmes to combat this problem. In this way, instead of problematizing the predominant images of external 'liberal peacebuilding' interventions, in a sense I contributed to their maintenance.

Conclusions

This chapter discussed doing fieldwork with elite participants and their networks working on intervention and focused on two main themes. First, it discussed the positioning of an individual researcher and its links with gaining access to policymakers and the networks working on intervention policy. As this section illustrated, different strategies of gaining access have an impact on the positioning and roles of an individual researcher. I make use of private contacts and recommendations as well as digital media tools to negotiate access. However, both of these strategies require that I utilize my various identities in terms of my nationality, gender, educational and career background, and my performances as scholar and expert. Also, all these strategies require a long-term commitment to the space of intervention and engagement with my contacts, which further exacerbate the blurring of distinctions between my roles as scholar and expert.

The second part of the chapter focused on the consequences of this type of access to elites working on intervention for my knowledge production about intervention and conflict. I discussed dilemmas of access and knowledge production I encountered during research, and what they may mean for theorizing about peacebuilding intervention. The reality of peacebuilding is that as a space of intervention it is messy and ambiguous, and it is through knowledge production and image hierarchies and scales that we assemble order to make a sense of it. As this section showed, the more one navigates access to the messy details of the intervention space, the harder it becomes to write about it and challenge the existing imaginaries of organizations and processes due to personal connections to actors involved in the process.

In hindsight, it was only the passage of time, change in interveners' network constellations and the securing of my academic existence as a senior researcher with a permanent contract, which allowed me to critically engage with the topic of policy experts in intervention and knowledge production. In the process, choices have to be made and consequences to be considered, and these are not universal but depend not least on the specific personal and career circumstances of the researcher as well. In this sense, intervention research can never be considered truly 'neutral' or 'objective', as our lives are intimately entangled with what we do in critical qualitative intervention research.

References
Autesserre, S. (2014) *Peaceland: Conflict Resolution and the Everyday Politics of International Intervention*, Cambridge: Cambridge University Press.
Bliesemann de Guevara, B. and Kostić, R. (2018) *Knowledge and Expertise in International Interventions*, London: Routledge.
Coles, K. (2007) *Democratic Designs*, Ann Arbor: University of Michigan Press.
Comaroff, J. and Comaroff, J.L. (2006) *Law and Disorder in the Postcolony*, Chicago, IL: University of Chicago Press.
Chandler, D. (2006) *Empire in Denial: The Politics of Statebuilding*, London and Ann Arbor: Pluto Press.
Fazlić, M. (2013) 'Bosanski Watergate: propast najvažnijeg Američkog "igrača u BiH"', *Slobodna Bosna*, Sarajevo, 22 August, pp 4–5.
Goetze, C. (2017) *The Distinction of Peace*, Ann Arbor: University of Michigan Press.
Höglund, K. and Oberg, M. (2011) *Understanding Peace Research*, London: Routledge.
International Crisis Group (2012) *Bosnia's Gordian Knot: Constitutional Reform*. European Briefing no. 68, Sarajevo/Istanbul/Brussels: ICG, 12 July.
Kostić, R. (2014) 'Transnational think-tanks: foot soldiers in the battlefield of ideas? Examining the role of the ICG in Bosnia and Herzegovina, 2000–01', *Third World Quarterly*, 35(4): 634–51.
Kostić, R. (2017) 'Shadow peacebuilders and diplomatic counterinsurgencies', *Journal of Intervention and Statebuilding*, 11(1): 120–39.
Käihkö, I. (2018) 'Conflict chatnography: instant messaging apps, social media and conflict ethnography in Ukraine', *Ethnography*, 54, online first, https://doi.org/10.1177/1466138118781640.
Leander, A. (2014) 'Embattled expertise: the knowledge–expert–policy nexus around the sarin gas attack in Syria', *Politik*, 17(2): 26–37.
Leroux-Martin, P. (2013) *Diplomatic Counterinsurgency*, Cambridge: Cambridge University Press.

Shore, C. and Wright, S. (1997) *Anthropology of Policy*, London and New York: Routledge.

Stone, D. (2019) 'Transnational policy entrepreneurs and the cultivation of influence: individuals, organizations and their networks', *Globalizations*, online first, https://doi.org/10.1080/14747731.2019.1567976.

US Department of Justice (n.d.) 'The International Criminal Investigative Training Assistance Programme', available online: www.justice.gov/criminal-icitap.

Wedel, J.R. (2009) *Shadow Elite*, New York: Basic Books.

Wedel, J.R. (2012) 'Rethinking corruption in an age of ambiguity', *The Annual Review of Law and Social Science*, 8: 453–98.

3

Interpretivist Methods and Military Intervention Research: Using Interview Research to De-centre the 'Intervener'

Casey McNeill

On the train from Stuttgart, I worried about how my interviews at the US Africa Command (AFRICOM) had gone. It was not that I had not gotten a lot of material. I had. But it was not the kind of material I was looking for. The phenomenon I *thought* my PhD research was going to analyse—shifts in US military strategy and tactics toward population-centric interventions in Africa—was not showing up. My reading of publicly available policy documents and reports about AFRICOM, created in 2007, suggested that it was designed to be a cutting-edge 'new kind of command' tailored to *preventing* 'new' security threats emerging in so-called underdeveloped contexts. AFRICOM is the newest of the US military's six geographic combatant commands, which have authority over military planning and operations in their defined 'areas of responsibility'. Prior to 2007, most of the African continent fell in the European Command's area of responsibility. The creation of a separate Africa Command was widely assumed to signal a more interventionist US foreign policy on the continent.

For my part, I saw AFRICOM as a case to research how this 'new kind of command' was reshaping how traditional security actors like the military were engaging with 'non-traditional' security issues and environments. This could be, I anticipated, a useful contribution to a growing literature in my field of International Relations on the ways in which conditions of 'underdevelopment' were being targeted with various kinds of security interventions in the context of the 'Global War on Terror'. My interviews, though, were making it clear that these discourses about a new kind of military command had limited correspondence with AFRICOM's actual strategy and practice, which seemed to have a much narrower and seemingly more conventional focus on the military's capacity to *contain* (rather than prevent) conflict and other threats. Anxiously I wondered, could I write a whole PhD thesis on how AFRICOM was *not* actually new and interesting?

These anxieties of course were largely misplaced: finding something surprising is almost always interesting, and not hearing what I expected raised new and productive questions for my research. In this chapter, I draw on my research experience to reflect on how interview research can be used to analyze, interpret and explain cases of military intervention. First, I discuss the influence of interpretivist methodology on my interview research with personnel at the AFRICOM and how it advanced my project in unexpected ways. Second, I reflect on the limitations of interview research for making sense of the situated *effects* of military intervention, and how other research strategies can be used to supplement fieldwork data. Overall, I make a case for the importance of multi-sited research when studying cases of international intervention as means of de-centring the 'intervener'. I argue that diversifying research sites does not necessarily mean working in multiple geographic locations, but also engaging with source materials across disciplinary boundaries and genres.

Seeing like AFRICOM: interpretivist interview research on military intervention

When I was first developing my research proposal, I encountered some scepticism from other political scientists about the value of trying to interview personnel at AFRICOM. The logic here was that anything that interview subjects would be willing to talk to me about would be publicly available, and anything that *was not* publicly available I would not get from an interview. My methodological orientation to my research, though, led me to largely dismiss advice that interviews with US military personnel would be a waste of time. My approach to fieldwork was informed by interpretivist and ethnographic research methodologies within political science (Schatz, 2009; Wedeen, 2009, 2010). Accordingly, I assume, as James C. Scott puts it, that 'If you want to understand why someone behaves as they do, then you need to understand the way they see the world, what they imagine they're doing' (cited in Glenn, 2009: B14). I took the scepticism expressed to be relevant to someone with a more objectivist and/or rationalist methodology, that is for whom interviews are a tool for collecting data points about rational actors' objective interests, decisions and actions. From an interpretivist perspective, however, I saw interviews as useful to the extent that they shed light on how apparently rational interests or actions (which are presented as such in policy rhetoric) emerge in relation to ideas, assumptions and worldviews that *are not* transparent in official policy texts and rhetoric.

More specifically, the goal for my interviews was to discuss with practitioners how they understood the relationship between their day-to-day work and AFRICOM's broader strategic objectives, and how they applied the latter objectives in dealing with challenges and contingencies as they came up. It made sense to me that for a researcher who did not want to problematize the strategic objectives or interests informing AFRICOM, interviews might indeed be redundant to analysis of other policy texts.

But my findings from interview research suggest that interview research can be an important corrective for *any* policy researcher because it is difficult to assess what policy strategies or directives are actually most relevant to policy practice. As noted, I found a discrepancy between publicly available narratives about AFRICOM's objectives and its actual priorities and practices, and this was not because the 'true' policy objectives were classified. Instead, most of what I ultimately gleaned from my interview research *was* consistent with publicly accessible information on US military and security strategy (specifically in published US military doctrine). It is just that before conducting interviews I had a largely mistaken sense of where AFRICOM fit within the expansive terrain of US foreign policy discourse and strategy.

So how did interview research help with this analysis? Here, I think that my interpretivist methodological approach was useful for reasons I did not initially anticipate. As noted, what I *thought* my interviews would help me do was to make sense of how AFRICOM's broader strategic imaginaries—which I thought were already relatively transparent to me—actually materialized in the day-to-day practices of AFRICOM personnel. To get at this, I used an open-ended interview roadmap consisting of a range of 'introductory' questions to introduce the themes I was interested in (for example, 'Can you tell me about...', 'Can you describe in detail a time when...') and 'structuring' questions (for example, 'I'd like to move on to another topic...'), with the bulk of the interview spent on probing and follow-up questions based on the examples that my interlocutors introduced (for example, 'Can you be more specific...', 'Can you describe that to me...', 'What was your reaction...') (see Kvale and Brinkmann, 2009: 135–40).

In applying this roadmap, I quickly found that the themes I was interested in (for example, how diagnoses of 'underdevelopment' shape AFRICOM's practices) did not have much resonance with my interview subjects' work. This was disconcerting, but I was prepared to improvise in line with my underlying objectives: the whole point of doing interviews was to collect data on how policymakers and practitioners see the world and what they imagine they are doing. Even if I did not understand how this would relate to my initial hypothesis, I had to trust that investigating these basic questions would bear some fruit.

And they did. Open-ended interviews gave me substantial data from which I could revise my understanding of how AFRICOM's work related to and reflected shifting interpretations of US interests in Africa. Most significantly, commonalities across these interviews, analyzed in relation to other policy documents, revealed how a variety of sometimes competing policy ideas and programmes materialized in a hierarchy of strategic objectives that was clear to practitioners (whether they agreed with this hierarchy or not) but not transparent in policy discourses themselves. In this way, my interviews accomplished almost the opposite of what I expected. Instead of interview research revealing how (already identified) strategic imaginaries materialize in day-to-day policy practices, attention to the latter helped me inductively identify the former.

I think my experience points to some broader lessons that can be drawn for researchers who analyze policy discourses in general and intervention discourses in particular. Polished policy narratives, rhetoric and talking points depict a rational coherence to policy that is unlikely to correspond to rational coherence in policy practice. This makes it risky to answer questions about interest, legitimacy, authority and so on from these sources alone. Where researchers *do not* have ways of triangulating 'official' or quasi-official (for example, talking points) discourses with other sources, they risk ascribing much more coherence to policymaking and policymakers than actually exists.

Interview research offers one method of triangulation under certain conditions. Interviews obviously depend on access. This is not a given, especially in research related to security issues and even more so with state militaries. Based on the experiences of non-American colleagues who, I am aware, have sought and been denied access to AFRICOM's headquarters, I believe that my ability to conduct interviews there was contingent on my citizenship, and perhaps also on the fact that I could present myself as a student (a PhD candidate). I also benefitted from blind luck and biographical privilege (specifically, having been an undergraduate at a private American university in Washington, DC). My first contact at AFRICOM came after I happened to run into a former professor of mine who, in a new job at the US State Department, worked with someone who could introduce me to people at AFRICOM. After this initial introduction, I had minimal (though some) difficulty setting up interviews at AFRICOM headquarters. I suspect, though cannot know for sure, that this may have been further helped by my physical presentation as a petite, young-looking, white woman; other bodies may have presented as more threatening or suspect case to those who initially vetted me.

Had interview research not been possible, other forms of triangulation could similarly de-centre and complicate the seeming coherence of official policy discourse. Another approach that would have been beneficial if I could not get access to do interviews would be to systematically collect and analyze publicly available information aimed at different audiences. In my case, my research revealed that particular Department of Defense strategies and practices dominated AFRICOM, such that its advertised 'whole of government' approach (and integration of State Department and US Agency for International Development strategy and practice) did not really materialize. In addition, publicly available information about AFRICOM and US policy toward Africa (as opposed to more technical reports on military doctrine) are often written (more or less successfully) to avoid backlash from African leaders and allied interest groups in the US. Triangulating analysis of a wide terrain of these discourses alongside reporting on AFRICOM's activities on the continent (comprehensive accounting of which is not available) may have led me to similar conclusions even without interviews, but interviews certainly got me there faster.

Limitations of, and supplements to, interview research in intervention sites

Exaggerating policy coherence has particular downsides in research on international intervention. The political geographer, Gillian Hart, has been influential for my thinking on this problem. In several papers, Hart (2001, 2002, 2004, 2006) critiques what she calls the 'impact model' of global political analysis, in which the analyst presents 'inexorable forces of global capitalism bear[ing] down, albeit unevenly, on passive "locals"' (Hart, 2004: 91). Hart primarily engages with political economy and international development research, but her critique of the impact model applies just as well (or even more so) to research on global security and international intervention. Especially within the discipline of International Relations, analyses of international security are, more often than not, based on interpreting the interests, decisions and actions of powerful state actors or, less frequently, wealthy international organizations. The impact model that thus emerges characterizes international security practices and their effects as the relatively straightforward outcome of these interests and decisions.

While this can occlude recognition of a whole range of empirical phenomena, what Hart is most interested in is how it prevents recognizing the 'local' as a site where 'global' processes are actually *constituted* as such. In other words, she argues that we should not assume that local 'cases' of 'development' or 'intervention' are best analyzed as instances or variations of 'globalization' or 'international security'. Rather, we should be equipped to see how what we conceptualize as 'globalization' or 'international security' is *produced* in 'local' sites, including in ways that unsettle, contradict, rework, and so on the interests, decisions and actions of 'global powers'. Applying Hart's insights to my own project, I concluded I needed to have ways of analysing how AFRICOM's policies and practices were actually materializing in concrete times and places. Otherwise, I would be implicitly depicting a world in which global security practices are formulated in the complicated sociopolitical worlds of the interveners, but then produce effects in relatively empty, uncomplicated, ahistorical and apolitical sites of intervention.

Toward this end, I planned to carry out research in the Sahel region, an area that US security strategists targeted as a priority site for 'preventive' interventions in the context of the 'Global War on Terror'. I wanted to conduct research into security conditions and practices in the Sahel spaces that US strategists and policymakers commonly described as 'ungoverned' and 'insecure'. The goal was to analyze how US policies related to and intersected with these conditions and practices, and with what effects. I judged that the best way to do this would be to spend an extended period of time in the Sahel (specifically in northern Mali and/or Niger, which have been key 'partner' states of AFRICOM), but early on I decided not to pursue this based on fears about hostage taking. As an alternative, I planned to conduct interviews (in 2014) with people displaced by conflict in northern Mali in 2012, thousands of whom were living in Bamako and Niamey, the relatively safe capitals of Mali and Niger.

This leads me to reflect on the limitations of interview research, for example, as compared with more immersive fieldwork strategies. While valuable in the ways discussed earlier in this chapter, my interviews did not accomplish some of the ambitious goals I had for my fieldwork as I was first developing my PhD research.

As noted earlier, my objectives for fieldwork were shaped by interpretivist and ethnographic methodologies: I wanted to observe and analyze security practices and effects as they materialize in situated 'interrelations between objects, events, places, and identities' (Hart, 2006: 998). For the interpretivist—who holds that the social and political world is produced intersubjectively (Wedeen, 2009)—immersive fieldwork strategies, like participant observation or 'soaking and poking' (Fenno, 1990: 55) are valuable here, to the degree that they make it possible for the researcher to situate actors' claims, actions and worldviews within an intersubjective historical, geographical and socio-political context. In relation to Hart's critique of the 'impact model' this kind of fieldwork has analytic and political-strategic importance where it reveals how 'global' phenomena are constituted in relation to 'local' conditions, practices and struggles, thereby recognizing the latter as sites of political agency and potential transformation.

Practical constraints led me away from adopting these methods. In addition to security concerns, I was also only able to secure funding for a six-month period of fieldwork in Mali and Niger (I applied to, but did not get, two grants that would have funded 9–12 months of research). In the end, I decided to divide my time between Bamako and Niamey, with a brief trip to Mopti in central Mali. Given the fact that this was my first trip to these locales (so I did not have a network of existing contacts), this fieldwork plan meant that most of my time and energy would be devoted to developing contacts and setting up as many interviews as I could, with as diverse a set of relevant actors as I could.

This raised the question, to what extent could this kind of interview-based research design accomplish research goals informed by ethnographic methodologies? Put another way, how much could guided conversations reveal about the concrete processes and practices I was interested in?

In my experience, interviews in Mali and Niger, as well as just *being* in Mali and Niger while I had focused time to think and reflect on my project, were highly productive and, like my experience at the AFRICOM headquarters in Stuttgart, inductively reshaped my research in fruitful ways. But there were also ways in which interview research was *not* well suited to my goals. Some of these goals I had to abandon. Specifically, I could not offer a detailed account of specific, contemporary Sahel security practices in particular spaces and communities.

In what follows, I elaborate on where interview research fell short, and then discuss how I worked with these limitations.

First, interviews with people displaced from northern Mali were challenging, and sometimes an outright failure, largely due to my inadequate attention to the context of these interviews. Specifically, I did not adequately anticipate and address how interlocutors would respond to me, a privileged outsider, as being a potential lifeline in a desperate situation. Given the traumas that these populations had experienced and the sensitivity of talking about perpetrators of violence, the questions I raised in these interviews did not focus on the conditions of peoples' displacement. Instead, I asked about daily life and changes in security conditions in the ten years leading up to the 2012 crisis in Mali. But for many people I interviewed—especially the most desperate, for example single mothers living in makeshift, temporary shelters—discussing anything other than the traumas of the crisis and their current vulnerabilities and desperation was almost, if not entirely, impossible. Regardless of what I asked, some simply repeated that they had received no assistance from the government or aid agencies and were desperate for some form of aid (see also Bjørkhaug, in this volume).

This experience raised not just research-related concerns, but ethical ones to the extent that these interviews constituted a further drain on vulnerable populations' limited energy, with minimal benefit (I tried to mitigate this by compensating displaced interviewees for their time with research funds) (see also Jennings, in this volume). A lesson I took from this was that essentially dropping in on vulnerable populations to conduct one-off interviews is likely inappropriate. Had I instead introduced myself and what I was doing on multiple visits to communities of displaced persons, I believe these issues would have diminished.

For example, there were a few occasions on which I was able to join groups of displaced persons in non-interview contexts and then later follow up with them after having already established some rapport. In one case, I attended a training in Bamako aimed at displaced persons and later followed up with many participants at their residences. In another, an acquaintance invited me to a group meeting of a savings collective run by refugees in Niamey. I made other contacts attending a public *fête* at a Tamasheq cultural centre. In all cases, conducting interviews on a second or third meeting led to a much more candid and open conversation (see also Göransson, in this volume).

This highlights the value of extended immersive fieldwork as opposed to a systematic collection of discrete interviews, especially in unfamiliar contexts. Ultimately, and not surprisingly, my interview-based fieldwork, primarily in state capitals, just could not substitute for time spent in northern Mali and Niger. This meant that my fieldwork did not produce near enough data about contemporary northern security practices for me to try to draw detailed conclusions about how the latter are relating to changing US and international security strategies and practices in the Sahel, which had been an early goal.

Nevertheless, interviews with displaced populations, with Malian and Nigerien scholars, journalists, activists, and state and military personnel pointed me toward other strategies to de-centre the security theories and practices coming out of AFRICOM. These interviews helped me situate contemporary security politics in relation to broader historical and political dynamics of state-periphery relations in the Sahel; specifically, to practices of territorialization and their relationship to security conditions and contestation over security practices. Attention to the historical, geographical, cultural and political dynamics of territorialization in the Sahel became an alternative vantage point (as opposed to a closer study of security practices in a particular field site in northern Mali or Niger) from which I could problematize how AFRICOM strategists and other state actors are conceptualizing security in the Sahel.

A focus on ideas and assumptions about how territorial and security practices are related helped me tease out key differences in actors' diagnoses of security conditions in the Sahel. From here, I looked for relationships between these diagnoses and different approaches for producing security, and relationships between these approaches and changing security conditions for Sahel populations over time. Much of this research drew on textual resources rather than interviews, including policy documents, journalists' and NGOs' reports, and especially other scholarly research particularly in history, geography and anthropology.

Interviews facilitated this in a number of ways. For example, several older individuals who had been displaced from northern Mali attributed the decline of security in the north to 'democratization' beginning in the 1990s. These responses led me to a literature on democratization, decentralization and conflict that both contextualized and verified these responses. Interviews with military and government personnel and policy advisors revealed a focus on the development of fixed territorial infrastructure as a means of improving security in the Sahel, which prompted me to dig into the political and historical context of this common assumption. Putting these literatures—one on case studies of relationships between decentralization and local conflicts and another on a longer history of efforts to territorialize political and economic order in the Sahel and their effects—in conversation with one another was instrumental for drawing informed hypotheses about how US policies toward so-called 'ungoverned spaces' in the Sahel was likely to intersect with existing conditions. Based on this, I could investigate these hypotheses in relation to other researchers' and reporters' accounts of developments in northern Mali and Niger. Ultimately, these avenues led me to a key finding. While AFRICOM's strategy in the Sahel has equated security with territorial control, security practices in northern Mali and Niger have commonly been organized around securing capacities for *mobility*, rather than capacities for controlling territory. Efforts to increase states' territorial control in the Sahel have often been disruptive to existing security institutions and practices, which helps shed light on why recent increases in international security interventions have correlated with deteriorating security conditions in many parts of the Sahel.

Conclusion

In hindsight, I can apply a logic to the messiness of my fieldwork experience and narrate how it ultimately contributed to a successful PhD. This logic of course was not obvious at the time, and the gap between what I thought I was supposed to be uncovering in my research and what I was actually doing produced a great deal of anxiety, both during fieldwork and as I was analyzing my data and contextualizing it with other research. I think that my interest in and borrowing from ethnographic methodologies helped me adapt and improvise, in spite of my anxieties. I held on to the idea that 'obstacles can be a source of knowledge for ethnographers' and 'every happening' is 'a potential moment for evidence gathering and/or rethinking the project's premises' (Wedeen, 2010: 256). And I intentionally tried to cultivate what Ellen Pader calls an 'ethnographic sensibility' across my research: not only in my daily life during fieldwork, but also in my reading of other sources (Pader, 2006: 170–5). What I mean by an ethnographic sensibility is that I tried to approach the entirety of the research experience not as the gathering of discrete pieces of data but as a process, the particularities and contingencies of which themselves could offer up new questions and evidence about the ideational, social and material contexts of my objects of study. For example, why did I start with the questions I started with and not others? Why is particular information harder to access? How do(es) expat culture(s) impact my own and other foreigners' experience of living and working in Mali and Niger? How are the questions I am raising approached differently by political scientists versus historians versus anthropologists? And so on.

I agree with Pader that immersive, ethnographic fieldwork is one of the best ways, but not the only way, to cultivate an ethnographic sensibility and apply its analytic benefits. She suggests that this can also inform reading and analytic practices even without fieldwork (Pader, 2006: 172–3). As I discussed earlier, I could have gleaned some similar insights to those that my interview research provided using publicly available textual evidence, depending on the questions that I brought to the analysis. Likewise, while just *being* in Mali and Niger for several months was invaluable in terms of gaining some familiarity with social and material contexts important to interpretation—hanging out with US military personnel during fieldwork was valuable for the same reasons—if travel was not possible due to funding constraints or other barriers, reading practices could have substituted for fieldwork in some ways. The biggest impact that fieldwork had on my research was less in the specific data I gathered in interviews but in the different—and, I think, more interesting—research questions that it inspired. Readings of other scholars', journalists', community leaders' and so on writing and commentary (for example, through publications, social media presence, or by making personal contact online) could have pushed my research questions as well, though probably in different ways.

My experience affirms both the analytical and political importance of de-centring the theories and practices of the 'interveners' within research on international intervention. By de-centring I mean accounting for the fact that theories and practices of intervention (for example, theories of international security informing US foreign policy) will always produce effects in relation to theories and practices rooted in intervention sites. Research methods must have tools for contextualizing these theories and practices within the historical, geographical and political contexts in which they are produced and materialize. This is not only important for anticipating more accurately the conditions and effects of intervention, but *also*—and maybe even more importantly—for recognizing minoritized theories and practices as playing a vital role in *revising* how we understand global politics.

References

Fenno, R.F. (1990) *Watching Politicians: Essays on Participant Observation*, Berkeley: University of California Institute of Governmental Studies.

Glenn, D. (2009) 'The power of everyday life', *Chronicle of Higher Education*, 56(5): B13–B14.

Hart, G. (2001) 'Development critiques in the 1990s: *cul de sacs* and promising paths', *Progress in Human Geography*, 24(4): 649–58.

Hart, G. (2002) 'Geography and development: development/s beyond neoliberalism?', *Progress in Human Geography*, 26(6): 812–22.

Hart, G. (2004) 'Geography and development: critical ethnographies', *Progress in Human Geography*, 28(1): 91–100.

Hart, G. (2006) 'Denaturalizing dispossession: critical ethnography in the age of resurgent imperialism', *Antipode*, 38(5): 977–1004.

Kvale, S. and Brinkmann, S. (2009) *InterViews: Learning the Craft of Qualitative Research Interviewing* (2nd edn), London: SAGE.

Pader, E. (2006) 'Seeing with an ethnographic sensibility: explorations beneath the surface of public policies', in D. Yanow and P. Schwartz-Shea (eds), *Interpretation and Method: Empirical Research Methods and the Interpretive Turn*, New York: Sharpe, pp 161–75.

Schatz, E. (ed.) (2009) *Political Ethnography: What Immersion Contributes to the Study of Power* (1st edn), Chicago, IL: University of Chicago Press.

Wedeen, L. (2009) 'Ethnography as interpretive enterprise' in E. Schatz (ed.), *Political Ethnography: What Immersion Contributes to the Study of Power* (1st edn), Chicago, IL: University of Chicago Press, pp 75–94.

Wedeen, L. (2010) 'Reflections on ethnographic work in political science', *Annual Review of Political Science*, 13: 255–72.

4

The Interview as a Cultural Performance and the Value of Surrendering Control

Markus Göransson

In 2013 and 2014, I spent seven months in Tajikistan speaking to veterans of the Soviet–Afghan War for my PhD thesis, which examined the emergence of the Soviet–Afghan War veterans as a discursive group in the late Soviet period and involved oral history and archival research.

I had not been to Tajikistan before and had only a limited number of contacts in the country. Much of my time in Tajikistan was therefore spent forging connections with Soviet–Afghan War veterans and others who could assist me in my research. I soon realized that in this process my initiative and pro-action were less important than factors that were outside of my control. Serendipity and the willingness or unwillingness of individuals to speak to me shaped my research process in a basic way, forcing me to shed a number of assumptions that I had imbibed from methodological literature. This was particularly true for collecting oral historical data. Beholden to luck and the need to interact with respondents on their terms, I was in most cases not in a position to insist on formal interviews. Nor would it have been ethical to do so, as this chapter will point out.

This chapter suggests that some of the assumptions about good interviewing that are mainstream in Western methodological literature were inappropriate for, and even harmful to, my research in Tajikistan. Early on in my research I realized that attempts to adhere to established standards of interviewing caused my respondents' discomfort, weakened their trust in me as a researcher and indeed jeopardized their anonymity.

In the course of my research, I came to view the interview as a culturally and socially situated performance that was not necessarily suited to the research context that I encountered in Tajikistan. My learning process in Tajikistan involved finding methods of work that took their cue from established forms of interaction among my respondents; in doing so, I found myself surrendering part of my ability to direct the research.

Collecting oral information in unfamiliar contexts

My first exchange in Tajikistan was with Rustam, a well-dressed taxi driver who spoke an uninflected Russian and drove a beat-up Opel in the inner districts of the capital of Dushanbe. I made his acquaintance after stumbling into his car on a rainy day while looking for a quick ride to an important appointment. After some polite chitchat, he told me he had been in the Soviet reserves in Termez, Uzbekistan, near the Afghan border, just as the Soviet invasion of Afghanistan had been getting underway in December 1979. With his hands on the steering wheel, he drove us through Dushanbe's tree-lined streets and told me he remembered well the troop movements that had taken place in the base in Termez. He described vividly the wounded, sometimes crippled soldiers who were brought back from the battlegrounds.

When we arrived at my destination our conversation came to an end. But I was excited that, a mere week into my stay, I had met someone who was closely associated with the Afghan War. I asked Rustam if he would give me an interview, to which he graciously agreed. So, we exchanged phone numbers and met a few days later in an outdoor *shashlik* (kebab) restaurant in front of the Dushanbe opera.

My interview with Rustam was the first of my stay in Tajikistan, but it was also the worst. As might have been expected, there was only so much that an ex-reservist who had not set foot in Afghanistan could tell me about the war. He offered colourful descriptions of life in Termez and the wounded soldiers who returned from Afghanistan, but he knew little more about those who had fought in the war than did other Tajiks of his generation. If anything, the interview gave a sense of the remoteness of the Afghan War even among former Soviet citizens who had resided in close proximity to Afghanistan and the troops who had been sent there.

Yet other problems, more pertinent to discuss here, also marred the interview. Prime among them were a number of mistakes on my part, which offer a point for discussing a number of broader issues related to conducting interviews in unfamiliar contexts. The mistakes included the following: 1) Before and during my exchange, I repeatedly referred to it as an 'interview' (*interviu* in Russian). 2) I formally introduced myself as a university-affiliated researcher and explained the purpose and objectives of my research. I also asked for Rustam's formal consent to participate in the interview and for me to record it. 3) I met Rustam in a place of my, not his, choosing. I did so because I wanted to select an open and public place close to where we had met the first time (which was a few hundred metres from the opera). I also wanted it to be one that we could both find easily and where I could buy him a meal or a drink as a thank you.

In hindsight, I believe these actions framed my exchange with Rustam in an unfortunate way. They established me as the researcher who was in charge of the encounter and Rustam as the respondent who was expected to submit to my questions. Judging by Rustam's reactions, they caused him unease. During the interview, he appeared uncomfortable and deflected or gave only sparse replies to many of my questions. My use of a voice recorder seemed to add to his discomfort, even though I had secured his formal permission to record the interview. This is illustrated by the following interchange:

Me: "So, after Termez, you started working as a driver?"
Rustam: "Yes, I was a driver… [long pause] Nothing will happen to me, right?"
Me: "What?"
Rustam: "The recording, the recording. Nothing will happen to me, right? No one else will…what I am telling you?"
Me: "No one else will hear this. Only me."
Rustam: "Ah. Everything I am saying is correct. Everything. You are a friend to me."

If Rustam was uncomfortable with my démarche, he was unhappy also with the venue. He made this clear by asking that we move to a different table to remove ourselves from the other guests and, sometime later, by suggesting that we relocate to his car that was parked nearby. Although he had consented to participating in the interview and agreed to meet me in the restaurant, it was clear that he was not at ease during the meeting. I was not a novice at interviewing, having previously undertaken other interview-based research and worked in journalism. Yet it was painfully obvious that I had managed the encounter poorly and shown scant sensitivity to Rustam's wants and wishes.

The interview illustrates a number of broader points about collecting oral information in unfamiliar contexts. One is the obvious importance of luck for accessing opportunities. Despite the errors I committed, my meeting with Rustam was not without value. He proved to be a well-connected person who was friends with several Afghan War veterans in Dushanbe. He kindly introduced me to three of them, who I interviewed in succession over the subsequent two weeks. They provided me with valuable information. Hence, my choice of taxi on that rainy day, one week into my stay in Tajikistan, put me in touch with a fixer of sorts. Similar strokes of fortune accompanied my research on other occasions. Just as I stumbled into Rustam's taxi, so I later made accidental contact with other individuals who lent me assistance. My most fortuitous encounter was with Ibragim Yatimov, a former platoon commander, who approached me at a Soviet–Afghan War commemoration in Dushanbe and lent me a great amount of support over the following months. Later, a minibus driver in the Pamir Mountains in eastern Tajikistan offered to drive me through the remote Wakhan Valley in his vehicle for a small fee, finding respondents for me on the way. Also, in the Pamirs, a kind young student introduced me to a veteran in his home village and two other veterans in a nearby locality. There were many similar instances. Opportunities appeared; they were rarely created. Having only paltry networks in Tajikistan, I depended on the helpfulness of others and the serendipitous moments that arose. Usually, I was on the receiving end of other people's kindness. Rarely, I found myself in a position to return favours, except by giving small gifts and lending small measures of assistance.

But if my interview with Rustam near the opera led to further opportunities, more subtly it also illustrates my limited ability to steer the research process. My attempt to take charge of the interview backfired, as Rustam resisted my efforts. In trying to adhere to what I understood to be good standards of interviewing, I inadvertently sought to impose a way of interacting on him, which seemed to cause him unease. The result was a tense exchange that put Rustam off and brought me little valuable information.

Spontaneity and informality

The difficulty of trying to direct interviews was evident in many other exchanges that I had with Soviet–Afghan War veterans in Tajikistan. From selecting the time and place of the conversations to deciding how long they would last, or even sometimes what issues they would address, my ability to lead them was limited. Few meetings were scheduled ahead of time. Most of them occurred spontaneously when people who I encountered on the street or approached in their homes or workplaces agreed to sit down with me over tea or sometimes vodka.

On a number of occasions, people phoned me to let me know they were available a short time later, sometimes no more than ten minutes. If I could, I dropped what I was doing and threw myself into a taxi. When I travelled through the Wakhan Valley and the mountainous Murghob district in eastern Tajikistan, I visited people in their homes. Invariably, they invited me for tea and an informative chat.

Unlike my stuttering start with Rustam, many of these later exchanges had a spontaneous and informal character. Accompanied by food and drink, they were friendly conversations, not formal interviews, where I as the researcher tried systematically to extract information from my respondents. I soon learned that the very notion of the interview was uncongenial to many of my respondents who raised their guard when I mentioned the Russian word *interviu*. The word seemed to connote formalism and officialdom, things my respondents preferred to avoid. One veteran who had served as a conscript in Afghanistan met me several times and spoke quite freely to me about his experiences during the war. But when I asked him for permission to conduct an interview, he declined. Trying a different tack, I asked him if he would be happy to talk to me about his time as a soldier in Afghanistan and let me use the information that he shared with me in my thesis. "Yes, but I don't want to give you an interview", he replied. Other respondents, too, appeared to shift into a different mode, becoming terser and more reserved, when I asked them for interviews. For example, a group of veterans who spent their days in a souvenir shop in Dushanbe were friendly enough to me until I asked them for an interview. Then the owner of the shop, also a veteran, said "no" outright and began to treat me coldly. I returned a few times to try to mend relations but without success. One of the other veterans explained to me that the owner thought I might be a Western spy. While many veterans were reluctant to speak to me at all (I was accused of being a spy on several occasions), the word *interviu* seemed to send up particular red flags.

Rustam's reaction on the opera square should have prompted me to change my approach to interviewing sooner than it did. However, it took some time before I broke free of unhelpful assumptions about appropriate interviewing that I had absorbed from literature on research methods. In many cases, that literature contained guidelines for undertaking interviews that were designed to help researchers to protect their respondents, secure their consent and increase the transparency of the research process. Not all these guidelines were appropriate for the research context that a researcher is likely to encounter in Tajikistan. The UK-based Oral History Society, for example, advises that 'Informed consent is best acknowledged by means of a Recording

Agreement, often called a "Consent" or "Clearance Form", which should be completed and signed face-to-face at the conclusion of the interview but which should be shown before any recording begins' (Oral History Society, 2019). This assumes a degree of faith in the legal system, a familiarity with the research process on the part of the respondents and their acceptance of the interview as a legitimate method of work. None of this may be present in areas where the legal system inspires little public trust and where the interview may connote official monitoring and scrutiny.

Breaking free of methodological assumptions required a reckoning with the research training that I had undergone as a doctoral student. This training had often been formalistic and had tended to ignore challenges linked to context. The validity and reliability of data was identified more with the sophistication of the research design than with its appropriateness for the research context. There was an apparent underlying assumption that the research—just like the research training—was to be undertaken in the UK, while discussions of ethics tended to merge with discussions of legality (see also Russo and Strazzari, in this volume). It seemed to be entirely beyond the scope of the course to address principles of good research without linking them firmly to particular research methods.

In my early weeks in Tajikistan, I clung to the lessons that I had learned in the research training and from the methodological literature, much to the detriment of my research. But with time I realized that brandishing forms and asking for signatures on documents was certain to make respondents feel uneasy. This was for good reason. Not only did my respondents know little about the UK legal system that pretended to protect them, but putting their signatures on forms would also have provided written proof of their participation in my research and allowed the authorities to identify them should the forms fall into their possession, for example during a search at border security. My promises of anonymity to those who preferred not to be named would then have meant nothing.

More sensitive to the situation and concerns of my respondents was to introduce myself to veterans, explain the scope and purpose of my research and secure the veterans' consent informally. This could be done during informal conversation, for instance over a meal or a drink or when we attended festivities and other events together. Such occasions gave me opportunities to introduce myself and explain what I was doing in the course of friendly and relaxed conversation. At such times, I avoided posing as a formal interviewer and did not ask for respondents' written consent. Learning to interact with my respondents on terms other than those prescribed by methodological literature was part of my research journey in Tajikistan, and one that entailed revisiting assumptions about proper approaches to oral historical research. One anecdote that illustrates this is taken from the early months of my stay in Tajikistan.

Informal conversations over cups of tea

Some of my most valuable interlocutors in Dushanbe were a group of friends who I came to know in May 2013. We met at an event dedicated to Tajiks who had fallen in the war in Afghanistan. The people who were part of the group were all military veterans and all but one of them had served in Afghanistan. Two of them had served in the same unit in northern Afghanistan. It was a tight-knit collective who regularly met and spent time together, eating and drinking and helping each other with small tasks, including renovation work on their houses. They took an interest in me and my research and started to invite me to their gatherings, most of which took place in one of their homes on weekends or during public festivities on holidays. I was delighted to spend time with them and seized the chance to try to speak to some of them.

Soon I realized that it was very difficult, if not impossible, to arrange meetings with the veterans outside of these friendly gatherings. When I suggested to individuals that we schedule one-on-one meetings, they often told me they were too busy or gave a non-committal reply. Some stopped answering my calls after I had phoned them on repeated occasions to try to book a time. One person agreed to meet me and then did not turn up at the agreed time. The problem, I realized, was not that they were unwilling to speak to me about their experiences in Afghanistan. They were generally very forthcoming when I asked them questions about their service as we sat together on the *kurpatchas* (quilts used as seating), drinking a pot of green tea or eating a meal. But they rarely seemed to want to go out of their way to set up a meeting with me for the purpose of talking to me about my research. Perhaps such a meeting would have smacked too much of the formal interview, as well as removed them from the safe and familiar company of their friends.

I was frustrated at first but decided to make the most of the situation. Instead of insisting on meeting veterans individually, I tried to use the occasions when we were gathered as a group to talk to people who were present. During the gatherings, when we had finished our meals and were lounging on the *kurpatchas* with small cups of tea in our hands, Russian TV flickering in the background, I sometimes turned to the person next to me and asked if he would be happy to answer some questions about the Afghan war and let me record it. More often than not, he agreed, and I took out my voice recorder and began the exchange. Many of my exchanges with veterans were conducted in similar settings. They were unplanned and took place in the company of others in contexts of normal everyday interaction.

This was a helpful way to get people to talk to me. It also allowed me to ask my questions in settings that were familiar and agreeable to my respondents. In contrast with the interview that I had conducted with Rustam in the kebab restaurant, I did not decide the time or setting of the exchanges, nor indeed who I would speak to. I talked to those who happened to be present, often to those who were seated next to me. I did not ask respondents to leave their usual contexts and I was mindful not to disrupt the flow of the exchange to avoid evoking the formal interview, even when it came at the price of omitting certain questions.

Many of these informal exchanges were conducted with other people around, while food and tea were being served and other conversations were going on around us. Sometimes, people interrupted us to bring us more to eat or drink or to offer their points of view. A number of times, the exchanges were cut short when a person in the group suggested that we move to another place or to call it a day. Phone calls, invariably answered, were also disruptive, as was the arrival of more friends, neighbours and family members. On one occasion, when I was talking to a former conscript in his workplace in Dushanbe, one of his colleagues was putting together a kebab grill on the floor behind us. The colleague was using a saw and a mallet that left heavy imprints on the tin and the interview recording. Naturally, these distractions affected the exchange and limited the questions that I was able to ask. The presence of other people during the conversations may have caused respondents to self-censor (although my impression was that many were more comfortable in the company of their friends than they would have been alone with me). Nevertheless, by asking my questions in the context of established forms of social interaction, I was able to gather information for my research without causing apparent discomfort to my respondents. Needless to say, I was fully transparent about my intentions and role as a researcher.

The anecdote illustrates how established patterns of social interaction may complicate attempts to maintain a conventional research relationship with interlocutors. My initial wish to conduct conventional interviews was frustrated by the reluctance that some of my respondents displayed to participating in them. Perhaps I would have remained more firmly in the driving seat had I insisted on conducting formal interviews, that is controlled conversations where I and the respondent occupied well-defined roles. But this is likely to have made my respondents uncomfortable—as happened in the case of Rustam—or deterred some of them from speaking to me in the first place, as happened with the veterans in the souvenir shop and several others. I was not in a position to set the tune. In most cases, I needed to adjust my approach to the forms of social interaction that were established and congenial to the people I met.

Of course, not all exchanges with veterans were informal. At times, I prebooked appointments with individuals and asked them questions prepared and even written down in advance much in the way of the conventional interview. Some Tajik Soviet–Afghan War veterans were comfortable with this. A number of them had previously taken part in interviews or had themselves conducted interviews or other research. Some had studied at university, worked as researchers or as journalists and were familiar with interviews as a research method. In the case of these individuals, the formal interview often proved an expedient means for gathering information. Yet other respondents were not equally versed in the interview as a performance.

Much has been written about oral history as a methodology (see for example Smith, n.d.; Lynd, 1993; Thomson, 1994; Perks and Thomson, 1998; Summerfield, 1998; Green and Troup, 1999; Portelli, 2003; Green, 2004). Yet little has been said about the challenges of gathering oral information in situations where the researcher has only limited control over the research process. Much of the methodological literature assumes that the historian will be more or less in control and able to direct the interviews in accordance with his or her research priorities. In his seminal interview-based work on Australian First World War veterans, *Anzac Memories*, the oral historian Alistair Thomson describes how he contacted his respondents by sending them carefully worded letters in which he introduced himself as a university historian and explained his reasons for wanting to interview them (Thomson, 1994: 229–30). He then met the veterans in their homes and asked them questions on themes preselected for his research. Throughout the interviews, he writes, he tried to maintain a professional demeanour and strove not to surrender 'the powerful position of interviewer' (Thomson, 1994: 236). While his attempts to direct the interviews were sometimes frustrated when respondents digressed or 'rode roughshod over my questions and asserted their own interests and emphases', he did not doubt his basic control over the interview.

Thomson describes an interviewer–respondent relationship where the interviewer is active and searching and the respondent mainly reactive. This is the relationship as commonly imagined. Numerous manuals and textbooks in oral history and qualitative social science research methods advise researchers to take charge of the interview. A brief handbook on oral history techniques from Indiana University encourages researchers to send 'the interviewee a list of your questions or a summary of the topics you'll be asking about' and to 'make sure the place [of the interview] is quiet and away from outside distractions' (Truesdell, n.d.). Other texts offer taxonomies of interview types, including 'questionnaire-based interviewing', 'semi-structured interviews', 'unstructured interviews' and 'focus groups', inviting the researcher to select the type most suited to their project (Matthews and Ross, 2010; cf. Terre Blanche et al, 2006). While it is acknowledged that challenges and distractions may arise, it is often assumed that the researcher is in a position to direct the research project and that the power of initiative lies firmly in his or her lap.[1] The importance of luck for the research process and the role of social and cultural practices in shaping the dynamics of the interview are given less attention.

Conclusions

Interviews are highly structured exchanges. They are also culturally and socially situated and rely on both parties being versed in the performance. In Thomson's interviews with Anzac veterans, the roles that he and his interlocutors occupied were rarely challenged or even scrutinized, as both interviewer and respondent seemed to fall naturally into them. In contexts where interviews are less well established as a performance or connote other things than they do in Australia, respondents may resist or subvert the exchange. This was my experience in Tajikistan where the notion of the *interviu* seemed to send up red flags among respondents who associated it with unwelcome things. A more fruitful form of exchange for my purposes was the friendly and informal conversation, often accompanied by food and drink. Not only did it help me to build trust with veterans and gain more opportunities to gather information for my research, it was also more sensitive to the wishes of my respondents, who seemed more comfortable to speak to me in these settings.

Of course, some individuals still kept a distance to me. One member of the tight-knit veteran community in Dushanbe refused to answer my questions flat-out and did not hide the fact that he distrusted my intentions. In other cases, a number of individuals refused to meet with me. But others were more at ease with my presence. They invited me to share in their memories, which were often rich and complex, and many expressed their appreciation for the fact that I spent time with them. To some, my efforts to gather information about their past seemed secondary to the fact that I shared in meals and drink with them. Visiting them in their homes and joining them at the *dastarkhan* (food spread out on a tablecloth on the floor) was viewed with kindness. The questions that I asked about the Soviet–Afghan War seemed less important.

My research in Tajikistan was a methodological journey that destabilized some of my assumptions about methods, particularly interviewing. As a doctoral student from a Western institution, I was steeped in methods that held a different resonance for Soviet–Afghan War veterans in Tajikistan. I also understood that I had little power of initiative or control over the research process but was beholden to the inclinations of other people and indeed to serendipity. Developing a research approach that was productive and ethical in this context required learning and adjusting to modes of social interaction that were well established among the individuals I met. In doing so, I needed to surrender assumptions of control and unhelpful conventions of interviewing.

Note

[1] One common piece of advice is for researchers to conduct their interviews in quiet and preferably private places. As the UK-based Oral History Society puts it: 'It is best to find a quiet and undisturbed location for an interview, usually the interviewee's home, though sometimes they may prefer another place' (*Oral History Society*, 2019).

References

Green, A. (2004) 'Individual remembering and "collective memory": theoretical presuppositions and contemporary debates', *Oral History*, 32(2): 35–44.

Green, A. and Troup, K. (1999) *The Houses of History. A Critical Reader in Twentieth-Century History and Theory*, Manchester: Manchester University Press.

Lynd, S. (1993), 'Oral history from below', *Oral History Review*, 21(1): 1–8.

Matthews, B. and Ross, L. (eds) (2010) *Research Methods: A Practical Guide for the Social Sciences*, Harlow: Pearson Education.

Oral History Society (2019) 'Is your oral history legal and ethical?', www.ohs.org.uk/advice/ethical-and-legal/.

Perks, R. and Thomson, A. (eds) (1998) *The Oral History Reader*, London and New York: Routledge.

Portelli, A. (2003) *The Death of Luigi Trastulli and Other STories: Form and Meaning in Oral History*, Norwell, MA: Kluwer.

Smith, G. (n.d.) *The Making of Oral History*, The Institute of Historical Research: www.history.ac.uk/makinghistory/resources/articles/oral_history.html.

Summerfield, P. (1998) *Reconstructing Women's Wartime Lives*, Manchester: Manchester University Press.

Terre Blanche, M.J., Durrheim, K. and Painter, D. (eds) (2006) *Research in Practice: Applied Methods for the Social Sciences*, Cape Town: University of Cape Town Press.

Thomson, A. (1994) *Anzac Memories. Living the Legend*, Oxford, Auckland and New York: Oxford University Press.

Truesdell, B. (n.d.) 'Oral history techniques: how to organize and conduct oral history interviews', http://citeseerx.ist.psu.edu/viewdoc/download;jsessionid=677459CA04177DA46133F3086D61B1B4?doi=10.1.1.305.1755&rep=rep1&type=pdf.

5

Unequal Research Relationships in Highly Insecure Places: Of Fear, Funds and Friendship

Morten Bøås

Researching conflicts as they unfold is challenging and usually necessitates the reliance on local contacts, researchers and fixers. As a member of the community of globally mobile conflict researchers—those who mostly live in Europe or North America—I depend a lot on these persons. This is particularly true for my research in the Sahel, where independent access to conflict-affected areas has become almost impossible due to high levels of insecurity, which turn the question of trust in local brokers into an essential one that relates not only to academic careers but importantly also to personal security (Bøås et al, 2006). In a highly insecure context, who can we trust regarding data and information? Who can we trust for sound security advice? And how does money influence our research relationships?

These questions are a constant part of the daily negotiation of fieldwork-based conflict and intervention research, and I also grappled with them in earlier research in insecure places, such as the Mano River Basin, northern Uganda and the DR Congo (DRC). Yet they have never felt as acute as when I started working in Mali and the Sahel in 2007. The reasons for this lie in the deep uncertainties and fears that are brought about by a combination of insecurity and the near impossibility of accessing the most research-relevant parts of these territories. While the research situation was also highly insecure at times in the other conflict zones I worked in, my research teams and I were never the direct target of attacks. This is different in the Sahel, where jihadist insurgencies attack hotels to create spectacular dramas for international media coverage, and international hostages are much sought after, leading to a severe decrease of fieldwork-based research in these areas. This situation is concerning because we are in danger of losing a grounded understanding of the social landscape of these areas based on independent third-party empirical observations in the field. Some of the security concerns causing this retreat from the field are very real, while others are motivated by risk-averse universities and funders (see Russo and Strazzari, and Heathershaw and Mullojonov, in this volume). While we can possibly do something about the institutional risk averseness, conducting research in high-risk contexts is something we need to become better at dealing with.

In the Sahel, the research that does take place is often conducted under a certain degree of suspense and suspicion, if not outright paranoia. Field visits are infrequent and usually short, making the development of a systematic data set based on first-hand data collection nearly impossible. This leads to a dependence on a combination of more anecdotal evidence and more data collected by sources such as journalists or intelligence officers whose reliability is uncertain—not because these data are bad or biased, but because we often know neither their quality nor for what original purpose they were collected, analyzed and framed in a certain way. Parts of this problem can be tackled by triangulating as much data as possible (see also McNeill, in this volume). The other strategy often employed by Northern researchers is working with a local partner, be it an individual researcher or a research organization, who will do the data collection in the risky areas, while the international researcher remains in the capital or another relatively safe part of the country, if not entirely attempting to control the research process remotely 'from home' (see also Kušić, in this volume).

In an ideal world, relationships between foreign researchers and local assistants would be based on trust, respect and eventual friendship, turning the researcher into what Geertz (1983: 56) calls the 'myth of the chameleon fieldworker, perfectly tuned to his exotic surroundings, a walking miracle of empathy, tact, patience and cosmopolitanism'. My own experience suggests, however, that while relationships with local assistants and researchers, fixers and brokers may eventually evolve into trustful friendship, relationships that work over an extended period of time mainly function not despite of but due to their unequal nature. While friendship may evolve, the fact remains that Northern researchers are almost exclusively the part that brings funding and opportunities, controls the research process, and spends a considerable part of the project funding—and this has an impact on the relationship.

In this chapter, I argue that this general trend is even more salient in highly insecure places where the international community tends to live in garrisons to which local researchers rarely have the same privileged access as researchers from the Global North (Büscher and Vlassenroot, 2010). There is undoubtedly an element of fear in intervention-related research in highly insecure places. Working in a place where I am a potential target has caused me at times to have second thoughts concerning the loyalty of those I work with and to have concerns about their security advice. Are they making the right decisions, and to what degree is the fact that I am here influencing these decisions? Are they willing to take more risks than they would otherwise do? Are they setting up risky meetings just in order to serve my research agenda?

This chapter is an attempt at critically thinking through how I have attempted to navigate these lines between fear, funds and friendship, also reflecting on those moments when I ignored such issues and just carried on hoping that everything would be fine in the end. Acknowledging that the issues, questions and doubts discussed here are something I should have thought through critically much earlier, I wonder whether the reason for this may be that 'we'—that is, researchers like me who have made fieldwork-based conflict research their career and livelihood—have created a social environment where we hardly ever talk about fear, distrust, wrong-doings and paranoia. Do we collectively cultivate an image of an ability to get things done against the odds, in which we become the 'heroes' of our own stories with no room for doubt and fear? I know that I have been guilty of this in my branding of myself and my 'field adventures'. This chapter is therefore also an attempt to more strongly acknowledge the relationships with those who have helped build my career: the local researchers, fixers and brokers.[1]

In the following, I use three vignette stories for my personal reflections. The first is about a fieldwork in 2007 in which I 'inherited' a local network of interlocutors, and discusses how (not) to treat information given in the trust of someone else. The second and third vignettes are taken from more recent visits to the field. The second vignette is an attempt to discuss how the feeling of being let down by a local research partner I had known for a long time had consequences not only for the research carried out in that case, but for our future relationship. The third vignette zooms in on the question of how money may influence personal security in asymmetrical research relationships in highly insecure contexts in risky ways.

'Will we ever be friends?'

My first encounter with Mali and the Sahel came relatively late in my career. The institute I was working for at the time had been contacted by a client who needed a political background analysis of Mali, including conflict and crime. As this institute also employed a researcher that had done a huge amount of work in Mali, but never on the intersection between politics, crime and conflict, it was decided that the two of us should work together. We both thought this was a good idea: we had worked together in the past elsewhere and knew how to draw on our respective strengths. In this case, these consisted in my colleague's general knowledge about Mali and local networks and contacts acquired over an extended period, and my presumed ability to quickly understand the links between politics, crime and conflict and to write an interesting report.

Our small fieldwork mission was implemented and it went very well. Through my colleague's contacts and networks we were able to get access to almost everybody, from well-placed ministers to former leaders of various parts of the Tuareg insurgency of the 1990s. It felt as if these people considered my colleague an old friend who had finally returned to Mali, and we got a wealth of information about politics, new small-scale insurgencies and the various criminal networks that were materializing in the Sahel and connected Bamako to the peripheries in a different manner than before. The fieldwork we did together—assisted by my colleague's old network of fixers, interlocutors, friends and former colleagues—was a very positive experience. I still remember fondly the many hours we spent sitting on the floor with Tuareg leaders, sipping endless amounts of bitter-sweet tea, talking about politics, people and places. After the end of this project, we attempted to raise follow-up funding for our collective work, yet the fact that Mali was a relatively peaceful country at the time contributed to the failure of these attempts. In 2007, the conflicts of the 1990s between the Tuareg minority in the north and the black majority population that mainly lives south of the River Niger were supposed to belong to a bygone era. This view would soon be proven wrong.

What changed the conflict landscape was the fall of Gaddafi in Libya in 2011 and the repercussions it created throughout the Sahel, but particularly in Mali (Bøås, 2012; Bøås and Torheim, 2013). As Tuaregs who had been in the service of the Gaddafi state were forced to leave Libya for marginal livelihoods in Mali with little to bring with them except the arms they carried, a new rebellion broke out in 2012. This time the Tuareg rebels, organized in the Movement for the National Liberation of Azawad (MNLA), not only demanded increased autonomy but independence for Azawad, their acclaimed homeland in northern Mali. The MNLA was initially successful in pushing the Malian army out of the way in the north. When unrest in the army led to a coup in Bamako, it even looked as if the rebels would succeed in gaining territorial control over the north. However, since their governing capacity was extremely weak, mayhem and plunder followed and northern Mali became an area of chaos and disorder. Jihadist-inspired insurgents like al-Qaeda in the Islamic Maghreb (AQIM), Ansar ed-Dine and al-Mourabitoun took advantage of this power vacuum. Through a combination of their military discipline and their generally more predictable behaviour towards the civilian population, they were able to push the MNLA aside and gain territorial control of most of northern Mali (Bøås, 2015; Bøås and Torheim, 2013).

The jihadi spectre that materialized in northern Mali teleported the country from obscurity to international high politics. Suddenly, there was a lot of interest from clients and funding bodies, and I was on my way back to Mali, this time on my own, to work with the network of local contact points I had 'inherited' from my former colleague. On the plane to Bamako I wondered: Would I end up on the same friendly terms with them as my colleague, even though we did not have the same shared past together? This was a totally counter-factual question that could not be answered, as by then the whole context had changed dramatically. The conflict that engulfed Mali in 2012 was not the usual type of Tuareg rebellion—a centre–periphery conflict—that the country had seen its fair share of in the past. This was a jihadi-inspired insurgency with clear lines regarding its enemies: foremost the Malian state, but also people like me who were seen as part of an international coalition of crusaders.

The Mali that I was returning to was therefore a country with a very different security situation to the one I had left in 2007 and, with hindsight, it is obvious that I failed to fully grasp this. What I was entering into was not a case of 'inheriting' a network of friends, but an unequal working relationship in a highly insecure place, in which issues of trust and friendship would also be influenced by the money involved. At this point you may ask what is wrong with a normal professional relationship, and the answer is that it is perfectly alright. However, what will also become obvious from this chapter is that, as we engage with a field over an extended period, we also tend to engage with many of the same persons. As such, it is quite natural that we want to be someone they prefer to talk to, someone they trust, respect and, yes, even consider a friend.

The 2012 context in Mali was not ideal for starting to work with a relatively large group of people who did not know me very well and therefore did not have much reason to trust me. Our talks and discussions seemed forthright and my hosts where just as welcoming as almost six years ago, but 'we' were not old friends. For them our relationship was a short-time business association, something that would only last while there were clear tangible benefits. We would never become friends—we were something else. And this was also the case for my assistant and interpreter. He and I had met back in 2007 and had stayed in contact but, as much as he was genuinely happy to see me return to Bamako, this was a working relationship. I did not realize that he wanted to please me to ensure more work, but our hosts read the situation more realistically than I did. They clearly saw this as 'work', as an arrangement made for an economic relationship, and this set limits to what they were willing to share. Most of the information received this night and later from this group of people turned out to be imprecise, partly wrong, and some of it even damaging for some people.

Luckily I never used much of that information, but what this episode shows is that we may read 'friendship' into relationships that are essentially about work, and that personal relationships with local interlocutors are not just something that one acquires automatically, something that grows around the international researcher as people attach themselves to this person out of trust, friendship and general altruism (see Carrier, 2004; Wolff, 2004). Nothing materializes out of nothing. Fieldwork relationships are not only about 'hanging out' at a certain site long enough. Usually somebody makes introductions and, while there is always an element of chance involved, most often things happen for a reason which is usually some sort of previous knowledge or contacts. This will frame initial inquiries as well as the range of possible local contact points. Such 'early-on decisions' have important bearings on the subsequent stages of the fieldwork and research process. The initial framing of a case may continue to shape research in each location for years to come—even as the situation in that location changes, like in the Malian case—as initial contacts, fixers, and local researchers turn into an expanding, but relatively circular network. More often than not, these networks have little to do with friendship—which is less surprising when we take interlocutors seriously as people with their own ideas, interests and agendas who choose who they bestow information, trust and friendship on.

'Respect me!'

If the quest for friendship with local research assistants and interlocutors is mostly a dream in vain, then what about respect? What does being respected mean in this particular social relationship between an 'international' researcher and their local counterparts? Which role does mutual trust play in this? I had to learn the hard way that respect does not necessarily come with the position and privilege of the international researcher, but is something that we must earn. When I returned to Mali in 2014, I assumed I would be working with the local researcher who had assisted me before. I also assumed that, since this local researcher and I had known each other and worked together for a while, our relationship was based on a certain degree of respect. I felt that I respected him and the various positions and interests he had, and expected that he understood and respected what I needed from him. In my perspective, we had, if not friendship, then at least contractual relations, and contracts where to be honoured (see Vanderstaay, 2005). What I completely failed to understand was that respect is more than just words in a contract, and I felt seriously let down when I returned to Mali in 2014.

The 2013 fieldwork had been quite successful overall, despite the issues discussed in the first vignette. It had led to several new articles and reports co-authored with Malian scholars. I was therefore quite optimistic when I returned to Bamako a year later that my local research partner and I would work well together again. Much to my surprise, however, I soon found out that he was not going to work with me. He had taken up a different contract and just told me that another person from his network would be my point of contact, a person I had previously heard about but never met. This new working relationship did not go well: the fieldwork was a series of misunderstandings, cancelled meetings and interviews with people I already knew and whose viewpoints had barely changed since our last encounter. I was therefore quite disappointed with the whole affair and particularly with my initial research partner who I thought had shown me very little respect by doing things this way.

What I failed to understand, and what became much clearer to me when we met up to discuss another contract during my trip to Bamako, was what respect entails in fieldwork in general and in a highly insecure research environment like this one more specifically. I was after all quite a newcomer to this field: I had just come for one trip in 2007 and then returned when the political situation deteriorated in 2013. To the local researcher I was somewhat of a vulture, returning to Bamako and Mali to feast on the dying corpse of the Malian state, writing about state failure without the credibility of having done research there for a much longer period. Why, this being the case, should he respect and trust me? Additionally, the issues that I wanted to research were by now highly securitized and therefore sensitive. While I could leave whenever I wanted or needed to, he was stuck in this insecure situation and had absolutely no illusions that, if things went bad or our joint research started to unsettle somebody high and mighty, I would come to his and his family's rescue. Thus, as I had not yet come to earn his respect, he saw me as someone who could bring some benefits in the form of money, but who potentially also posed a security risk. His way to balance benefits and risk was simply to take a part of the 'cut' for organizing a research assistant for me, but without having to be deeply implicated himself, and just wait and see how this arrangement would play out.

When I finally understood his way of reasoning, I also understood his positioning and behaviour towards me. At the same time, however, that initial feeling of having been seriously let down and of a lack of respect did not disappear swiftly. Reflecting on my continuing disappointment, I wonder whether we may have to learn how to live with our 'fields' not only when 'friendship' is lacking, but also when—rightly in this case—little respect is paid to us. Perhaps lack of respect is even a good thing as it keeps us on our toes with regard to the question of how the combination of an increasingly deteriorating security environment and money may influence the researcher–interlocutor relationship. While in this case the local researcher chose to distance himself from the potential risks I represented and thus opted for safety at the cost of more money he could have made, the following vignette is an example of how the combination of my quest for new data and the money involved in the research relationship can turn this relationship toxic, putting everyone involved at risk.

'Hey ho, let's go!'

I have always taken pride in a rule I used while working in the Mano River Basin, the DRC and Northern Uganda: that nobody working with me should be allowed to take risks that I was not prepared to take. This meant that if I did not feel comfortable travelling to a certain place or meeting somebody, so should no one else. In fact, I have even written about this and about the danger that the access to funding that people like me represent may lead local researchers and research assistants to take higher risks than they normally would (see

Bøås et al, 2006). It is a seemingly easy rule, but not necessarily one I have always abided by. The increased difficulties in accessing the field that I encountered in Mali after 2012 almost inevitably led me to start making some compromises in this regard. As researchers, we want as accurate data as possible and to be the ones with the most interesting and novel pieces of information. Thus, the temptation will always be to try to push through, thinking 'Hey ho, let's go!' This is precisely what I did one night.

I should confess that I find insurgents like Mokhtar Belmokhtar fascinating. I am not just fascinated by his role as the man behind the attack against the In Aménas gas plant in Algeria in 2013 that made him the most famous and most wanted jihadi in the Sahel, but by his full life trajectory—how as a young man he left Algeria in the 1980s to fight in Afghanistan, then returned and played a role in the Algerian civil war in the 1990s, followed by his time as bandit, smuggler and insurgent roaming northern Mali and other Sahel peripheries, until he cast all his criminal networks aside and became what he is today: the mythical face of Sahel jihadism. Thus when one morning, during a discussion about which informants to interview in the coming week and where, one trusted broker told me that it could be possible to meet a recently returned fighter who had spent some time with Belmokhtar's insurgency, al-Mourabitoun, I was thrilled. I told him that if it was possible to set up such a meeting, he should go ahead. He said he would try. A few days later I was told that this former fighter was willing to meet us at a place on the edge of Bamako. The broker who had provided this contact and I talked this through—just the two of us, as I felt that involving others could jeopardize this opportunity or even bring it to the attention of security forces, and then the whole encounter could turn very bad. We talked for a while, debating pros and cons. Was it real? Would it be possible? Would this person show up? Could we verify what he would tell us? We also discussed our own security, and I asked my broker if he felt secure and comfortable going through with this meeting. He said it was fine, that it would not be a problem.

Thus, in the evening of that very day we prepared to leave. It was just the two of us and a driver who only knew where he was supposed to take us but nothing more. As we started to approach the meeting point at the edge of town, it was dark and few people were to be seen. I could sense tension starting to build up in the car but chose to ignore it. We entered through some dark buildings into what seemed like an abandoned small yard between three old shattered houses. As we parked the car but left the lights on and the engine running, my broker started to get restless and became even more nervous when not one but four persons emerged out of the shadows, telling us to stop the engine and turn off the lights. It was abundantly clear that we were in a place where we should not have been. The person we were supposed to meet was not alone. He was together with three other men. Were they friends, former fighters, or something else? We never really understood, but they were aggressive and angry and demanded money. What I had hoped would be an interesting event that would provide novel insights into the inner life of al-Mourabitoun ended up in an attempt by us to navigate ourselves out of this encounter as best we could. After lengthy exchanges that seemed like negotiations, we finally agreed to give two of them a lift to another destination on the outer boundaries of Bamako and, when we got there, they just left the car and disappeared into the shadows of the darkness. We never understood what this was about and never talked much about this thereafter—both of us seemingly happy to brush this aside as just a 'bad day' in the field.

It was only much later that I started to reflect on this and came to understand that this was not just the case of a broker making a bad decision, but very much about me. Those who I worked with knew what I was interested in and, on this occasion, this knowledge pushed one of them to do something that he clearly otherwise would not have done. I should have seen this. I should have recognized that what drove this decision was an unequal relationship based on the hierarchy of power that I held by controlling funding and representing global connections through co-publishing and other things of interest to a young aspiring researcher like him. I had misunderstood the situation, not realizing that, in his attempt to please me and grow closer to me and global connections that I represented, my broker had ended up doing something that he would never have done, had it not been for me.

Field research is always about money or about capital of some sort. Without money we cannot travel, get accommodation or hire local researchers. There must be something in it for the local partners. This should be obvious, but it is often the 'elephant in the room' of field research, hardly ever mentioned in books or articles based on field research or in manuals supposed to prepare students and young researchers for the field. We prefer not to talk about it as it would throw into sharp relief the obvious power hierarchies that exist between 'international' and local researchers. Money has serious implications for research relationships: local researchers in the violent and closed contexts discussed in this book desperately need funding for research and for their salaries, and this may very well affect what they are willing to do, the risks they are willing to take. There is no perfect antidote to this problem or dilemma in this type of setting. The only thing we can do is to become better at talking honestly about them.

Conclusion

The way global academia is organized means that local researchers, research assistants, informants, fixers, brokers, interlocutors or whatever we call them will never enter the centre-stage of international research. We will never reach a level of equality as there will always be differences in skills, opportunities and connections. What we can become much better at, however, is acknowledging these hierarchical research relationships and the dilemmas they create, and coming to terms with how unequal partnerships in highly insecure places will always inform working relations between international researchers and their counterparts on the ground.

We all make mistakes, we all have feelings of suspension, fear and distrust during fieldwork, and this should be acknowledged as normal. We are not machines, but people with emotions and attachment to ourselves. The real problem is the silencing around these dilemmas. We have created an environment where we do not speak about the most basic elements of field research in highly insecure places, but rather spend time and energy on theorizing our positionality and intersectionality. Parts of this debate have clearly been much needed and useful, but it has also become a way of letting ourselves off the hook with a certain degree of grace, as it is much easier to discuss difficult questions through conceptual lenses than directing them towards ourselves in plain language. Maybe we should rather try this for a while and see where it will take us.

Note

[1] Molony and Hammett (2007: 292) note that searches in academic databases for material on the ethics of employing research assistants most often only turns out acknowledgements, dedications or corrections (in the latter case an author that apologises for an 'error' made by an assistant). Turner (2010: 206) finds that the limited work that exists mainly comes from the health sciences and then usually involves discussions about the use of interpreters.

References

Bøås, M. (2012) 'Castles in the sand: informal networks and power brokers in the northern Mali periphery', in M. Utas (ed.), *African Conflicts and Informal Power: Big Men and Networks*, London: Zed Books, pp 119–34.

Bøås, M. (2015) 'Crime, coping and resistance in the Mali-Sahel periphery', *African Security*, 8(4): 299–319.

Bøås, M., Jennings, K.M. and Shaw, T.M. (2006) 'Dealing with conflicts and emergency situations', in V. Desai and R.B. Potter (eds), *Doing Development Research*, London: Sage, pp 70–8.

Bøås, M., and Torheim, L.E. (2013) 'The trouble in Mali—corruption, collusion, resistance', *Third World Quarterly*, 34(7): 1279–92.

Büscher, K. and Vlassenroot, K. (2010) 'Humanitarian presence and urban governance development: new opportunities and contrasts in Goma', *Disasters*, 34(2): 257–73.

Carrier, N. (2004) 'Surviving Ali: the trials and tribulations of an anthropologist–informant relationship', Paper presented at the 5th Annual Researching Africa Day Workshop, St Anthony's College, University of Oxford.

Geertz, C. (ed.) (1983) *Local Knowledge: Further Essays in Interpretive Anthropology*, New York: Basic Books.

Molony, T. and Hammett, D. (2007) 'The friendly financier: talking money with the silenced assistant', *Human Organization*, 66(3): 292–300.

Turner, S. (2010) 'Research note: the silenced assistant. Reflections of the invisible interpreters and research assistants', *Asia Pacific Viewpoint*, 51(2): 206–19.

Vanderstaay, S.L. (2005) 'One hundred dollars and a dead man: ethical decisions in ethnographic fieldwork', *Journal of Contemporary Ethnography*, 34(4): 371–409.

Wolff, S. (2004) 'Ways into the field and their variants', in U. Flick, E. Kardorff and I. Steinke (eds), *Companion to Qualitative Research*, London: Sage, 195–202.

PART II

Security and Risk

Developments in ethics procedures, risk assessment, insurance regulations and legal frameworks (such as counter-terrorism legislation) have drawn attention to the security- and risk-related aspects of fieldwork-based research in violent and closed contexts—and they have affected intervention researchers' access to 'the field' and to data/information. In addition, the characteristics of the field itself, which may be controlled by authoritarian states or violent groups, who target researchers, research participants or both, have contributed to a shrinking of space for fieldwork-based research. The authors in this part of the book discuss practical issues emanating from this situation, ranging from how to approach research ethics in a less procedural–bureaucratic and more vocational–practical and context-specific way, to how researchers deal with questions of their own safety and that of their national collaborators and research participants and informants, to the effects that the alleged 'duty of care' of Western research institutions for their employees has on academic knowledge production about international intervention. The research underpinning the reflections in this part was conducted across a range of institutional research boards and research ethics committees in Europe, as an international–national research collaboration in Tajikistan, among communities in central and northern Mali, with armed groups in the eastern Democratic Republic of the Congo (DRC), and under close surveillance by state security agencies in the south Caucasus and Central Asia.

6

The Politics of Safe Research in Violent and Illiberal Contexts

Alessandra Russo and Francesco Strazzari

As higher education communities and facilities are increasingly targeted by attacks,[1] a transnational debate has arisen among academics and practitioners about how knowledge is produced under conditions of growing risk for researchers who are committed to site-intensive methods, fieldwork and/or dissemination in circumstances of limited academic freedom.

On the one hand, it is a known fact that—especially in times and zones of violent conflict—university campuses and colleges are systematically targeted by various forms of armed attacks. While violence directed at university sites stems from insurgent groups' radical rejection of the idea of 'Western education', schools are an easy, soft target not only for 'terrorists' but also for aerial and artillery bombing on the part of governments.[2] On the other hand, authoritarian regimes and police states tend to deploy repressive measures to monitor researchers and patrol their activities. University institutions and personnel are increasingly seen as objects of attack in and of themselves, targeted in the effort to intimidate or silence dissent. Launched as retaliatory measures for having somehow challenged the one official, institutionalized narrative that is permitted and accepted, these attacks vary from killings and disappearances, wrongful prosecution and imprisonment, loss of professional position and expulsion from study, to improper travel restrictions. 'Having knowledge—having data—is extremely threatening' (Cooley, quoted in Kumkova, 2014): state authorities and officials are often keen to act as the sole gate-keepers, and they seek coercively to ensure that 'alternative narratives' are not able to emerge.

Several episodes have drawn the attention of the transnational scholarly world to the fact that research and academics are under attack. The brutal murder of Giulio Regeni in Egypt made international headlines in February 2016 and can be seen as one of the most evident cases in point:[3] an Italian citizen enrolled in a PhD programme at the University of Cambridge, Regeni was in Cairo to carry out ethnographic field research on trade unions and labour rights as a form of political opposition when he disappeared on 25 January 2016. When his corpse was found a few days later, dumped by the side of a motorway and bearing clear signs of torture, a lengthy international controversy was kindled. Three years later, the five Egyptian officers who were formally accused by Italian prosecutors have enjoyed substantial impunity in Cairo; meanwhile, conducting political research in Egypt has become virtually impossible, and a broad community of scholars who were investigating post-2011 events has left the country.

It would be misleading to consider the phenomenon of attacks against and constraints applied to (social science) research(ers) as limited to the non-Western world. The quality and accessibility of academic work, instruction and research is subject to limitations in the Western scholarly environment as well. Research is not only monitored, policed and ultimately securitized in conflict-affected contexts or under authoritarian regimes: suffice to consider the *etat d'urgence* in France or counter-radicalization legislation in the UK and note their impact on research agendas in the social sciences (Russo, 2017). Further, technology plays an ambivalent role in reshaping research routines and protocols: research standards not only value but formally call for the full disclosure of sources to make research outputs fully accountable, transparent, traceable and 'truly scientific'. These requirements, however, often amount to a tangible threat for the safety of research participants (interviewees, respondents, informants) whose data and personal information are exposed to circulation and unintended manipulation thanks to their digitalization and virtual ubiquity. In other words—and as paradoxical as it may sound—in addition to the forms of restriction, sanction and repression typically associated with highly unstable, repressive and authoritarian contexts, researchers today face new and more subtle challenges in which their conduct appears to be administered and governed through the introduction of research techniques, protocols and procedures originally intended to make research safe, compliant, lawful, ethical and responsible.

The social and political sciences have recently (re)discovered the value of fieldwork-based research, site-intensive and immersive methodologies, and ethnographic endeavours to foster the study of transnational phenomena and global–local encounters. The increasing relevance of interpretivist approaches and emergence of the so-called 'practice turn' as well as a renewed scientific interest in 'the local' and 'the grounded' has brought the researcher's subjectivity and ethics to the forefront of methodological debates. How are researchers positioned within research settings, especially those settings that may be defined as violent, risky and dangerous? This question is currently being contemplated by a plethora of actors engaged in the regulation of research practices, including research institutions, funding bodies and donors, and university bureaucracies. Whilst contemporary social and political phenomena seem to demand more fieldwork-based research agendas and respond most fruitfully to 'frontier research', the space in which scholars are free to use such ethnographic instruments seems to be increasingly delimited. Institutional concerns about protecting researchers deployed in field missions in high-risk zones or countries have been amplified in recent years, with European and North American universities intent on designing safety protocols. Although little harmonization is visible as yet, it is a fact that new measures are being adopted everywhere and, we argue, these measures can be seen as emerging or embryonic security regimes.

Our reflections on these dynamics and trends are based on multiple empirical founts and data sources. Since 2015, we have been involved in a research project focusing on the duty of care principle—that is, how universities and research institutes govern their research staff during missions abroad. As part of that framework we have been in contact with several (junior and senior) researchers as well as research directors and heads of departments, which has given us the opportunity to look into different emerging practices across Europe with regard to researchers who travel to high-risk areas and countries. Alongside this data source, we also draw on some auto-ethnographic accounts. The Giulio Regeni 'case' mentioned earlier has prompted intense debate in Italy (and across Europe), and we have been involved in that debate at different levels.[4] In 2016, we were appointed as members of a task force called on to design a fieldwork research policy for our home institution. The experience led us to both survey a core sample of Italian (Frediani, 2017) and European research institutions to compare and contrast their in-house fieldwork research policies (if any) and to reflect upon the procedures through which these policies are established. Finally, in 2017 we joined the SAFEResearch initiative[5] as part of which we attended several trainings on digital security and hostile environment awareness, eventually contributing to the collective writing of a multi-authored handbook on fieldwork research safety (SAFEResearch, n.d.).

This experience has led us to analytically distinguish between two different logics affecting research in risky contexts: on the one hand, its securitization (Strazzari and Peter, 2016) and, on the other, its bureaucratization/judiciarization.[6] The securitization of research typically occurs when emergency measures and extraordinary procedures are invoked in the name of research security, aimed at the safety of both researchers and research materials/data. This logic rests on unstable and controversial definitions of 'zones of danger'—that is, areas into which Western travellers, including researchers, should not venture without adopting a proper code of conduct. The logics of bureaucratization and judiciarization of research, *par contre*, does not entail the same sensationalism and calls for urgent action that usually characterize securitization. Rather, it consists in the proliferation of internal institutional and disciplinary practices that apply to fieldwork research, research missions abroad and projects featuring site-intensive methodologies and ethnographic endeavours.

In this chapter we argue that—especially in the absence of an open debate and evaluation—the combined effect of these processes is that knowledge production is opened up to a number of paradoxes and, potentially, vulnerabilities. The move to anchor researchers' routines to concepts that are in themselves debatable (that is, research safety, dangerous research settings) ultimately ends up regimenting social science research through indirect surveillance and discipline mechanisms. Our aim here is not to suggest how effective security/safety regimes for carrying out fieldwork research should be designed; rather, we would like to draw attention to the rationales and effects of this emergence of security regimes, the resulting constraints of which are often scarcely visible and rarely reflected upon. Our experience suggests that, given the relational and context-specific nature of security, unilateral, unidirectional and univocal protocols are highly problematic; indeed, the impact of readily available standard formulas, 'best practices', and field manual prescriptions on research and knowledge production need to be evaluated.

Instead of hoping to identify one 'risk assessment arrangement' or procedure that works better than others, we believe that it is important to learn research techniques 'through a kind of informal apprenticeship in a fraternity of researchers' (Ahram and Goode, 2016: 839). Context-specificity translates into an intersubjective definition of dangers, risks and safety, and it therefore follows that only a multi-stakeholder, multi-phased decision-making process to which researchers, supervisors, project coordinators, funding bodies and all other relevant actors contribute can meet standards of appropriateness. By relying on expertise and knowledge produced 'from within', this process should limit or even avoid the usual reliance upon prepackaged indexes, indicators, maps, cartographies and other tools that are provided by actors located outside of specific research routines and practices. Most importantly, this process should be 'Janus-faced': on the one hand, it should establish requirements and asks for risk-mitigation measures before and during the research mission. On the other, it must offer collegial moments of self-training and instruments of capacity-building, with cognitive schemes being collectively constructed by and shared among the researchers themselves as part of this framework (see also Sangaré and Bleck, and Verweijen, in this volume).

The following two main sections of this chapter shed light on the way research is being made (allegedly) safer by establishing security regimes that are themselves based on certain regulations, codes and protocols, and how these security regimes may in turn impact researchers' practices and processes of knowledge production in the social sciences in problematic ways.

Regulating research

According to our preliminary study, as of 2019 relatively few European research institutions had adopted regulations and/or policies addressing the question of 'safe (fieldwork) research'[7] on the basis of self-reflective debates involving scholarly communities. There certainly are institutions that have established (or are in the process of establishing) specific procedures regulating research trips to high-risk zones; however, this process seems to feature a number of problematic elements.

First, the process is crisis-driven rather than being based on broader, documented trends. Unfortunate and dramatic events in which Western researchers or institutions came under threat while employing site-intensive methods have triggered reactions within research institutions. This reactive attitude is likely to result in extemporaneous procedures aimed at assigning responsibility in order to fill a legal vacuum and avoid issues of liability.

Second, the process is other-directed, as it is stems more from funding bodies' requirements than from collegially questioning the conditions of knowledge production under critical circumstances. In particular, universities' reliance on EU funding for research can be considered a crucial factor for the adoption of policies and guidelines for regulating fieldwork research in the social sciences.

Third, the process can be considered part of broader reform templates inspired by a new public management approach that is increasingly pervasive in the higher education sector. Managerial logics calls for auditable and calculable knowledge to be benchmarked and measured through indicators,[8] often at the expense of the principles of free enquiry and autonomy. In many cases it is the employer or dean who takes top-down measures, frequently in consultation with legal advisors. As a result, fieldwork research practices are organized according to general regulations regarding university staff on missions abroad; at the same time, however, research activities are micro-managed, as they are obliged to meet demands of recording, monitoring, transcribing and codifying research.

This situation is not entirely new. In the US, institutional review boards have monitored and regulated social science research (specifically research involving interactions with human subjects, and thus also ethnographic work) since the 1960s. In that context, not only have social scientists been excluded from rule-making (ethical standards developed for biomedical and psychological subjects were applied to social sciences), but they have also been impeded from doing 'controversial' fieldwork research: as a matter of fact, institutional review boards have the power to deny funding, degrees or promotion to those scholars who refuse to adjust their research proposals according to the ethics committees' recommendations (Schrag, 2010).

At present, the role of ethics review committees appears to be functionally integrated into the development of regimes for safe research. In principle, their main purpose is to ensure the integrity and transparency of scientific research, with special attention to privacy protection and the collection, usage and storage of sensitive data. Thus, existing 'ethical clearance procedures' seem to focus on the methodological soundness and formal correctness of research activities rather than the safety of research participants as well as researchers. In a number of universities, however, the mandate of these committees extends to assessing the risk of undertaking a research project (especially when the project is carried out by a postgraduate researcher/PhD student), requiring modifications to mitigate the risk and even denying university authorization to pursue projects perceived as risky. Thus, boards and committees' assessments may be deployed according to actuarial calculations about the riskiness of research projects, with the result that universities' immediate priorities tend to shift from advancing science to measuring and mitigating risk factors vis-à-vis expected benefits.

On average, university administrators and members of these committees expect researchers to collect a priori information about the research setting and to display it as evidence of the safety or riskiness of a given location. One common requirement in several departments across Europe, for example, is that researchers refer to the indications and travel guidelines provided by various diplomatic offices and ultimately the ministries of foreign affairs. Information inferred from ready-made cartographies of danger is used to evaluate the authorization and ethical review forms that PhD students and research staff are required to fill out before beginning data collection. Such reliance on risk maps officially compiled by ministry officials and bureaucrats often proves to be inconsistent, however, with the rapidly evolving realities of fieldwork research. There are at least two reasons for this. First, several researchers admit that their main source of information about the places they plan to visit is their own personal set of handcrafted, trusted local networks made up of colleagues from local universities as well as other expats and informants. Secondly, institutional reports and indicators of potential threats inform risk assessment procedures, with the final authorization decision being made by boards of professors who not necessarily have any expertise in the specific topics or areas investigated by the proposed research project. In the effort to obtain approval for their applications, researchers are typically quick to learn specific techniques of strategic box-ticking, wording and phrasing, thereby de facto voiding the process of thoughtful challenge and consideration.

In addition to ethics review committees, some universities have equipped themselves with guidelines on the safe planning and management of research activities conducted off-site and in remote locations (that is, far from conventional academic facilities), as well as with fieldwork safety risk-assessment forms and templates. These toolkits often draw on documents that are developed and published by collective bodies comprising university administrators;[9] in other cases, they are ratified by governing bodies such as academic senates.

Regulations regarding safe research are not solely a response to increasing concerns about risk: another factor leading to their development is the recently minted legal obligation of duty of care, a principle of which universities are increasingly aware concerning the protection and safeguarding of personnel travelling abroad on behalf of their employer (de Guttry and Capone, 2017). In abiding by this principle, universities have imported regimes and policies developed by multinational enterprises and international organizations. Indeed, these latter are subject to a legal obligation to ensure the well-being, security and safety of their employees deployed abroad, an obligatory 'duty of care' that extends to contractors, volunteers and related family members. Duty of care is anchored in the EU normative framework, specifically a 1989 Council directive on safe and secure workplace environments,[10] which the Court of Justice applied to missions abroad as well. As such, this principle is about the prevention and minimization of risk and the organization and provision of medical services for staff (and family members) in emergency situations. Organizations—research organizations included—are asked to adopt sound administrative procedures, including properly functioning internal investigation structures. Employers that fail to provide adequate information about the danger of a mission and adequate training for such dangers may be legally liable.

However, mechanisms deriving from this recognition of the duty of care appear to overlook three important points regarding the way research is practised. First, while risk mitigation for employees—that is, personnel organically related to (research) organizations—appears to be a core concern, the safety of locally hired staff and research participants contributing to research activities as drivers, interpreters and fixers, as well as informants, activists and so on, remains somewhat marginal. In other words, the duty of care seems to presuppose a clear-cut division between the researcher and the researched: only the well-being, safety and security of the former is included within the perimeter of diligence the research organization deals with. Once that has been ensured, the organization is much less concerned about the context in which the research will be conducted and the relations that constitute the researcher's environment.

Second, duty of care is caught up with categories that reflect specific notions of citizenship, nationality and the formal organization of labour that largely fail to capture the multiform reality characterizing present-day research practices. There is no doubt that the employer has a duty of care vis-à-vis its employees; however, it is common for the terms of researchers' employment contracts to vary quite widely. The nature of the research itself, its workflow and source of financing all play an important role in causing this variation. In France, for example, fixed-term, early career researchers are considered equivalent to public officials, while in Italy they hold a legal and fiscal status comparable to apprentices or students with scholarships.

Third, research does not always unfold according to a predictable workflow. Not only do research organizations host multinational research teams,[11] they are also imbricated in complex webs of collaborative projects involving other institutions whose status might or might not be homologous. A case in point would be research consortia that include universities from very different countries, as well as think tanks, individual practitioners, officials, governmental agencies, NGOs and consultancies. When carrying out a specific research task as part of these multi-institutional research projects, it is difficult to identify in what capacity the individual researcher is acting. In collaborative research projects that are based on ad hoc university partnerships and consortia, do project leaders and coordinators have special responsibilities vis-à-vis all research participants, regardless of their formal affiliations? This question is particularly important when some of the research partners have executive tasks of data collection and analysis. Moreover, peculiar configurations of responsibility may develop in situations of supervised research (that is, PhD candidates and postdoctoral researchers): although supervisors are not liable for the research conduct of the scholars they personally supervise, they are expected to train, advise and mentor supervisees and to equip them with methodological toolkits and awareness. Yet, '[s]upervisors are not safety experts' (Academics Anonymous, 2016), and the entire university body would seem to be called on to deploy its various structures and teams to provide training and support in these cases (for example, the information technology offices may be involved in digital security training). Hence, duty-of-care requirements for universities might end up pushing frontier research towards less regulated (frequently business-oriented) contexts through dynamics that resemble those characterizing the privatization of the security and military industry (for example Amoore, 2001).

In light of these conditions, the extent to which funding bodies should be held accountable for demanding grant recipients to ensure research participants' safety and security remains an open question. However, the fact that many junior and senior researchers depend on research grants that are awarded from outside their home institutions has given rise to mechanisms that are similar to those PhD students and early-career postdocs enact when submitting ethical review applications to evaluation boards. For example, applicants to EU-funded research schemes and grants are required to plan all aspects of data collection in detail well in advance of the research project's start date and to comply with the ethics appraisal reports released by European Commission experts for every EU-sponsored research project. The application package thus includes an ethics self-assessment, a questionnaire based on sets of guidelines 'designed to help applicants in getting your proposal "ethics-ready"'. The questionnaire is not specifically conceived for one discipline or another; it includes questions about researcher interactions with 'human participants', 'personal data collection and/ or processing' (although the notion of personal data itself has rather different meanings in different scholarly fields) and 'the involvement of non-EU countries' (this latter seems to point to social science fieldwork). EU guidelines acknowledge that social science research often involves working with human participants and particular methodological tools (such as interviews, focus groups, observation, surveys, and ethnography); they also include a rather advanced statement[12] that may reflect researchers' reluctance to see their practices increasingly disciplined by the proliferation of 'codes of conduct': 'The kinds of risk to researcher safety vary according to the nature of the discipline, the topic and the research site. Only the "researcher in the field" can fully assess safety concerns and/or their willingness to tolerate risks' (European Commission, 2019: 30).

However, other instructions resulting from the guidelines do replicate the mentioned disconnect between the external requirements researchers are asked to follow and their actual practices. For example, they specify that written informed consent—a practice that is clearly derived from the medical field but often impossible to even conceive while doing fieldwork in the social sciences—be obtained as a precondition for interacting with human participants. Exemptions must be thoroughly justified and, in any case, 'consent must be formally documented and independently witnessed' (European Commission, 2019: 8). Furthermore, sending researchers to non-EU countries entails specific risk-assessment procedures and the adoption of safety measures such as insurance coverage, 'no lone working, contact points via phone, [and] counselling support' (European Commission, 2019: p. 27). A list of 'health and safety' indications is specifically provided by the European Commission (2019: 31) for 'research "in the field"':

- keeping careful notes of all research engagements;
- ensuring projects are adequately staffed;
- using mobile phones to keep in touch with the research base;
- conducting full risk assessments of fieldwork sites;
- formally notifying authorities of research being conducted in an area;
- carrying authorised identification;
- researcher preparation and training covering techniques; for handling conflict, threats, abuse or compromising situations;
- debriefing after field research with an assessment of fieldwork safety; and
- reporting any health and safety incidents.

Moreover, research carried out in a non-EU country is required to comply with that country's legal obligations, a requirement that deserves at least some attempt at problematization if we consider the increasing number of countries in which scholarly activities are sometimes considered a threat to national security if not explicitly criminalized. Legal obligations in destination countries often vary quite a bit, and not necessarily in a way that any researcher, or supervisor, would be able to detect: for example, some countries targeted by multiple research initiatives have introduced the requirement that scholars secure and carry a 'research permit'[13] through a procedure that typically involves listing local partners, but experience has shown that the how, where and when of obtaining such permits may depend on who you ask: cumbersome bureaucratic procedures and local facilitators do not necessarily contribute to anyone's safety.

While we acknowledge that guidelines and codes of conduct may potentially contribute to researchers' endeavours to reflect on their role and position in research activities, and we certainly do not seek to encourage foreign researchers to bypass local administrative regulations, attempts to regulate research remain controversial. More specifically, we believe that it is high time to problematize the nexus between researcher safety, on the one hand, and the growing regulation and traceability/accountability/auditability/predictability of research routines, on the other. Our experience seems to confirm that researchers are likely to rely on the informal habits they developed by imitating practices already modelled by senior colleagues/supervisors. Furthermore, for a significant number of researchers we have interviewed/contacted, the main risk they encountered while conducting fieldwork comes directly from local security apparatuses and their surveillance/policing practices; therefore, researchers quite often prefer to keep as low a profile as possible while in the field (see also Driscoll, in this volume). Unfortunately, regulatory codes seem to conflict with researchers' preferred reliance on informal habits and discreet behaviours in requiring that everything happening in the field be 'reportable', a state of affairs that is not always either feasible or advisable. For example, in some fields the safest way to travel is to be escorted by a local fixer—a figure that the cited regulatory frameworks certainly have not taken into account (see also Bøås, in this volume). From a broader, epistemological perspective, the move to delimit fieldwork research to a 'special domain' calling for tailored health and safety requirements might actually feed ongoing patterns of essentialization, exoticization/orientalization and fetishization of 'the local' (on the different reasons for and effects of the problem of access to insecure areas, see also Peter, in this volume).

Side effects of regulation

The regulation of fieldwork research seems to be implicitly related to other emergent aspects of organizing research trips and missions, while at the same time ensuring the security of researchers and research participants. As mentioned, informal acquaintance-type relationships with individual fixers appear to be less and less compatible with the ethics and health-and-safety requirements demanded by university boards and funding agencies; however, travel security services are often outsourced to private providers for trusted-traveller programmes, consular facilitation, logistical assistance and so on. Therefore, fixer agencies might slowly replace individual fixers in providing field assistance (interpreters, translators, drivers) and a wide range of other services from arranging accommodation and transfers to research sites to setting up interviews, liaising with local networks and contacts, and offering insights on political, social and economic issues—and they will issue an invoice for it (Strazzari and Peter, 2016). The increasing involvement of these academic travel agencies and tour operators has the potential to transform fieldwork research into safely packaged ethnography, or at least lead to the homogenization of targeted interlocutors as well as site saturation. Further, the development of a micro-political economy around foreign researchers' visits might amplify the forms of bias that already exist in the collection of self-reported data (social desirability bias, that is the tendency of respondents to answer questions in a manner that will be perceived favourably; the 'interviewer-expectancy effect').

Similarly to the fact that the role of on-site fixers becomes more and more professionalized, other venues and elements found in the field seem to be undergoing a parallel process of professionalization: on the one hand, the European Commission encourages funding recipients to appoint or recruit ethics advisors, that is experts who provide advice on research ethics to individual researchers, research groups or project consortium partners in the context of EU-financed projects (European Commission, 2012). As pointed out by Leese, Lidén and Nikolova (2012: 66), ethics advisors have been conceptualized on the basis of an odd definition of ethics, reduced to 'matters as legal compliance of technical activities and formalized aspects of research governance, such as informed consent agreements or data protection documentation'; at the same time, the move to bring in specialists to handle the critical dimensions of a research project confirm the already noted tendency to outsource and 'segment' the process of knowledge production.

In a similar vein, the European Commission's guidelines on how to complete a project ethics self-assessment recommend involving an appropriate data protection officer, a newly created practitioner tasked with supervising a research project's compliance with the General Data Protection Regulation (GDPR). The field of digital security is particularly emphasized as a focal aspect of research security. Needless to say, the adoption of the GDPR involves additional costs for research institutes.

A third instance of professionalization and outsourcing can be seen in the tendency for universities to decouple the procedure for securing permission or approval before going ahead with planned field research, making it into a two-stage process. On the one side, the ethics review process remains entangled in academic bureaucracies, continuing to be governed by the university itself; on the other side, insurance policy and risk management measures are subsumed under a 'health-and-safety perspective' and often outsourced to consultancies and private firms (for example, Drum Cussac, Control Risks). The latter deliver ratings based on country risk indicators, offer travel security advice, and provide intelligence and logistics services. Nonetheless, the resulting maps, databases and analyses appear to be produced by 'experts' who either rely on remote desk research or make use of knowledge generated by (local?) researchers whose own fieldwork in no-go areas is likely to lie in a grey zone in terms of duty of care. As a result, the researchers that we have interviewed unanimously complain about the shallowness of the risk-analysis reports associated with their mission requests on the part of external consultancies.

Overall, we can say that ongoing regulation tends to transform fieldwork research into a distinctive professional practice: for 'safety and security reasons', actual contact with the object of study might be reduced to short visits, predictable itineraries and encounters mediated by a host of service providers, thereby making gatekeeping functions into a business (Duffield, 2014). Given increasingly strict regulatory frameworks, 'research safety and security' may eventually come to represent a privatized and commercialized good; in addition, the obligation to comply with the administrative and bureaucratic requirements established by the host country add a further layer of complexity. While there is no doubt that research activities must be lawful in principle, it is not uncommon for state authorities, officials, security services and bureaucrats at different latitudes to increasingly deploy very different tools to deter and/or repress the freedom of research and, ultimately, ward off the scientific disclosure of certain areas, countries and sites. On the one hand, disregarding local rules may be a first source of fieldwork risk and mistrust among local acquaintances and networks; on the other, researchers specifically may be over-exposed to screening and profiling practices.

Conclusion

Our interactions with peers and colleagues and our own experience point to a generalized dissatisfaction among researchers vis-à-vis the regulations designed to make research less dangerous and more accountable. The emerging security regimes set up with the intent of making research safer do not entirely reflect the realities of social science research and/or researchers' perceptions and practices: for example, collaborative research seems increasingly to be the preferred format, both to attract resources and to achieve substantial scientific advancement. Research activities are thus embedded in and conducted across different regulatory contexts and asked to abide by a multiplicity of possibly conflicting protocols.

Moreover, the emerging safety and security regime appears to be disconnected from capacity-building and providing instruments that would enable researchers to develop ethnographic sensitivity and cultural awareness, as well as engage in collective self-reflection. The notions, concepts and categories used to design regulatory frameworks are either transposed from other disciplinary fields, accountable to external actors (funding bodies, insurance companies) or end up being imposed on researchers without continuously incorporating their feedback. Alternative concepts and instruments have been tentatively embraced by some scholarly networks and collectives; however, statisticians, accountants and actuaries calculating the risks of 'unsafe research' seem to enjoy more authority and legitimacy with university institutions, administrations, funders and international agencies than scholars do.[14] Still, notions such as 'responsibility to protect' applied to research and academic freedom might complement the adoption of the duty of care, mitigating its effects by making safe research a shared commitment rather than the mere output of a protocol.

While senior scholars' prior fieldwork experience and familiarity with university bureaucracies are valuable assets in muddling through authorization and assessment procedures, junior researchers and PhD students seem to suffer more from the over-regulation and regimentation of fieldwork research, not only because their research is conditioned by paperwork and assessed by reviewers who are not area specialists, but also because ethical-approval procedures are often one-sided. They are not living documents that can be adapted to the changing situations researchers may encounter while carrying out fieldwork. The resulting feeling of discomfort generates collective engagement and calls for flexible and tailored trainings as well as the provision of assistance during and after fieldwork (including, for example, psychological support to researchers exposed to post-traumatic stress disorder). The difficulty is that researchers' preferences are both costly and unwieldy in relation to the quantifiable indicators typical of risk-assessment procedures.

In looking at the way this field evolves over the long term, our criticism is therefore two-fold: on the one hand, research feasibility and riskiness are a priori assessed by statisticians, accountants and experts who promise to 'secure knowledge extraction, processing and production' but have little knowledge of how knowledge is extracted, processed and produced in a fieldwork context; on the other hand, fieldwork research seems to be increasingly moulded by self-encapsulation and bunkerization processes that can only result in the narrowing of its potential as a method to study social change, in the sense of both geographical and cognitive delimitation.

Notes

1. For updated documentation on recent and ongoing attacks, see Scholars at Risk, Academic Freedom Monitor: http://monitoring.academicfreedom.info.
2. Human rights organizations have documented systematic rocket or air strike attacks on schools in different armed conflict zones, including the Palestinian occupied territories, Syria, Ukraine, and—more recently—Yemen. It is widely documented that governmental armed forces as well as non-state armed groups and even multinational forces and peacekeepers have used schools and other education institutions for military purposes: armed personnel take over these places and 'use them as barracks, logistic bases, operational headquarters, weapons and ammunition caches, detention and interrogation centers, firing and observation positions, and recruitment grounds' (GCPEA, 2015).
3. A case displaying some similar traits is the one involving Alexander Sodiqov (see Heathershaw and Mullojonov, in this volume). Other recent cases raising similar concerns are those of Homa Hoodfar and Matthew Hedges, to just mention a few. In June 2016, Homa Hoodfar, an anthropologist at the Montreal-based Concordia University specializing in sexuality and gender in Islam and holding both Canadian and Iranian passports, was detained in Tehran's Evin prison. In May 2018, Matthew Hedges, a PhD student at Durham University, was arrested in Dubai and accused of espionage; initially sentenced to life imprisonment, he was eventually pardoned.
4. In May 2016, the Pisa-based university Sant'Anna School of Advanced Studies organized an event in support of Amnesty International's campaign 'Truth for Giulio Regeni' (workshop 'La ricerca accademica sul campo: rischi e responsabilità'). In October 2016, the workshop 'Riflettere e coordinarsi. Giornata di studio per la tutela della libertà di ricerca e dell'etnografia' took place at the University of Modena and Reggio Emilia. In January 2018, the workshop 'Conducting social science research in risky environments' was held at the European University Institute.
5. 'SAFEResearch' is funded by the Swedish Research Council and coordinated by Jannis Grimm (Freie Universität Berlin), Kevin Koehler (King's College London), Ellen Lust and Isabell Schierenbeck (Gothenburg University), and Ilyas Saliba (WZB Berlin Social Science Center).
6. For a broader consideration of these processes, see Cuono (2013).

7   As members of the task force set up by our home institution to design a fieldwork research policy, we examined a core sample of universities where some of our international research collaborations are based (so that we could gather information through directly accessible informants).
8   On the introduction of the 'audit culture' into universities see Strathern (2000); Shore (2008).
9   For example, in the UK, the Committee of Vice-Chancellors and Principals, the Universities and Colleges Employers' Association, the Universities Safety and Health Association, which respectively articulated the Code of Practice for Safety in Fieldwork, in 1995, and the UCEA/USHA Guidance on health and safety in fieldwork in 2005 and in 2011.
10 See Council directive 89/391/EEC.
11 This also derives from the fact that the academic job market encourages researcher mobility, a trend that in turn renders departments and research programmes increasingly multinational.
12 European Code of Conduct for Research Integrity (by the European Federation of Academies of Sciences and Humanities); Global code of conduct for research in resource-poor settings (whose development has received funding from the European Union's Horizon 2020 research and innovation programme through the project 'Trust: Equitable Research Partnership'); European Commission's Guidance note—Research on refugees, asylum seekers and migrants; Ethics in Social Science and Humanities (drafted by a panel of experts at the request of the European Commission); Code of Practice for the Safety of Social Researchers (by Social Research Association).
13 While not explicitly referring to 'research permits', Russian authorities appear to have recently ratcheted up bureaucratic pressure on foreign scholars. In 2015 four of them have reported having been fined, deported or threatened with these penalties while conducting academic research in Russia due to alleged visa violations, that is using business and tourist visas instead of humanitarian visas. While the former can be obtained quickly and directly from a travel agency, the latter require a host institution in Russia (Schreck, 2015).
14 One quasi-isolated example is the lecture delivered by Seyed Masoud Noori in October 2015, titled 'Global human rights today colloquium series: shared responsibility to protect academic freedom', (see Scholars at Risk: www.scholarsatrisk.org/event/shared-responsibility-to-protect-academic-freedom/).

References

Academics Anonymous (2016) 'Universities must do more to protect PhD students working in dangerous countries', *The Guardian*, 13 May.

Ahram, A.I. and Goode, J.P. (2016) 'Researching authoritarianism in the discipline of democracy', *Social Science Quarterly*, 97(4): 834–49.

Amoore, L. (2001) 'Data derivatives on the emergence of a security risk calculus for our times', *Theory, Culture and Society*, 28(6): 24–43.

Cuono, M. (2013) 'Bureaucratiser l'inégal, l'extraordinaire, le particulier. Paternalisme et dépolitisation à l'époque néolibérale', in B. Hibou (ed.), *La bureaucratisation néolibérale*, Paris: Éditions La Découverte, pp 177–202.

de Guttry, A. and Capone, F. (2017) 'Do universities have a duty of care towards their employees and students when they travel abroad on university business? A critical analysis of the state-of-the-art and the relevant practice', *Interdisciplinary Political Studies*, 3(1): 11–39.

Duffield, M. (2014) 'From immersion to simulation: remote methodologies and the decline of area studies', *Review of African Political Economy*, 41(1): 75–94.

European Commission (2012) 'Roles and functions of ethics advisors/ethics advisory boards in EC-funded projects', Brussels: European Commission.

European Commission (2019) 'Horizon 2020 Programme Guidance How to complete your ethics self-assessment', Brussels: European Commission.

Frediani, E. (2017) 'La valutazione del rischio da ricerca universitaria all'estero: un "problema" in cerca di regole', *Diritto e Società*, 1(1): 321–48.

Global Coalition to Protect Education from Attack (2015) *Lessons in War: Military use of schools and universities during armed conflict*, www.protectingeducation.org/sites/default/files/documents/lessons_in_war_2015.pdf.

Kumkova, K. (2014) 'Canadian researcher released after five weeks in Tajikistan jail', *The Guardian*, 24 July.

Leese, M., Lidén, K. and Nikolova, B. (2019) 'Putting critique to work: Ethics in EU security research', *Security Dialogue*, 50(1): 59–76.

Russo, A. (2017) 'Decontaminating the university — or the cognitive repression of radical thinking', *Security Praxis*, 6 April.

SAFEResearch (n.d.) SAFEResearch Handbook, https://gld.gu.se/en/conferences/saferesearch-handbook/.

Schrag, Z.M. (2010) *Ethical Imperialism: Institutional Review Boards and the Social Sciences, 1965–2009*, Baltimore, MD: JHU Press.

Schreck, C. (2015) 'Western scholars alarmed by Russian deportations, fines', *Radio Free Europe/Radio Liberty*, 31 March 2015.

Shore, C. (2008) 'Audit culture and illiberal governance: universities and the politics of accountability', *Anthropological Theory*, 8(3): 278–98.

Strathern, M. (2000) 'The tyranny of transparency', *British Educational Research Journal*, 26(3): 309–21.

Strazzari, F. and Peter, M. (2016) 'Securitisation of research: fieldwork under new restrictions in Darfur and Mali', *Third World Quarterly*, 38(7): 1531–50.

7

The Politics and Ethics of Fieldwork in Post-conflict Environments: The Dilemmas of a Vocational Approach

John Heathershaw and Parviz Mullojonov[1]

On 16 June 2014, Alexander Sodiqov was arrested by the security services while conducting fieldwork in Khorog, Tajikistan. He was interviewing an opposition leader who had been involved in a protest movement at the time he was arrested. Alex was subsequently charged with espionage offences and detained in a high security prison by the State Committee on National Security (SCNS) of the Republic of Tajikistan, a country which has seen intermittent political violence since the formal end of its civil war in 1997. At the time he was a PhD student at the University of Toronto and working with us on an Economic and Social Research Council (ESRC) project based at the University of Exeter studying conflict management in Central Asia. Having been charged under article 305 of the criminal code, he faced the likely prospect of a prison sentence of up to 20 years on his conviction. A global campaign was launched and, on 23 July, Alex was freed on bail but remained under investigation. On 10 September, he was allowed to leave the country and arrived back in Canada, where he still resides. While Alex was freed, the investigation was not formally discontinued; the repercussions of the case for his family and friends have continued and the chilling effect on academic research in particular and civil society in Tajikistan in general are still apparent.

The case proved to be a turning point in the relationship between local academic community and authorities. It was consistent with increasing authoritarianism in Tajikistan, which was apparent long before 2014, and from which, as Alex's case proved, academics are not insulated. However, after 2014 this repression apparently assumed a more organized and structural character. The international controversy and wider criticism caused by Alex's arrest appeared to change the state's attitude and policy towards the Tajik academic sector. As a result, the authorities have introduced a set of new restrictions on academic activities and structures in Tajikistan. For instance, field trips and research on the ground (such as opinion polls, interviews), have become the subject of severe control and excessive scrutiny. The government has considerably tightened and lengthened the process of approval and agreeing on conducting academic research. The investigation continued for several years—and may still be officially open. Alex was never formally acquitted and the security agency never admitted the illegality of his detention. Moreover, security officials continued interrogation of several specialists and young experts, both those connected to our project and those without any such links.

Alex's case raises questions of the ethical challenges and responsibilities of conducting fieldwork in post-conflict environments (PCE), broadly conceived as including conflict and potential conflict settings (Monk 2014). There has been exponential growth in the field of Peace and Conflict Studies since the end of the Cold War driven by a vast increase in development assistance and peacebuilding programming by Western agencies and a concomitant expansion of academic interest and research. This growth has been particularly acute in conflict-affected countries of the post-Soviet space as it was only in the late 1980s with the fracture and then break-up of the USSR that they opened up to aid and research. It is no surprise that such research may be viewed with suspicion and often through the prism of global geopolitics, especially by state officials. Funded by Western organizations, accessing PCEs through such organizations, asking questions that are only meaningful in Western academic and policy contexts, and working with locals as assistants and translators, the power relations of peace research are self-evident. In cases where researchers, either policy-focused or academic, are blithe to these dependencies and tensions, the hypocrisy is enormous. While aware of these issues in advance of Alex's arrest, and having taken measures to gain permission and consent for the research, as the principal investigator of the project, Heathershaw was partly responsible for the circumstances that led to his detainment.[2]

A growing number of authors directly address the profound political and ethical questions raised by such research. Yet for most researchers written reflections upon ethics are confined to the methods appendices of PhDs and brief notes in the introductions of monographs based on data collected via fieldwork in PCEs. In his 2009 book, Heathershaw provided the barest of ethical reflections and was subsequently and rightly challenged about his positionality in a forum on the book in a 2010 issue of the journal *Central Asian Survey* (Megoran et al, 2010: 227). 'Conflict and methodology are usually analysed as separate fields of interest,' remark Cohen and Arieli (2011: 423). 'Methodological aspects of field work in conflict environments have not been systematically analysed' (Cohen and Arieli, 2011: 423). Yet risks associated with ongoing political violence, poor levels of public health, weak or non-existent emergency services and (as in the Alexander Sodiqov case) uncertain and often predatory actions of political authorities are abundant (Nordstrom & Robben, 1996). Research on PCEs is increasingly demonstrating that, far from the liberal peace envisaged in the 1990s, an illiberal or victors' peace often ensues. For such states and their insecure governments, the control of knowledge and communication in and about the PCE is a key task. In such an environment, researchers may find themselves spuriously identified as enemies of the state.

However, this is not the only context in which research faces 'political', legal and ethical risk. All research on 'human subjects' at US and UK universities does. In recent years a debate has emerged in the academy over the status of the Internal Review Board (IRB) or Research Ethics Committee (REC) in approving (and disapproving) academic research. Critics have accused REC/IRB members of being ignorant of the culture and politics of the research site and therefore unable to make reasonable judgments (Clark, 2006; CESS, 2016), misapplying principles of natural or medical sciences to social scientific sciences (Yanow and Schwartz-Shea, 2008) and taking a risk-averse approach in order to protect the reputation and provide legal cover to the institution, among other failings. Such accusations particularly come from those conducting qualitative fieldwork outside of Western democracies and often in difficult political environments. Each of these accusations has some merit.

This chapter reflects on this problematic in light of the emergent literature on research ethics in PCEs and our personal experience during our fieldwork in PCEs, especially Tajikistan in 2014. Writing the paper together allows us to reflect together on differentiated risk faced by locally based researchers such as Mullojonov, compared to Western-based researchers such as Heathershaw, with the relative security afforded by their foreign passports and tenure at elite universities overseas. This chapter's source material includes a paper initially drafted by Heathershaw in the aftermath of the events of 2014 as well as Mullojonov's own reflections on those events. While this event was exceptional, and risk is differentiated, we argue that many of the ethical challenges faced by researchers in PCEs are simply slightly different and sometimes more acute versions of problems faced in all fieldwork in 'developing countries' and even 'advanced industrialised democracies'. Issues such as informed consent, confidentiality and anonymity, and research with children and vulnerable groups, pose ethical problems in all contexts. It is the argument of this chapter that ethical questions in research in PCEs are, like all other questions in these contexts, highly politicized questions. In general, in many post-conflict societies the risk is shared not only by directly engaged researchers but by the wider circles of partially or occasionally involved persons such as interpreters, assistants, helpers and participants. The authorities tend to view research projects as political projects, putting at risk all involved. It is this confluence of politics and ethics that throws up the tension between 'procedural ethics' and 'ethics in practice' and highlights that ethical questions remain fraught and unanswered throughout research rather than resolved by the institutional review processes.

Five ethical challenges that are particularly acute in the case of research in PCEs are elaborated across five sections of this chapter:

(1) *Safety* and the dilemma whether to conduct research at all (with a particular look at the use of travel advisories for researcher safety): Is the priority to do no harm (to ourselves or to others) even if this leads to seeing no evil?
(2) *Positionality* and the trade-off between access and impartiality: What are the responsibilities to communicate findings to the participants' community and what implications may that have for local researchers and the participants themselves?
(3) *Permission* and the tension between attained official approval and official surveillance: Should official approval be attained even if this endangers the anonymity, confidentiality and safety of research participants?
(4) *Consent* and the dilemma of overt versus covert approaches: How much do you reveal to your participants and do you provide information and seek consent in writing?
(5) *Collaboration* and the dilemma of meaningful co-production versus sensible distancing within teams of locals and foreign citizens: Do the ethical and practical maxims of collaborative research supersede the threat to local researcher safety that such collaboration brings?

Together these individual dilemmas raise a greater problem where acting ethically with respect to one question may require acting unethically with respect to another. The dilemmas are irreducible by formal ethics review procedures and can only be addressed contingently and imperfectly in practice.

Procedural versus practical ethics

Defenders of ethics committees and the bureaucratic approach offer a *procedure-based* account of research ethics in practice. They assert that procedures set the ethical parameters within which research is conducted and reduce the risk of unethical research. Specific context here is superseded by general standard. Farrimond (2013: 42, emphasis added) notes that, 'institutions often create *robust standardised ethical procedures* to avoid a committee having to discuss every single instance of very similar research'. Such proceduralist approaches are not abstracted from practice but, its advocates argue, 'something you do' (Farrimond, 2013: 14–15, 3). Procedure, it is implied, does not reduce this risk to zero but it diminishes any ethical dilemmas to questions that can be resolved via procedural measures.

Despite sharing fundamental objections to this context-free approach, during the detention of Alexander Sodiqov a more positive side of this procedural ethics was visible, where the ethics certificate achieved in the review process provided both legal cover and insurance for the university to devote hundreds of staff hours to securing the release of a member of our research team. However, both before and after the detention of Alex, the research team faced difficult ethical and practical challenges for which our ethics frameworks were either irrelevant or inadequate. In short, whatever the formal ethics review procedures achieved, they did not foreclose the ethics dilemmas of the research, which proved ongoing, immutable and unresolvable.

From the perspective of practice, 'ethics' may easily become a box-ticking exercise; quite the reverse of the stated intentions of ethics committees and responsible researchers. The nature of ethics in practice—the highly politicized context of research and the need for the use of discretion in the face of moral dilemmas—is rarely addressed. Carpenter comments critically on the role of REC/IRBs in assessing fieldwork in conflict zones: the process is largely designed not to protect human subjects, but to protect universities from malpractice suits, where 'neither the training nor the oversight is of much relevance to scholars conducting interviews among traumatized or violently divided populations in post-conflict societies' (Carpenter, 2012: 370;

cf. Bahttacharya, 2014; Marshall, 2003). These fundamental concerns about REC/IRBs are not confined to research in PCEs. Yanow and Schwartz-Shea (2008: 490) have argued forcefully that the medical ethics and experimental conditions presumed by review boards begin from premises that are simply inconsistent with fieldwork-based research that involves the researcher entering into the world of the research participant rather than the other way around.

To their critics, proceduralist approaches may create new risks, or be irrelevant to research in practice, but most importantly they are simply unable to reduce ethical dilemmas. These critics adopt a praxis-based approach to ethics. Ethics is both a practical and pragmatic activity that requires difficult decisions throughout the life-cycle of research. In this approach, contextual judgments of conscience and discretion supersede an abstract and general set of rules. The lawyer and theologian William Stringfellow (2004: 27) argues that 'ethical deliberation originates vocationally' whereby, 'any ethical system which is settled and stereotyped, uniform and preclusive, neat and predictable is both dehumanising and pagan'. With Stringfellow, and an emerging number of voices in the policy-practice and academic study of PCEs, we argue that a praxis-based approach to research ethics by scholars is necessarily vocational (Bush and Duggan, 2013; Fujii, 2012; Yanow and Schwartz-Shea, 2008). As Fujii (2012: 717) argues, 'ethics is an ongoing responsibility, not a discrete task to be checked off a "to do" list'. A vocational approach is attendant to wider political and ethical questions that lie beyond the formal requirements and, for example, may include the structural inequities of research funding and projects between Global North and Global South, as is apparent in Central Asian Studies (Kuzhabekova, 2020; Sabzalieva, 2020).

In the following, we discuss the five dilemmas identified, which indicate that procedure-based approaches to ethics have intended and unintended consequences, which can be both ethically positive and negative. Moreover, these procedures do not reduce, to any great degree, the need for difficult judgments to be made in practice and with conscience and discretion. However, there is a risk that scholars as responsible professionals may be left high and dry by an approach that disregards proceduralist approaches to ethics. The succeeding analysis therefore seeks to delimit the proper place of ethics committees in sanctioning research and sharing responsibility for it. As Bhattacharya (2014: 842) notes, 'the institution must share equal and, in some cases, greater responsibility in being reflexive about "how" individuals should be involved in research, especially in politically vulnerable areas across the world'.

1. Safety: 'do no harm' or 'see no evil'?

'Do no harm' is a principle applied from medicine to both humanitarianism and research but one that has been placed under threat by the radicalization of aid as most famously represented in the emergence of Médecins Sans Frontières from the International Committee of the Red Cross. In contemporary PCEs both aid workers and researchers entering the field are more likely to be associated with a political agenda and risk their research being used as 'intelligence' by that side (Black, 2003: 103). The fact that academia and journalism are both used as recruiting grounds and cover stories for some Western spies makes the accusation of espionage against them at least plausible (Lashmar, 2017). Moreover, their participants and collaborators face specific threats from being part of a project that is perceived in this way. For some journalists, and perhaps some academics, this must be balanced against the concern that risk-reducing strategies of staying in the capital, embedding with occupying forces or being escorted by host governments risk the concern of 'seeing no evil'. But this is a stylized debate that conceals more complicated dilemmas in practice. Wilson (cit. in Black, 2003: 99) argues that 'researching in an "ethical manner" seems not about proclaiming good and evil, but about enabling the reader to hear the voices and appreciate the actions of as many of the different people involved as possible'. Journalism and academia are both criticized for the 'extractive' nature of what they do in taking information from PCEs rather than providing assistance (Black, 2003: 100). There are also very real methodological weaknesses associated with this extractive exercise where confirmation and selection biases combine with an insufficiency of time and space for research (Haer and Becher, 2012; Jessee, 2011; Reed, 2012; Vlassennroot, 2006).

In the ethical and political environment in PCEs where there is a large presence by the 'international community' it may be the UN and major donors as well as the host government, one's scholarly community, funders and publishers that shape the professional environment. The ability to attain a visa and where one can travel in the country are often determined by security levels agreed between agencies and with local authorities. Foreign ministry travel advices against 'non-essential' travel are set accordingly and can make travel insurance and approval by REC/IRB difficult, if not impossible. Travel advisories are further politicized by the relations between the two states in question and risk adding many PCEs to fieldwork blacklists. 'Local knowledge', while much more specific and sometimes more helpful, can often contradict these advisories. It is also partial and limited, where one piece of local knowledge may quite frequently conflict with another (Helbardt, 2010: 351).

A brief summary of the circumstances immediately prior to and at the time of Alex's arrest in 2014 highlights some of the uncertainties around the assessment of risk in general and the use of travel advisories in particular. On 21–22 May 2014, while we were conducting research in a neighbouring region of Tajikistan, there was a violent incident in Khorog that led to two deaths. Foreign embassies in Tajikistan—fearful that the situation may worsen—advised their nationals not to travel and the government stopped issuing permits for the region. However, by early June, the situation had calmed, the government started reissuing permits and almost all foreign travel warnings had been lifted. The UK government position was the exception. On 11 June, the UK changed its travel advice again to advise against non-essential travel by British nationals (apparently due to a security warning the UK ambassador received personally on his own visit to the region on 10–11 June when he was asked to leave, with the stated reason being the situation in Afghanistan). The UK's was the only embassy to do so and foreign tourists, including some Britons, continued to travel to and be welcomed into the region.

However, it is perhaps the Tajik government's perception of threat that is most relevant in assessing risk to researchers.[3] We may identify three sources of heightened fear. First, one of the government's long-standing concerns, which was been heightened during and since 2014, has been the deterioration of the political and military situation in northern Afghanistan, where several thousand Central Asian radicals have established their military bases and strongholds. Second, the deepening social and economic crisis that resulted in a shrinking of labour migration and unprecedented reduction of international remittances has also increased their threat perceptions. Finally, the tendency to see geopolitics as a 'Great Game' of intrigue and counter-intrigue—long a feature of elite political imaginaries—has perhaps been accentuated by the confrontation between Russia, its former imperial power, and Western states, from which most research projects involving Tajik academics hail. As a result, the Tajik authorities have undertaken a number of measures aimed at increasing control over society. One of the government's measures is to restrict academic freedom that it regards as a potential source of destabilization. In this regard, intellectuals, experts and academics are placed under specific scrutiny and pressure. This is especially relevant with regard to conflict studies and explorations of that social and economic situation in the country where any deviation from official interpretation is rarely tolerated.

This heightened threat perception makes the arrest and detention of our colleague in 2014 more explicable. Unfortunately, however, procedural approaches are unable to assess shifting and hard-to-ascertain threat perceptions of host authorities. There are three versions of the reasons for the case proposed by our local colleagues in Tajikistan. First, Alex's arrest was the initiative of the Khorogh (Kuhistani Badakhshan Autonomous Region, GBAO) branch of the Tajik SCNS undertaken without properly informing the central office in Dushanbe. The leadership of local SCNS office desired the kudos of disclosing an 'international spy network' without taking into consideration potential outcomes and international complications. Second, some civic activists in GBAO believe that the Tajik authorities were preparing a large-scale police operation in GBAO aimed at destroying local opposition and arresting several senior informal leaders. Allegedly, the police operation was scheduled in June—just prior Alex's arrival to the region. The proponents of this version believe that the primary goal was not Alex but the person he was meeting—Alim Sherzamonov, one of the local civic leaders. According to this version, the SCNS sought to accuse Sherzamonov of working for foreign intelligence. The subsequent international scandal and attention have forced the authorities to release Alex and to drop the charges against Sherzamonov—as well as to cancel the police operation. The third version is that Tajik authorities used the case as a pretext to increase pressure on civic institutions and especially on local academic and expert society. In this regard, the case was just a part of the more profound and long-term process of squeezing public space and academic freedom in the country.

This summary of the case and its possible explanations highlights several aspects of the dilemma of assessing risk. The general level of violence in the region was low and the politically motivated targeting of researchers in this region of Tajikistan was unprecedented. Uncertainty over the travel advice, and its highly politicized nature, make it a poor mechanism for the assessment of risk, which is often highly contingent. Had all research by all members of the team, regardless of their nationality, been abandoned, the arrest would not have occurred. In hindsight, this would have been the better option. However, we had spent many months preparing for the work and only had a matter of weeks to conduct a few dozen key-informant interviews. Expedience trumped caution—wrongly in this case.

Hindsight is a wonderful thing. On the other hand, its nearest equivalent in real time, cautious counterfactual reasoning, provides a recipe for inaction in a PCE. If all the attention of ethical consideration is focused on reducing harm to researchers and participants to negligible levels, then the ethical imperative of 'enabling the reader to hear the voices and appreciate the actions of as many of the different people involved as possible' would once again be stymied. Indeed, if travel advisories were rigorously followed, most fieldwork-based conflict research would be impossible and vast swathes of the world would be out of bounds to ethnography. The consequences of this for our ability to understand political violence by state and non-state actors would be catastrophic, as academic research would essentially be confined to an analysis of fragmentary secondary sources of journalists and diplomats or macro-scale data analysis. There is of course a danger here of presenting research as heroic and one's own work as particularly important (Helbardt et al, 2010). Improving our knowledge of PCEs is both an academic and ethical imperative but not one that can simply be balanced against the countervailing ethical requirement to do no harm in our research.

2. Positionality: access to the field versus partiality of research

A related problem to that of whether to conduct research at all is that of how one is politically and ethically positioned once one is at work. Positionality is a particularly acute concern in PCEs. The distinction between independent academic and contracted policy-practice researchers is often hard to maintain given that academic researchers often rely on non-academic bodies for letters of invitation, liaison with the authorities and logistical support, thus sacrificing their independence (Black, 2003: 98, 102). As discussed under #1, the risk environment of academic research is determined as much by the bureaucratic processes of international donors and agencies as by 'objective' risk factors. Research always goes ahead in warzones and PCEs, but it does so according to these professional parameters. Even in so-called 'forgotten conflicts' with a high level of violence, like Liberia in the 1980s and 1990s, policy-practice research goes on and often provides the data and interviews used by academic researchers of PCEs (Black, 2003: 100–2). As such, the positionality of the researcher reflects the appointments one accepts and relationships one builds in order to gain access to the field. These inevitably compromise the impartiality of the research, as the findings are a product of both what one is able to observe and ask and how one is perceived by the participant. We should admit to bias—that is, make it visible—argue Helbardt et al (2010: 365), not claim to act with neutrality or even impartiality.

The politics and political struggles of research became acute during our experience of 2014 and, often unwittingly, in previous periods of fieldwork. The research team subsequently discovered that we had been under surveillance for, at least, several days before Alex's arrest and that at least one of our interviews in the capital Dushanbe had been observed and photographed by agents. For the security services of many post-conflict states, and particularly in post-Soviet political contexts, it may be assumed that a 'research project' is espionage on the part of foreign governments and civil society organizations that are seeking to oust their government. The complete failure to understand what academic research has repeatedly demonstrated—that the key actors in such revolts are always locals and that foreigners play a secondary role at best—is part of the rationale for this paranoid state thinking.

Our attempts to retain impartiality were further complicated by the impact agenda of UK funding agencies, including the ESRC which funded our project, and the Research Excellence Framework (REF). Our project was expected to influence policy and establish a variety of knowledge exchange relationships both in the UK and in the field. We had good connections with the UK Foreign and Commonwealth Office (FCO) and, given the impact agenda and risks of research, decided to attain visas for the two visiting UK researchers through the UK embassy in Tajikistan. During our research in country and on the project, we were introduced to senior Tajik officials by the ambassador and met with the locally recruited Tajik FCO and UK Department for International Development (DfID) staff. At the same time, we were working with a UK NGO and small Tajik NGO—both of which had been placed under a certain amount of bureaucratic pressure by the authorities in recent years. In the period 2000–2007, at the height of Western aid and the UN peacebuilding mission to Tajikistan, such activities and partnerships were commonplace and uncontroversial, but this had changed by 2014. Nevertheless, by operating above board and with a variety of different parts of government and civil society we had hoped to achieve something which the ESRC and the REF would count as 'impact'. Today, approval of all research projects not just by state educational institutions but by the law-enforcement agencies is routine. While nominal 'impact' can be claimed through these partnerships, such collaboration with foreign governmental and local law-enforcement agencies has the effect of making independent research difficult or impossible.

3. Permission: official approval versus official surveillance

REC/IRBs and ethics procedures often require researchers to gain permission from the relevant authorities. Gaining governmental permission for a multi-sited social science study is complicated; in most countries it is not legally or practically required and in some PCEs it is not practically possible. In some PCEs there are clear mechanisms in place for authorizing research, but these come with permission attached. Fujii recounts an example of this problematic from her field research in Rwanda where, on presenting her letter of authorization to the local authorities in one region, she was assigned a minder to accompany her on all her interviews. She was immediately put in a difficult position at her first interview with a person she had previously met and knew to be a person who 'would report to his superiors all that we had discussed'. Small talk took place in lieu of an interview and the field trip was curtailed (Fujii, 2012: 721).

Our project conducted research in five non-Western states: Russia, China, Kyrgyzstan, Tajikistan and Uzbekistan—in the latter three of these, work was conducted in PCEs. Mostly, this involves a number of short visits to each country rather than a sustained period of ethnographic fieldwork. However, we specifically requested visas for research and typically worked with local partners that formally and/or informally disclosed the purpose and some of the details of our research to the authorities. In Kyrgyzstan, our approach was more informal and localized. In Tajikistan, it was necessary to get a business visa for research and, in this case, a permit for Badakhshon. In Uzbekistan, explicit official authorization from three different parts of the state was required in order to conduct research. After meetings with the Uzbek embassy in London, and requests sent through the Academy of Sciences in Tashkent, our initial application was blocked before, after three years, being given official permission. By this time, our project, and its research funding to support the trip, was about to end.

Where official approval is attained, further problems of participant safety arise. State agencies often demand to see a list of interviewees and even make the arrangements for the interviews themselves. Such measures immediately endanger REC/IRB stipulations about anonymity and confidentiality. Authorities often insist that researchers receive an escort or work with certain assistants (handlers). The Central Asia specialist Shirin Akiner (2005) was allowed access to the Uzbek city of Andijon in the company of the region's governor, just days after a localized rebellion and massacre by state forces, to conduct an 'independent study', which became known in the academic community for the series of concerns it raised about access and impartiality. Participants who speak critically of the government out of bravery and/or political disposition may place themselves at great risk. In the worst-case scenario, a tightly delimited official permission may be used against research teams who have inadvertent contact with a non-approved person and most acutely against that person. This could be taken as prima facie evidence of deception and, therefore, espionage. Working in such circumstances, with permission, research either becomes invalid (as in Akiner's case) or puts participants at risk; in some cases, both may occur.

4. Consent: overt versus covert approaches to research

Informed consent is a fundamental principle of research ethics, which is often deemed inviolable by review boards. This creates problems for experimental research and ethnographic observations where informed consent is either inconsistent with those methods or practically impossible. Moreover, such an approach often assumes that an individual has the autonomy to enact consent. Ethics committees often insist on written consent from participants, a procedure that in many contexts reduces rather than increases trust between researcher and participant (Bhattacharya, 2014: 840). Obtaining informed consent constitutes a dilemma of research that extends across all research with human subjects, but is merely made more acute during fieldwork in PCEs.

Written consent forms seem to be much more about providing evidence to satisfy an audit culture than actually respecting the wishes, preferences and welfare of the research participant. 'Asking people to sign forms not only presumes literacy of certain kinds and degrees', Yanow and Schwartz-Shea (2008: 490) note; 'it also assumes that doing so is itself not potentially harmful including to the researcher who now possesses, in certain circumstances, potentially dangerous documents'. Such an expectation, they note, 'assumes "Western" middle class values as universal to participants in all research settings' and is apparently ignorant of how documentation is perceived by citizens who see documents used and abused against them by state authorities (Yanow and Schwartz-Shea, 2008: 490). Clark's (2006: 419–20) survey found a reluctance to use consent forms and even introductory letters, with snowballing and intermediaries more often used to make contacts and arrangements in conflict zones of the Middle East and establish trust.

In our research practice, we typically rely on oral informed consent and only use written consent forms with citizens of Western democracies who may expect such things and are unlikely to be placed at risk by them. In effect, as would necessarily be true for all but the most small-scale research, our topic is framed differently for different participants and audiences. For the ESRC project research in Tajikistan in 2013–15 we chose an overt approach of providing information sheets to participants and local officials, where appropriate, but specifically avoided requesting and keeping consent forms, which we felt may deter our participants and, in the worst-case scenario, put them at risk. As it turned out, the information forms about the project carried by Alex were used against him as evidence of espionage by interrogators, but the lack of written materials from interviews proved crucial in protecting prior interviewees. Many researchers undertaking their research in Tajikistan—and in similarly difficult research environments known to us—follow a similar approach in protecting the personalities and data of interviewees.

In 2003–05 in Tajikistan and Uzbekistan, during an earlier period of research when the political environment was more conducive and the research environment less constrained, Heathershaw refrained from using written consent forms and practised anonymization with his local participants. However, with regard to expatriate NGO workers, he did use consent forms and, with their permission, used their names in his published work (Heathershaw, 2009). Like Fujii (2012), he now regrets these decisions, which caused some concern in one prominent NGO, several of whose staff members were quoted and identified in a book that was, by implication, critical of some aspects of the NGO's work. While the ethical concerns with regard to expatriate participants may be less acute, the core responsibility to do no harm to their livelihoods and careers remains.

5. Collaboration: co-production of knowledge versus sensible distancing

A final dilemma is that of team-work and collaboration. The power imbalance between researcher and researched is immediately apparent for those doing ethnographic work with citizens in PCEs (Fujii, 2012: 718). But how power imbalances work against certain researchers or within a research team is less often acknowledged. This can be acute in PCEs where research is often commissioned by international organizations and donors. We are aware of cases where international organizations have cancelled contracts with local researchers at the first sign of their potential prosecution or suppression by the authorities, seeking to insulate themselves from political risk while wholly abandoning their legal and ethical responsibilities to local researchers. An ethic of research that is particularly prevalent in communities of Area Studies that have been informed by a postcolonial sensibility is to acknowledge the imbalances between 'foreign' and 'local' researchers, whose position differs in terms of pay, immigration status, evacuation opportunities, language skills and the social capital to navigate oneself to safety in the face of an emergency. While acknowledging this imbalance, it is possible to begin to attenuate it via co-production of knowledge from research design through to publication. In particular, controversy arises where foreign scholars fail to fully acknowledge support from research assistants and/or fail to give them credit and responsibility by including them as co-authors where their contribution and abilities make this appropriate.

However, one informal tactic used by locally based researchers who face the prospect of state intimidation, or even career damage in their role as a consultant for international agencies, is to deny or downplay their role in a piece of research that has been deemed controversial and received with some hostility following publication. At other times, it may be necessary for the principal investigator (typically a foreigner) to withhold certain findings from the publication in order to protect the co-author (as well any research participants). This raises difficult questions of the 'no harm' vs 'no evil' dilemma once more. Many academics may baulk at omitting examples of state violence and corruption, for example, while others may consider it a professional responsibility to think through how inclusion of such examples effects collaborators and co-authors.

In our own research, we have typically gravitated between co-production of knowledge, authoring together several times (most recently, Heathershaw and Mullojonov, 2018), and sensible distancing. Several colleagues based in Russia and Eurasia were involved in the project from early stages to completion. At the same time, local colleagues in Tajikistan were occasionally interviewed by the security services and asked about the project and Heathershaw's wider research activities. In these circumstances, we have come to an understanding where locally based colleagues disclose whatever is appropriate about the movements and purposes of foreign colleagues while, at the same time, discussing together how to protect themselves and our research participants. Despite several cases that must remain confidential where the safety of local team members has been protected, we are aware that public association with the project and with Heathershaw has become a burden for many Tajik colleagues and that his critical stance may have indirectly worsened their predicament. He has distanced himself from some of these colleagues in order not to increase this risk. For others, he has written letters of reference to support applications to the US-based Scholars At-Risk and the UK's Committee for At-Risk Academics among other bodies. The environment for academics in Tajikistan—particularly those working on topics deemed political— remains precarious.

Conclusions

This chapter has argued that a vocational approach to fieldwork in PCEs is preferable to one that relies excessively on the tick-box approach of REC/IRBs. A vocational approach supersedes the proceduralist approach in that at times it will involve action in keeping with but in excess of the requirements of the REC/IRB; at other times, it will require action that directly contravenes the general requirements and perceived 'best practice' of REC/IRB. The five ethical dilemmas discussed—of safety, positionality, permission, consent and collaboration—demonstrate some of the most significant topics with which a vocational approach to fieldwork must contend. While there are obviously certain extreme practices that are always ethically unacceptable (those which involve wilful misrepresentation of findings or wittingly doing harm to participants), appropriate action must always be assessed *in context*. A general framework may provide questions and dilemmas to concern rather than instructions and even parameters. In some cases, such as survey experiments, deceit may be acceptable. In other cases, a covert approach—that is, withholding or concealing information from the legal and/or political authorities in a particular place—may be warranted in order to protect sources and confidentialities. In many cases, as in our case in Tajikistan in 2014, mistakes and misjudgments will be made.

To advocate that deceit and covert strategies may be appropriate in some circumstances may be considered controversial. However, it is first and foremost a recognition of the fact that certain ethical requirements (for example, confidentiality of data) run up against others (for example, operating within the law) in the practice of doing research in PCEs. Any academic who has really reflected on the approval process of the REC/IRB will have noticed the manifold areas of potential internal contradiction. This is not to dismiss the role of the REC/IRB, demand exemptions for fieldwork, or even call for its wholesale reform—a move that is unlikely to be successful given the legal and bureaucratic constraints on action (cf. Hauck, 2008). Rather, it is to suggest that we must recognize what the REC/IRB is and is not. It is an approval process through which, in a worst-case scenario such as we faced in 2014, institutional support and insurance payments can be approved to arrange emergency evacuation, fight legal battles, conduct a campaign and negotiate solutions with political authorities. It is not a body that determines the practice of ethical research. In this regard, the approval process for REC/IRB may raise some of the dilemmas listed earlier but it will be only one of a series of inputs into these practical and vocational judgments made by the research team.

The post-conflict environment is not a *sui generis* type and many of these dilemmas may be found just as acutely in difficult political environments, including authoritarian states that are stable and largely free from political violence. But the PCE is a particularly challenging environment because of the presence of an international community that offers a precarious 'third space' (between the rule of the REC/IRB and that of the host government) in which research takes place. Without the active maintenance of this third space, research may be impossible and, therefore, its possibilities and constraints may be unavoidable for the PCE researcher. A vocational approach to research recognizes that the PCE context affects every choice made by the researcher; equally, every choice made has an implication for research and research ethics. Where to live, where to eat, who to make friends with, and related questions may be more significant choices than whether to use snowballing to identify interviewees, whether to work with a particular NGO, or gain a letter of introduction from a particular local university or government agency. Vocational fieldwork is ethical fieldwork to the extent that all these choices are made with regard to the potential harm to others and to oneself. Ethical fieldwork is not that which avoids all harm and controversy but that which takes reasonable measures to mitigate such harm both before and after it arises. None of us is perfect in this regard and we must all be prepared to admit our misjudgments and mistakes in order for ourselves and our colleagues to learn how to be more responsible, both politically and ethically, in our fieldwork. Research ethics in practice is about negotiating dilemmas not following rules.

Notes

1. We acknowledge the constructive comments of Alexander Sodiqov, Catherine Owen, David Lewis, Emma Sabzalieva, Nick Megoran, Safaroz Niyazov, the anonymous reviewers and the editors. Our thanks are particularly extended to Alex for consenting to our discussion of his case in some detail and in print.
2. For a different and constructive summary of the case and the issues it raises see Niyazov (2017).

³ We thank Safaroz Niyazov for prompting us to explore why the threat perception of elites in Tajikistan may lead to academics being targeted.

References

Akiner, S. (2005) *Violence in Andijon: An Independent Investigation*, Johns Hopkins Central Asia-Caucasus Institute paper.

Bhattacharya, S. (2014) 'Institutional review board and international field research in conflict zones', *PS: Political Science & Politics*, 47(4): 840–4.

Black, R. (2003) 'Ethical codes in humanitarian emergencies: from practice to research?', *Disasters*, 27(2): 95–108.

Bush, K. and Duggan, C. (2013) 'Evaluation in conflict zones: methodological and ethical challenges', *Journal of Peacebuilding & Development*, 8(2): 5–25.

Carpenter, C. (2012) '"You talk of terrible things so matter-of-factly in this language of science": constructing human rights in the academy', *Perspectives on Politics*, 10(2): 363–83.

CESS (Central Eurasian Studies Society) (2016) *Taskforce on Fieldwork Safety: Final Report*, 5 March.

Clark, J.A. (2006) 'Field research methods in the Middle East', *PS: Political Science and Politics*, 39(3): 417–24.

Cohen, N. and Arieli, T. (2011) 'Field research in conflict environments: methodological challenges and snowball sampling', *Journal of Peace Research*, 48(4): 423–35.

Farrimond, H. (2013) *Doing Ethical Research*, Basingstoke: Palgrave MacMillan.

Fujii, L.A. (2010) 'Shades of truth and lies: interpreting testimonies of war and violence', *Journal of Peace Research*, 47(2): 231–41.

Fujii, L.A. (2012) 'Research ethics 101: dilemmas and responsibilities', *PS: Political Science and Politics*, 45(4): 717–23.

Haer, R. and Becher, I. (2012) 'A methodological note on quantitative field research in conflict zones: get your hands dirty', *International Journal of Social Research Methodology*, 15(1): 1–13.

Hauck, R.J.-P. (2008) 'Protecting human research participants, IRBs, and political science redux: editor's introduction', *PS: Political Science and Politics*, 41(3): 475–76.

Heathershaw, J. (2009) *Post Conflict Tajikistan: The Politics of Peacebuilding and the Emergence of Legitimate Order*. Abingdon: Routledge.

Heathershaw, J. and Mullojonov, P. (2018) 'Rebels without a cause? Authoritarian conflict management in Tajikistan, 2008–2015' in *Tajikistan on the Move: Statebuilding and Societal Transformation*, edited by Marlene Laruelle, Lanham: Lexington Books, 33–61.

Helbardt, S., Hellmann-Rajanayagam, D. and Korff, R. (2010) 'War's dark glamour: ethics of research in war and conflict zones', *Cambridge Review of International Affairs*, 23(2): 349–69.

Jessee, E. (2011) 'The limits of oral history: ethics and methodology amid highly politicized research settings', *Oral History Review*, 38(2): 287–307.

Kuzhabekova, A. (2020) 'Invisibilizing Eurasia: how North–South dichotomization marginalizes post-Soviet scholars in international research collaborations'. *Journal of Studies in International Education*, 24(1): 113–30.

Lashmar, P. (2017) 'Putting lives in danger? Tinker, tailor, journalist, spy: the use of journalistic cover', *Journalism*, 1–17, online first.

Marshall, P.A. (2003) 'Human subjects protections, institutional review boards, and cultural anthropological research', *Anthropological Quarterly*, 76(2): 269–85.

Megoran, N., Atkin, M., Abbas, N., Harris, C., Jeffrey, A. and Heathershaw J. (2010) Author–critic forum: the politics of peace building in Tajikistan, *Central Asian Survey*, 29(2), 219–230, DOI: 10.1080/02634937.2010.499729.

Monk, D.B. (ed.) (2014) *The Post-Conflict Environment: Investigation and Critique*, Ann Arbor: University of Michigan Press.

Niyazov, S. (2017) 'Fieldwork as socially constructed and negotiated practice', in, *Reimagining Utopias: Theory and Method for Educational Research in Post-Socialist Contexts*, edited by Iveta Silova, et al, Rotterdam, Boston and Taipei: Sense Publishers, 119–39.

Nordstrom, C. and Robben, A.C.G. (1996) *Fieldwork Under Fire: Contemporary Studies of Violence and Culture*, Berkley: University of California Press.

Reed, R. (2012) 'Researching Ulster loyalism: the methodological challenges of the divisive and sensitive subject', *Politics*, 32(3): 207–19.

Sabzalieva, E. (2020) 'Negotiating international research collaborations in Tajikistan', *Journal of Studies in International Education*, 24(1): 97–112.

Stringfellow, W. (2004) *Conscience and Obedience: The Politics of Romans 13 and Revelation 13 in Light of the Second Coming*, Eugene: Wipf & Stock.

Vlassenroot, K. (2006) 'War and social research', *Civilisations*, 54(1): 191–8.

Wood, E.J. (2006) 'The ethical challenges of field research in conflict zones', *Qualitative Sociology*, 29(3): 373–86.

Yanow, D. and Schwartz-Shea, P. (2008) 'Reforming institutional review board policy: issues in implementation and field research', *PS: Political Science and Politics*, 41(3): 483–94.

8

Challenges of Research in an Active Conflict Environment

Boukary Sangaré and Jaimie Bleck

Conducting research in active conflict zones presents specific challenges to social science researchers. Insecurity and uncertainty in the context of data collection require them to be flexible but transparent in their methodological choices. This chapter specifies some challenges we have faced working in Mali between 2012 and 2017, a context characterized by the presence of violent extremists, ongoing communal conflict and limited state capacity. Since the outbreak of the 2012 crisis, we have conducted collaborative and individual research projects on issues related to governance, armed actors and youth. Like many Sahel countries, Mali faces immense challenges in terms of political and security governance. Since 2012, Mali has been hit by unprecedented crises ranging from a secessionist rebellion to violent inter-communal conflict. The rise of violent extremism and the inability of the state to cope with the problems of insecurity have led to mass popular frustrations. Despite the international community's commitment, non-state armed groups are gaining ground and offer alternatives in terms of governance, security and justice, which respond to gaps left by the state since independence. This crisis began in the north of the country, but the turmoil has spilled over to the centre and now envelops more than two thirds of Mali's geographic territory. This article is informed by our experiences of adapting our research to this challenging research environment. It describes our attempts to adapt methods and techniques in this context and stresses that these challenges have both pragmatic and theoretical implications.

We build on previous reflections on research in conflict zones (Ayimpam and Bouju, 2015; Bouju, 2015; Boumaza and Campana, 2007; Lamarche, 2015; Wood, 2006), but try to focus our discussion on the specific challenges relevant to the Sahel: operating in environments characterized by, first, a multitude of non-state armed groups (NSAGs) including violent extremists and actors engaging in communal conflict; and, second, weak state capacity, limited infrastructure and ongoing conflict. While the guidance we provide stems directly from our own experience, we hope that some of the lessons may resonate in other highly politicized weak states with an ongoing conflict.

Our chapter is structured in response to a series of methodological and pragmatic questions: how should academic researchers assess risk and ethical challenges in environments of insecurity? How can research be flexible enough to adapt to the challenges of the field and yet continue to respect the methods and techniques that make the research academically viable and valid? And how can a researcher negotiate his or her fieldwork in a context of occupation by armed groups? We address these questions in the context of the two sets of parameters relevant to the areas where we do work—environments characterized by 'violent extremism' and communal conflict, and by weak state capacity. With regard to the former, the politicization of the 'War on Terror' means that researchers working in contexts with 'violent extremism' need to be especially conscious of the ethical and safety implications of their research and future publications on themselves, their collaborators and research team, their respondents and the broader communities where they work. This task is further complicated by the presence of community-level conflict, which is always rooted in very specific and complex histories. We have been confronted with the logistical realities and ethical challenges posed by both settings. Second, in the context of weak state capacity and ongoing conflict, we stress uncertainty and the inability of researchers to rely on pre-established infrastructure or to predict security and governance challenges down the line. This reality impacts research logistics, but also requires a longitudinal thinking about the impact of research and publication as it affects stakeholder communities in evolving security situations.

Safety and research ethics

Working in an environment characterized by violent extremism and communal conflict requires tremendous awareness of context. Context knowledge is key to risk assessment when asking questions like: what research is feasible where? What types of questions can be asked? And how to approach research subjects? It also directly informs awareness of the ethical challenges posed by the research environment. In this context, we have found it essential that foreign researchers work in collaboration with those who are living and working in the country of research. That collaboration can take the form of a collaborative research project between co-PIs (principal investigators), working with local research assistants, or outsourcing data collection to a trusted local firm (Bleck, Dendere and Sangaré, 2018; see also Bøås, and Kušić, in this volume). In these contexts, any researcher entering a new environment, or even returning to a previous research site, should do their 'homework': even foreign researchers who have long-standing relationships with the country of research, or local academics based in the capital with vast historical, cultural and linguistic knowledge, will be confronted by shifting security challenges and social cleavages, requiring real-time analysis of the situation at hand.

Given precarious security parameters, we have found it immensely useful to consult with trusted local colleagues and other country-based researchers with experience in a specific geographic area to see whether a proposed study is feasible and safe. We both frequently draw on our network of contacts, particularly those who are actively conducting research in geographic zones of interest, to make security assessments, and have found this vital as conditions change constantly and places that were previously accessible become unsafe. If, based on the initial security assessment, the team choses to embark on the research mission, we have also found it critical to have a local decision maker on the ground who has the authority to make immediate adjustments to the research protocol as the security situation evolves, and that the entire research team receives trainings on project goals and research ethics and knows that they can raise their voice to the team leader if they feel that the research mission could potentially endanger the team or the community in any way.

The responsibility here is not only to think about the immediate security of the lead researcher and their team; in our projects we have taken care to think through the implications of research processes and publishing for multiple constituencies: the lead researcher, local research partners, the broader research team, respondents and the broader communities where data is collected. In the institutional review board (IRB) process, we typically conceptualize the responsibility to protect as focused on respondents,[1] and we have found it extremely important to be wary not only of adequately protecting ourselves and our research collaborators, but also to take into account the wider set of tremors that our research might inflict on the community where we conduct our research. Deciding which places and populations 'can be accessed' can be difficult, however, as security needs or risk assessments need to be weighed against the value of obtaining information from these areas/populations.

In this context, we have learned that it is essential to vet the on-the-ground reality with the proposed research question. The process of 'iteration', or vetting an existing research question with the realities of the 'field' (Kapiszweski et al, 2015), may include questions around issues such as: what types of questions can I ask in this politicized setting to ensure that I will not put anyone in danger? Is the framing of my question appropriate and does it reflect the realities of the research environment? Does my question resonate with the understandings of the context by actors on the ground? How do we ensure that the diversity of perspectives is taken into account, given trade-offs between accessibly and truly representative and inclusive responses to research questions?

Leveraging relationships in the research process: understanding the parameters

The question of the relationship to 'the field' is essential to any ethnographic fieldwork but investigating 'difficult terrain' requires even more thoughtfulness about the implementation and renewal of adaptation strategies. Each researcher will develop their own design based on their research experience, prior knowledge of the field, their ability to adapt and their own social arrangements. The difficulties of accessing highly insecure places may be more easily overcome by a person who has a strong bond with this area, either because they were born there, live there or have some other familial ties (but see also Verweijen, and Muvumba Sellström, in this volume).

Drawing on or building relationships with members of the study group or the surrounding population can minimize hazards and risks. However, these relationships also raise the question of the risk of instrumentalization of the researcher's work or of the researcher themselves, who can be erected as a spokesperson for the group they are studying or rejected as a potential whistle-blower of the group's practices and discourses. In some instances, however, a researcher may be in a position to provide advocacy for a local population, and this commitment could go beyond mere moral support and involve the conscious choice of the position of an advocate. For example, in February 2019 an informant one of the authors had been working with in the Malian municipality of Mondoro (Mopti) since 2009 called in frustration to alert the researcher about mass graves of 24 Peul civilians. He explained that the community had issued repeated warnings about abuses committed by Malian soldiers in the context of anti-terrorist operations in the municipality, but with no response. After triangulating this information, the author felt obliged to intervene on the community's behalf and alert international human rights organizations, since he estimated that these crimes would continue if the information was not relayed.[2] This was not the first time he had advocated on behalf of the population he was researching. In 2013, he had shed light on Peul pastoralists arbitrarily arrested during military operations to reconquer formerly occupied areas.[3] Given his previous engagement with and knowledge of this specific community, he felt compelled to get involved in order to advocate for the release of people wrongfully arrested and sometimes tortured or killed by the military. Such choices to be an active advocate, however, have to be carefully considered and thought through (see also Bjørkhaug, in this volume). The researcher has to balance the desire to shed light on a violent situation, based on an objective analysis supported by a solid and transparent methodology, with the imperative not to fan the flames of a conflict through their actions and, in both cases, deep knowledge of the context and triangulation of information was essential to the decision to act as advocate.

Indeed, research agendas that engage with difficult social issues such as human rights violations must increasingly navigate the media hype that often accompanies such issues. We as researchers have to deal with other information mediators including local NGOs, international agencies, social workers, journalists and so on—not just to coordinate information, but also in terms of advocacy and decision making about policy on the ground. The complex and multidimensional connections of the field generate obligations and connections between the researcher and the informant: they share a space of inter-subjectivity in which they co-construct ethnographic knowledge. However, the patient construction of a space of inter-subjectivity between the researcher and the research participants can be quickly 'undermined' in the context of violent conflict (Albera, 2001). Co-construction can be dangerous for the researcher, the participants and the broader population being surveyed; much like being exposed to an improvised explosive device, the foundation of this relationship can crumble and be fatal for the researcher and the study.

Negotiating access

In negotiating access to the field, we have found it crucial to understand the diversity of actors and the cleavages within a local population, including both respect for different traditions but also being wary of whose narrative is representative of what group—especially when there are feuding groups in a village or different caste concerns within a 'group'. The Fulani people in Mali, for example, are a very diverse society with a hierarchical social organization, divided into nobles, the local elite, agro-pastoral categories, lower caste men (*griots*) and former slaves. A certain social tension regulates the relations between these different categories and social groups. When conducting research in Fulani communities, we have had to take into account this social complexity in order to negotiate our access to the field by knowing who to address first and what questions to ask to which actors. In addition, in an environment characterized by such cleavages we also constantly had to think about our own positionality: how could we avoid being perceived as closer to one party than the other? How could we avoid (unwittingly) using politicized words? How could we manage relations in a tense and devolving climate? During the period of study, what should be our projected identities?

In our own work in rural settings in Mali in general, it has been useful to make initial scouting trips to negotiate with traditional authorities, distribute kola nuts as a sign of respect, explain the project goals and assess security—before returning with a research team. As it proved impossible to circumvent village chiefs, we had to consider what the research plan would have to look like to gain their consent, while acknowledging that not all data gathered would be consistent with their experiences and perspectives. Given the collectivist and communal nature of consent structures—often starting with the chief and then the head of household before accessing less powerful individuals—we have found it particularly important not to force participation and to give an extra emphasis on volunteerism within the context of the consent speech.[4] Given security challenges, we have also relied more on open-ended questions that allow subjects to bring up sensitive issues themselves and without direct prompting, if and when they felt comfortable and safe to do so. We have also tried to be conscious of questions that could be triggers for local respondents' discomfort or fear, for example by vetting questionnaires thoroughly with the help of members of those communities before using them widely.

Since operating in these contexts has often required drawing on broader relationships with enabling (international) organizations and actors, we also found it necessary to understand how the people and organizations that we associated ourselves with shape the information we gather. For example, if we are travelling with a UN convoy, what are the implications for who is willing to speak with us and for how interlocutors frame their narrative (see also Peter, in this volume)? In many developing world contexts, there is also a problem of academics being mistaken for development agents from NGOs or being associated with the ruling government (see also Clausen, in this volume). Piggybacking on these institutions in times of insecurity can make logistics easier but may, at the same time, further entrench respondents' perceptions of the researcher as biased, particularly in politicized environments. And it can generate research fatigue among respondents who await concrete results from previous inquiries (see also Lai, in this volume). In our collaborations with international sponsors, we have therefore found it important to think about balancing our long-term relationships with communities and their expectations with the immediate scope of work as desired by donors.

Preserving research quality: flexibility, methodological rigour and transparency in research design

The pragmatic security concerns discussed guide who we talk to and what we can ask. This necessitates a flexibility in research design and in the use of the information that respondents feel comfortable providing us with. Due to compromises in research designs—caused, for example, by the inability to reach all of the 'populations of interest', self-censorship, high rates of non-response or a heightened risk of social desirability bias—it becomes critical for researchers to think about how these compromises impact 'data validity' (in the words of positivist approaches) or contextualize the narrative that is being recorded (in ethnographic terms). Researchers can think through a set of questions that can help them to develop a counterfactual account, or at least how responses might have differed under different security conditions, with different informants or different data-collection methods. How would another group of people, who we did not speak to, have answered our questions? How does our relationship to our respondents and their relationship to broader power structures affect the answers that we have obtained? What are respondents not talking about that might also be of critical importance? By openly addressing these questions, academics are not merely acknowledging constraints to their initial research design in footnotes of publications, but actively thinking about how their adaptation to the research terrain has shaped both their research agenda and the information they have collected.

For instance, if a researcher can anticipate where the population they managed to interview sits on an ideological spectrum, it will help situate the claims they are making relative to the broader population. In one author's work, the research team was unable to access refugee camps, but was able to survey displaced persons living in Mali. Reflection on how the narrative of one type of vulnerable population who were interviewed (some displaced persons) sat along an ideological cleavage (all northerners who fled), helped this author and her colleagues to strengthen the argument, since they could describe critiques of governance as coming from a group that was relatively more pro-government as compared to peers in refugee camps, who they did not survey but knew to be more likely to be anti-government (Bleck, Dembele and Guindo, 2016).

Being transparent about the research process can help others to interpret our data and conclusions, and it can also provide important insight about how the realities on the ground differ from narratives of conflict that dominate international news media. In some instances, being confronted by the incongruence between respondents' priorities and those driving our initial research agenda can generate important theoretical breakthroughs. For instance, in one author's research with communities in Mopti during the initial period of rebellion, respondents' constant prioritization of health, agriculture, and food and water security made the research team rethink its narrow definition of the 'crisis' as linked solely to changes in governance (Bleck and Michelitch, 2015).

Our recommendation is that in writing up the research, academics should be transparent about constraints and consider what kind of bias was introduced into the data. This will help other researchers who were not present in the field to interpret the value of what we have contributed and also inform our own research design. This way, we can learn lessons about what is 'possible' in the current operating environment and also gauge possibilities for future research designs to complement the communities, spaces and questions that were broached in previous work.

Operating in environments of weak state capacity and ongoing conflict

While context knowledge and long-standing relationships are always critical to fieldwork-based research, these prerequisites may carry life-or-death consequences in conflict-affected areas. Conducting research in environments characterized by communal conflict, violent extremism and lack of control by the state requires that researchers develop personalized approaches and rely on existing networks (see also Verweijen, in this volume). Negotiations with influential community members can potentially provide cover during research. These people can be traditional, religious or locally elected leaders, or influential business people. Sometimes even something like the 'right' choice of transport service can help a researcher avoid attacks and insecurity. In northern Mali, for instance, there are car rental agencies that have close relationships with armed groups and their drivers thus know the necessary codes to move through, and protect their clients in, areas occupied by those groups.

Sometimes, direct negotiating with armed groups to have access to certain geographic areas is feasible. For instance, in November 2014, one author was involved in a team conducting a study on the impact of communal conflict on the local population in the region Ménaka, a region that was the scene of communal clashes and fighting between various armed groups at the time. The author knew, from when they were at university together, a leader of the Coordination of Movements for Azawad (CMA), a coalition representing different armed organizations and the team contacted this CMA leader to make sure they could travel safely in the areas of Ménaka controlled by the CMA. The CMA leader put the team in touch with the military leaders in the area, who in turn provided assurance that they would not be touched and advised the different units along the way of the team's arrival. Once they had received this 'green light', the team were able to safely move from Ansongo to Ménaka, where they spent a week of research without any incidents.

Security situations can change rapidly, however, which makes it difficult to assess risk. For instance, in June 2015 one author went to Serma Camp (Hayré, circle of Douentza) as part of a study being conducted for an international NGO on the camp population's perceptions of insecurity and violent extremism. The research team knew the area from six months of previous graduate research in 2009 and 2013; however, by 2015 the security situation had deteriorated. The area of Serma had become the stronghold of a self-proclaimed jihadist groups affiliated with the Katiba of Macina and Ansaroul Al Islam. Knowing that this region was dangerous, the research team had tried to prepare for its arrival in the field by contacting interlocutors, yet since there was no adequate telephone network in the area the team had to go to the camp to notify them before starting its research. When it arrived in the camp, the team was welcomed and planned to spend the day and then go to the main town, Boni, to spend the night. After the traditional greetings, the team presented the purpose of the mission and received permission to conduct interviews; however, someone reported the research team, which had a female member, to the jihadists, who forbade that women and men mix in public spaces. In the middle of the day, the team was alerted of the imminent arrival of the jihadists, prompting them to leave the camp within minutes in order to get to Boni safely. They were later informed that the jihadists had abducted the people they had spoken with, in order to find out what they had discussed during the interviews. Fortunately, these people were later released after the jihadists had found the research questions benign.

This incidence highlights the high risk that researchers may not only put themselves in danger but may also unintentionally endanger their interlocutors. Due to the high degree of uncertainty in the field in a weak state characterized by ongoing violent conflict, it is not possible to control all the parameters, even if risk is minimized by taking the necessary culturally appropriate precautions and measures. Similarly, territory that was previously under government control can become occupied by armed groups. It becomes difficult to assess respondents' level of protection, if it is not possible to predict what the governance situation will look like in six months' time. Because of this, we recommend erring on the side of extreme caution and imagining what type of protection would be available for respondents if the area was suddenly overrun by a different armed group. If people are interrogated about what researchers asked them, they should be able to answer truthfully and without fear. This may mean substantial but necessary restrictions to a project. In research on youth recruitment to insurgent groups, for instance, we were very cautious in our attempts to locate and interview former and current combatants. We did not want to draw attention to these youths, since we would not be able to provide any kind of security guarantee for them after we had left. We were working with an international organization and this was their prime 'population of interest', but we had to draw a line to say that in most cases we did not feel that it was safe enough to include this population, as violent conflict in Mali was ongoing and state capacity weak.

This type of prudence is critical. If researchers or contractors are motivated by money in an environment of limited employment opportunities or lucrative contracts linked to 'understanding violent extremism', they might be willing to say they can accomplish a research task even when it requires them to assume greater levels of risk than they would typically be comfortable with (see also Bøås, in this volume). When bidding on a contract or consultancy, we cannot assume that other teams have thought through risk. Similarly, donors eager to gain access to important data might seek to outsource risk without thinking through the ethical implications of data collection as they affect all stakeholders immediately and over time. In our view it is our responsibility as researchers to think beyond our own safety to the safety of our team and the communities that respondents are embedded in and create limits for what we think is responsible research.

It is important to note that many academic research teams operate without the resources, infrastructure or security protocols provided by international organizations or even most NGOs. This enables us to 'fly under the radar', but simultaneously puts us at risk. We are often reliant on public transport, travel and live without security protection, and operate without formal security briefings. This places an extra burden on us to gather relevant security information to assess risk, but also to access resources and protocols available at our home universities. Many security procedures of universities are not common knowledge and thus need to be actively investigated. For instance, before departure a foreign researcher should understand what types of registration are required by their university, who they could call if there was an emergency, if the university offers any kind of insurance for them or collaborators (and, if so, what type), and how they might gain access to emergency funds (if available). This knowledge will help to clarify the parameters of research and understand the burden of risk the PI bears and that they are asking their collaborators to bear. In especially dangerous environments, it may be necessary to have co-PIs and collaborators sign an agreement regarding risk and responsibility.

We have found it essential to provide resources and decision-making authority to collaborators on the ground so that they can avoid risk and get out of dangerous situations, if they arise. For instance, it might be essential for teams to depart from an existing schedule to travel on market days when they are less conspicuous as newcomers or they might determine that an initially selected research site is too risky to pursue. When foreign researchers are involved in the research, they should defer to local collaborators in determining the scope of what research is possible and also what resources would be required to allow these researchers to pursue the research safely and without harm to any of the key constituencies. Ideally, the project needs to ensure that it has adequate levels of funding in order to manage risk, including emergency funds for evacuations and a flexible fund that can accommodate last-minute changes.

Conclusion

This chapter is not designed to instruct researchers whether or not it is 'safe enough' or ethical to embark on a particular field research project. Instead, it draws on our own experiences to offer readers a list of some issues that they will need to consider, if they do choose to embark on such types of data collection. We have focused our contribution on a research environment characterized by both communal conflict and violent extremism, but also one without adequate state control over territory—where violent conflict is very much evolving. This type of environment introduces a tremendous degree of complexity into navigating the various relationships in the field, but also uncertainty about security questions as they evolve over time.

We hope that our experiences of conducting research in Mali can be informative for other researchers, but also recognize that there is a diversity of experiences and range of identities that inform one's positionality, networks and, ultimately, research experience. We emphasize how this type of research environment requires that the researcher be transparent about the resources that they have access to, but also their deficiencies—as they will have both practical and methodological implications. Further, it is essential that the researcher think through the consequences of conducting research on themselves and their research team, but also the broader communities where they conduct research.

Notes

1. See an extended discussion in Sriram et al (2009).
2. Testimonies collected by telephone on 22–24 February 2019 and confirmed by Fulani IDPs met in Bamako on 6 March 2019.
3. These groups were suspected of allegiance to the Movement for the Unity of Jihad in West Africa.
4. IRB typically requires language that makes clear to respondents that they have the right to leave the interview at any time or to skip any questions they are uncomfortable with.

References

Albera, D. (2001) 'Terrains minés', *Ethnologie française*, 31(1): 5–13.

Ayimpam S. and Bouju, J. (2015) 'Ethnocentrisme et partenariat: la violence symbolique de l'aide humanitaire', Institut des Mondes Africains: www.researchgate.net/publication/290430007_Ethnocentrisme_et_partenariat_la_violence_symbolique_de_l'aide_humanitaire.

Bleck, J., Dembelé, A. and Guindo, S. (2016) 'Malian crisis and the lingering problem of good governance', *Stability: International Journal of Security and Development*, 5(1): Art. 15, pp 1–18.

Bleck, J., Dendere, C. and Sangaré, B. (2018) 'Making North–South research collaborations work', *PS: Political Science and Politics*, 51(3): 554–8.

Bleck, J. and Michelitch, K. (2015) 'The 2012 crisis in Mali: ongoing empirical state failure', *African Affairs*, 114(457): 598–623.

Bouju, J. (2015) 'Une ethnographie à distance? Retour critique sur l'anthropologie de la violence en République centrafricaine', *Civilisations*, 64(1): 153–62.

Boumaza, M. and Campana, A. (2007) 'Enquêter en milieu "difficile". Introduction', *Revue française de science politique*, 57(1): 5–25.

Kapiszewski, D., MacLean, L. and Read, B. (2015) 'Field research in political science', *Field Research in Political Science: Practices and Principles*, Cambridge: Cambridge University Press.

Lamarche, K. (2015) 'Quand les occupants défilent avec les occupés. Étude d'une coopération paradoxale entre militants israéliens et palestiniens', *Participations*, 12(2): 217–43.

Pulman, B. (1986) 'Le débat anthropologie / psychanalyse et la référence au "terrain"', *Cahiers Internationaux de Sociologie*, LXXX: 5–26.

Sriram, C.L., King, J., Mertus, J., Martin-Ortega, O. and Herman, J. (2009) *Surviving Field Research: Working in Violent and Difficult Situations*, New York: Routledge.

Taylor, A. and Charuty, G. (2016) 'Suite: Gradhiva au musée du quai Branly. Entretien avec Anne-Christine Taylor, réalisé á Paris le 31 août 2016', *Gradhiva. Revue d'anthropologie et d'historie des arts*, 24: 228–43.

Wood, E.J. (2006) 'The ethical challenges of field research in conflict zones' *Qualitative Sociology*, 29: 373–86.

9

On Assessing Risk Assessments and Situating Security Advice: The Unsettling Quest for 'Security Expertise'

Judith Verweijen

He was visibly nervous, perhaps traumatized. He had just been on a deployment to Afghanistan, and it looked like he had been having a rough time. The officers of the European Union Security Assistance Mission to the Democratic Republic of the Congo (EUSEC-DRC) had been sympathetic towards my research on the Congolese army, but they were concerned about my safety. And this officer in particular was worried about my plans to conduct research in remote rural areas with ongoing military operations. Taking another sip of his beer, he sketched the heart of darkness scenarios I would—in his eyes—inevitably be facing. He seemed convinced that my status as a woman would make my descent into the 'jungle out there' even more dangerous. "If they try to rape you", he explained in a way that I perceived as mansplaining, "tell them that you have AIDS". Was that sound advice or not? I did not get much chance to make up my mind, for a next thought popped into his head. Lowering his voice, he whispered, "If you like, I can get you a handgun, before you go out there, that's the only way to stay safe."

Looking back at this beer-drenched conversation, it is the starting point of the gradual erosion of my belief that those who we are socialized into seeing as 'security experts', notably professional (Western) military personnel, are actually knowledgeable about 'the security situation' in war-ridden eastern Democratic Republic of the

Congo (DRC). Imagining myself carrying a handgun, and the situations in which I would use it, I quickly concluded it would expose me to immense danger, not least as I was utterly incapable of handling such a device. Moreover, it would elicit potentially lethal reactions by provoking exchanges of fire, not to speak of the risks of being arrested and thrown out of the country on accusations of being a mercenary or spy. The more I reflected on this—unsolicited—advice, the more outrageous it seemed. But he had not been joking. He had been deadly serious. Perhaps his reasoning reflected his own sense of security as a trained military professional, feeling insecure without a firearm. But he also seemed to be reading the eastern DRC's security dynamics through a predefined grid of a 'war zone' that appeared strongly shaped by his experiences in Afghanistan.

The story of my field research in zones in the eastern DRC's Kivu provinces that were coloured red on the security maps of the United Nations peacekeeping mission in the DRC (MONUSCO)—facilitated by a light-touch approach to risks and ethics at the university where I was then based—is one of continuous engagement in finding, processing and assessing 'security expertise'. This process invited ongoing reflections on questions such as: what counts as knowledge on security dynamics? How is such knowledge constructed? Who is in its possession? How does this knowledge translate into guidelines for action? In this chapter I describe how in the course of 14 months of fieldwork for my doctoral dissertation between 2010 and 2012 conducted in three phases (for a detailed description, see Verweijen, 2015a), my understandings of who was a 'security expert' and what counted as 'security expertise' started to shift. Although initially unsettling, these shifts ultimately proved a fruitful avenue to enhancing awareness of how one's positionality and related biases shape readings of 'the security situation', and how these readings feed into the construction of 'security knowledge'.

MILOBS missing out on micro-dynamics

In the first two months of my research, I frequently interacted with foreign military personnel of different kinds, including EUSEC. Conducting research on the Congolese armed forces (FARDC) and their micro-level relations with civilians, I felt that there were perhaps distinctly 'military' dimensions that I would overlook as a 'civilian'. A trained military eye, I suspected, would be able to observe aspects of command and control, training, and military strategy and tactics that I might not be able to detect. In addition, I believed that military professionals might be well placed to assess particular aspects of the security situation, such as armed group activity. After all, they are trained in developing 'situational awareness', while having in principle a systematic approach to gathering what they call 'intelligence'.

Keen on talking to military personnel (and on lowering accommodation costs since conducting research on a shoestring budget), I seized upon the rather unanticipated opportunity to stay for some time in a team site of UN military observers (MILOBS) in North Kivu. MILOBS are unarmed military personnel deployed as part of the UN peacekeeping mission, charged with gathering and verifying information on security dynamics. It must certainly be strictly forbidden for non-UN personnel to stay in a MILOBS team site, but the Uruguayan officer who was in charge did not seem to be overly concerned. He was more worried about my safety, indicating which zones were, according to him, dangerous. These zones were subject to seemingly unpredictable events—armed group attacks on army positions, assassinations of local authorities and business people, frequent ambushes and, in some zones, kidnappings. Yet, as I would gradually find out thanks to a journalist from the area, the patterns this instability followed were not incomprehensible. To grasp these patterns, however, one needed fine-grained knowledge of local conflicts and power relations—knowledge that the MILOBS did not possess.

Within the zone where the MILOBS team site was located, I soon struck up a friendship with Emmanuel,[1] who shared an interest in comprehending the reigning insecurity due to his profession. We developed a close research collaboration, travelling to various surrounding villages to interview people. These interactions allowed me to gradually get a firmer grasp on who was targeted by whom, how and why. Due to recent military operations, armed groups had been displaced and thus cut off from their regular sources of income. Consequently, these groups were developing new strategies to access revenue, including kidnappings. Additionally, as armed groups had been driven deep into the bush, they incurred difficulties to access towns and villages. As a result, some economic operators working with their money, such as *cambistes* (money changers), traders and local shopkeepers, tried to default on their obligations to these groups, like not paying back outstanding debts or interests. In response, armed groups carried out revenge attacks against these civilian collaborators. Furthermore, since the army had now become the dominant force, seeking protection from armed groups was no longer an effective way of securing one's business. This prompted economic operators to try to switch loyalties, which elicited further revenge attacks. Another dynamic was the loss of power of those local political actors who had previously been backed by armed groups that were now no longer in control. Capitalizing on the changing power configuration, their political rivals sought alliances with the newly dominant armed forces to settle scores, sometimes in a violent manner.

In sum, confirming observations of the 'micro-dynamics of violence' school (for example Kalyvas, 2006), much of the insecurity in the zone stemmed from shifting and contested armed actor control. Yet, the MILOBS had not developed that analysis. They often lacked the details of particular security incidents, in particular how these incidents were related to the complex ties between civilians and armed groups. Furthermore, they analyzed events in isolation, not seeing wider patterns and underlying dynamics. From an 'ethnography 101' perspective, this ignorance is easily explainable. Of the seven MILOBS in the team site, only two spoke conversational French. In addition, the MILOBS did not spend much time outside of their team site. Their interaction with Congolese was limited to encounters during their car patrols. This situation made them heavily reliant on their Congolese interpreter to gather information. Yet their interpreter also lacked the fine-grained understanding of local power relations and politics needed to grasp the logics that inform security incidents. Not being from the area, he did not have the intimate connections—such as family bonds—that facilitate access to sensitive details. Many people in the area also distrusted MONUSCO, therefore likely withholding or manipulating information.

Aside from access to certain types of information, it occurred to me that the MILOBS were lacking a particular theoretical sensitivity that could have helped them make sense of the observed insecurity. The instability caused by contested armed actor control over the area, and the ways civilians harnessed these actors for personal purposes, were textbook micro-dynamics of violence stuff. This theoretical awareness had gone a long way in fostering my understanding of security dynamics in the area. But the MILOBS likely had not had similar exposure to theories highlighting the importance of revenge, jealousies and score settling within the production of violence. As a result, they may have tried to interpret events through the grid of grand conflict narratives, which posit relatively stable fault lines between well-delineated adversaries defined on the basis of political, ideological, religious or ethnic affiliations. Yet such narratives are not readily applicable to the convoluted political–military context of the eastern DRC, introducing uncertainties about armed actors' logics of action.

Kidnapping analytics

Increasingly aware of their limited appreciation of what was actually going on, I started to become reluctant to take the MILOBS's security advice at face value. On what basis, I wondered, did they call certain zones 'unsafe'? Did the fact that multiple security incidents occurred in a particular zone necessarily imply that I myself was at risk? For whom, exactly, were the zones they deemed 'unsafe' unsafe? Raising the question with Emmanuel and some of his friends, we started to comprehensively think through the observed dynamics. The targets of murders, attacks, kidnappings and ambushes were not random. They were carefully selected. These acts were meticulously planned, aiming at specific houses, vehicles or people. And as revealed by their timing and location, they were grounded in in-depth knowledge of people's routines and movements. It did not logically follow—or so it seemed—that a *muzungu* (white person) researcher rapidly visiting the area would necessarily run a high risk of being attacked, in particular when nobody was aware of her movements. These observations allayed my concerns to frequent zones deemed unsafe by the UN.

Towards the end of my stay, I raised with the MILOBS the idea of doing research in the Binza area, at that point a hotbed of kidnappings. They quickly brushed aside my plans as "totally crazy", stating I could get kidnapped myself. They considered my plans to go on a motorcycle particularly unsafe, emphasizing I could be hit by stray bullets. At first panicked by their statements, systematically reflecting on how they arrived at these conclusions together with Emmanuel allayed some of my fears. Perhaps the MILOBS did not fully understand how much advance planning the kidnappings required, with the target, time and location being so carefully chosen. Also, Emmanuel was convinced that going by car would in fact be more rather than less dangerous. Since car traffic in the area was relatively rare, and therefore highly conspicuous, it would immediately draw attention to the fact that there was someone with means in the zone. A motorcycle was much less visible. The car, so we concluded, offered a false sense of security. Even in the case of an ambush, what difference would being in a car make? Trying to flee would inevitably mean being shot at. It was perhaps that the MILOBS themselves felt safer in a car, not least as they were soldiers stripped of their common means of defence—the firearm. Yet reading the security situation through one's own predefined notions of 'safety' is not going to yield accurate risk assessments.

These assessments, I became convinced, could only be developed through logical reasoning, in particular reflections on the nature of perpetrators and their motives, targets and modus operandi. Such reasoning also provided me with a (perhaps mistaken) sense of security. It led me to believe that one could open and demystify the black box of insecurity, breaking the paralysing effects of blanket fear stemming from incomprehension. In addition, adequate analysis allowed one to develop accurate precautionary measures. Emboldened by these considerations, Emmanuel and I decided that we could in fact visit Binza, but with a carefully designed plan of action. First of all, since motor-taxi drivers were rumoured to often collaborate with kidnappers, Emmanuel would drive the motorcycle himself. Second, to mask my whiteness while on the road, I bought a full-face motor helmet, scarf and gloves to cover as much skin as possible. Third, we kept our travel plans completely secret, not informing anyone where we were going and when, aside for the MILOBS. Once arriving in the village where we intended to conduct research, we spread a false narrative on the length of our stay and our next destination. We told people we would move on to a village towards the east within two days. However, the next day, we suddenly returned to where we had come from, but not via the main road, where people could immediately see and report on our direction. Instead, we zigzagged among rows of houses in order to reach the main road at the outer edge of the village, then went full speed ahead.

We completed the mission without being kidnapped. However, this may have had as much to do with luck as with artfulness. How much our precautionary measures had reduced risk remains a wild guess. No matter how much I clung to analytics in order to navigate insecurity, I still felt an intense relief upon returning into an area deemed safe. Had I been religious, this would undoubtedly have been an appropriate moment to thank the Supreme Being.

Attenuating the barbarian syndrome

Compared to the MILOBS, I found another type of military actor that I initially interacted with—MONUSCO blue helmets—somewhat better informed. The officers from the Indian or Pakistani army I spoke with appeared to have a more robust awareness of armed groups and developments within the FARDC. Yet their analyses were often still limited. Heavily focused on the military side of things, they did not adequately grasp how and how deeply both state and non-state armed forces were embedded into civilian society. Furthermore, they readily highlighted the 'rag-tag' nature of these forces as an explanation for their behaviour. To substantiate that analysis, they would cite features of what from their vantage point appeared 'military unprofessionalism': unclear hierarchies, deficient logistics and a lack of discipline. For instance, one Pak-batt (battalion from Pakistani contingent) officer said about the FARDC: "If they want to clean their weapon they shoot in the air. There are not even checks whether they wear their uniforms properly, so even at the basic level there is no discipline." These observations did not only stem from their positionality as professionally trained military but, as I discovered, were also derived from certain biases towards Congolese society and 'culture' (see also, Verweijen, 2017). As one Ind-batt (Indian battalion) officer observed: "Whatever organization you have in the military, it is a reflection of society." Hence, the perceived deficiencies of Congolese fighting forces were mainly ascribed to the 'underdeveloped' nature of Congolese society. Implicitly, these analyses were infused with tropes of 'African barbarism', which frame the propensity for violence as an innate feature of 'Africans'.

Such assumptions are highly consequential for assessing insecurity and how it potentially affects oneself. If armed forces have tenuous command and control, the risk of falling victim to abuses by soldiers is potentially higher, depending on soldiers' norms and intent. In these cases, soldiers may for instance engage in burglary or road robbery without permission from their commanders. Where armed forces are highly disciplined and commanders have a firm grasp on their subordinates, by contrast, such acts would only occur when ordered or tolerated by the hierarchy. If commanders in these more disciplined forces have a virtuous character, maintaining good contact with them can be a way of enhancing one's safety. But, obviously, if one assumes that all army personnel are undisciplined and inherently violent, liaising with them will not appear a viable safety mechanism. Thus, MONUSCO blue helmets urged me to approach FARDC officers with caution. This advice created a dilemma as the nature of my research forced me to spend a lot of time with the Congolese army.

Lacking barracks and other infrastructure, FARDC personnel often stay in hotels or lodges when on a mission. In order to get to know officers, I decided to stay in the same places. In a certain town in South Kivu, this strategy panned out surprisingly well and I soon found myself interacting with a particular officer on a regular basis. Although having a slight alcohol problem, Major John was an intelligent and well-spoken guy with advanced knowledge of security dynamics. That was no coincidence. He was the so-called S2 (intelligence officer) of a FARDC brigade. He was thus tasked with collecting information on armed groups and monitoring security developments in the area. Through frequent discussions with Major John, I discovered that the knowledge of armed groups possessed by the FARDC—that supposedly rag-tag, unprofessional and undisciplined army—was far superior to that of the professional and relatively well-equipped MONUSCO forces. Major John appeared to have a good sense of the histories, size, revenue-generation strategies and local political connections of armed groups in the area. What's more, many of his observations were corroborated by other people I spoke to.

Major John did not only evolve into a so-called 'key informant' himself, he also brought me into contact with other members of his brigade. Through these regular contacts, I was able to mitigate what I have elsewhere (Verweijen, 2015b) labelled the 'Barbarian Syndrome' surrounding armed actors in the Global South. Having frequent informal conservations with members of the brigade, they started to become concerned about my safety. Some officers of the general staff would discourage me from going to certain places if they knew military operations had been planned there. I also had extensive discussions concerning the nature of insecurity in certain areas with Major John and one of his best friends, Major Zero Zero. For instance, we went to great lengths to grasp patterns of attacks in an area south of a particular goldmine. Ultimately, we drew the conclusion that this could not be the work of a highly organized foreign rebel group, the Forces Démocratiques de Libération du Rwanda (FDLR), as some had alleged. Rather, the attacks were more likely conducted by a group of bandits operating with the complicity of certain villagers. The implication was that travelling to that area was relatively unsafe. The foreign rebel group was not known for attacking and killing foreigners. However, that was uncertain for the group of bandits, whose level of discipline and objectives were unknown. Based on these conversations, I concluded that, at least in the case of this particular brigade, the FARDC was far more useful for navigating insecurity than any foreign military actor.

Imagining the ambush

While the FARDC seemed to have substantial 'security expertise', their narratives on security incidents could also be treacherous, as I learned from a human rights defender in the area. Becoming a key research collaborator, Hassan was by all means an impressive figure. Maintaining contacts with both armed groups and the army, he was always ready to go the extra mile to address human rights abuses, for instance pleading with army officers to liberate civilians they had unlawfully detained.

His dedication to human rights also seemed to render him fairly 'neutral', as he was not interested in covering up abuses and crimes by one side or another. Thus, his analyses contrasted sometimes sharply with narratives of abuses or incidents circulating among the security services or parts of the population.

In the Kivu provinces, it often occurs that attacks are not explicitly claimed by particular groups. Moreover, the identity of the attackers cannot always be read from their appearance and mode of operating. The result is 'blame games' whereby different groups point the finger at different categories of alleged perpetrators. The latter commonly include the FDLR, the Congolese army (or deserters thereof), 'Mai-Mai groups' (a generic name for armed groups framing themselves as engaging in community self-defence) or groups of bandits. This finger pointing is not only informed by groups' desire to wash themselves of any blame, it is also shaped by ethnic biases. For instance, when asked about the recurrent ambushes in what is known as the '17 forest' due to it being 17 kilometres long, interlocutors from villages in the surroundings blamed these incidents on FARDC soldiers speaking Kinyarwanda (often framed as 'foreigners' who would not be 'authentically Congolese'). At the same time, certain groups in the army saw too readily the hand of the Mai-Mai in these incidents, in part as the majority of Mai-Mai combatants were members of an ethnic group that they heavily distrusted. Given that many FARDC personnel deployed in the Kivus are from the provinces themselves, it is not surprising that their interpretation of security events reflects dominant conflict narratives.

By comparing different narratives on security incidents, I became increasingly aware of the biases in the information provided by Major John and his fellow brigade members. Nevertheless, some of the general knowledge they had provided on armed groups and their command chains became essential analytical tools for my security decisions. One of these decisions concerned whether to conduct research on a particular 'ambush rich' axis or not. As my most trusted collaborator, I discussed the situation extensively with Hassan, leading us to try to dissect the mechanics of ambushing. Up till now, ambushes had in principle not been accompanied by atrocities, as long as victims did not actively resist having their belongings confiscated. Rather, the main ambush scenario consisted of armed men trying to obtain people's belongings as quickly and efficiently as possible, before vanishing into the adjacent bush. Armed groups have different repertoires of violence, and killing, rape and kidnapping did not appear part of this particular group's repertoire. In addition, as the FARDC and Hassan suggested, the group was disciplined. This should reduce the possibility of the attackers inflicting additional harm during an ambush.

Based on this analysis, we thought systematically through what would happen in case we would fall into an ambush, imagining step by step how it would unfold, and how the perpetrators would act and reason. When ambushing was about quickly extracting belongings, so we concluded, it was best to facilitate that by not trying to resist and having a certain amount of cash at ready—sufficient for the attackers to rejoice at the booty and quickly withdraw into the bush. The thought exercise of 'imagining the ambush' and gauging the psychology of the attackers straddled the fine line between frightening and fun. It led us to coin the running gag of being 'ambush ready'. But it was not a joke, of course. The prospect of falling into an ambush remained all too real. Perhaps this form of psychological preparation could render a potential ambush less harmful, but it could not help preventing one. The fact that we managed to complete our trip ambush-less remained grace of Lady Luck. This ongoing fortune—travelling dangerous zones unscathed—was both a blessing and a curse. Without any incidents, how could I know whether I was pushing my luck too far?

Rape preparedness

Through what I labelled my 'ambush logistics', I came into contact with several humanitarian organizations. Each time I was moving into ambush-rich or otherwise dangerous zones, I would leave my valuables at the base of a humanitarian NGO. Being a regular appearance at some NGO compounds, I exchanged extensively with their staff, in particular logistics personnel, about the security situation. After all, they moved and worked in insecure areas, and sometimes had direct contacts with armed groups (even though they would rarely admit that). These regular conversations allowed me to discover that humanitarian logistics personnel grasped the security situation relatively well, including armed group dynamics. I generally took their security advice seriously—until the one time that I decided to ignore it.

My study design envisaged a comparison between, on the one hand, densely populated and accessible zones and, on the other hand, remote, isolated areas. I therefore planned a mission into the Hauts Plateaux mountain range. The area was not accessible by road, so I would need to go on foot. The decision to hike sparked concern among the UN blue helmets with whom I shared my plans. Apparently, going by foot was widely perceived as 'very insecure'. I would not be able to quickly access medical facilities, the blue helmets suggested, nor would

I have the possibility to rapidly get away in case hostilities broke out. Reflecting on these comments, it appeared to me that these conditions also apply when going by car to areas where roads are in an advanced state of dilapidation. Their arguments therefore did not convince me to abandon my plans. Moreover, according to my research collaborator Sibomana, who was born and raised in the Hauts Plateaux area and would accompany me into the mountains, the risks were not exceptionally high.

Ascending to the highest town in the mountains that could still be reached by motorcycle, we were invited to spend the evening at the base of a large humanitarian organization. Interested in their analysis of the security situation, I sat down with the security and logistics manager, who turned out to be an expat. The guy was unambiguous in his analysis, insisting that security in the area was bad, very bad. Two days prior one of their sub-stations had been attacked. "You are crazy to go into the mountains with just the two of you", he said, trying to discourage me from undertaking this mission. Out of the blue, he added: "I am pretty sure that you will get raped." He explained that his organization continually registered rape cases in the area, and was apparently convinced that I would be affected by the same dynamics. His words unsettled me. Was it really that dangerous to go into the mountains? And, if the risks were outrageously high, why would Sibomana have agreed to this mission? I had few indications he had been trying to mislead me nor could I establish what the motives for that could have possibly been. Yet I also decided that it was not sensible to take a decision on the basis of two strongly opposed opinions.

The next day, I went to the camp of a Mai-Mai group that was in the process of surrendering itself to the Congolese army, but were still deployed in their fiefdom. Talking to the deputy commander charged with intelligence and operations, I tried to elicit his assessment of security dynamics in the area. Aware that his analysis could be highly self-interested, the reasons he invoked to substantiate that the zone was relatively safe appeared credible. The army was not conducting any operations in the area. Since his group was still in control, banditry was minimal. Furthermore, one of the bigger rebel movements that had earlier destabilized the area had withdrawn deep into the forest. This assessment converged with that of a range of other sources that I contacted in the village, including an FARDC commander, customary chiefs, a human rights defender, elders and, at the market, people from different villages in the surrounding area. I also learnt from these sources that the attack on the humanitarian NGO had largely been a result of its own recruitment practices: they had hired no fewer than three people from the same (extended) family as security guards, and that in a region where employment is so scarce that the stakes of its distribution are extremely high.

Based on this information, I decided to leave the next morning with Sibomana, hiking towards the natal village of the Mai-Mai leader, with the approval of his colleagues at the camp. I did not say goodbye to the security and logistics manager, who I felt had misread the security situation. Yet despite my dismissing his analysis, I would eventually heed one piece of advice that he gave. Convinced that I ran a high risk of being raped, he had insisted that I would carry a so-called PEP (post-exposure preventive treatment) kit, a cocktail of medication one needs to take within 72 hours after rape to avoid pregnancy and the transmission of HIV and other sexually transmitted diseases. At that moment, sexual violence-related aid in the eastern DRC had reached a climax, and many humanitarian NGOs distributed PEP kits to health centres. This included health centres in very remote zones, as I found out when coming across one after two days of walking. Having to overcome shame and guilt for usurping something that was destined for women with much less opportunity for damage control than myself, I eventually dared to ask the doctor running the centre for a PEP kit. Carrying around this unusual load—a couple of plastic bottles filled with pills—was both uncanny, a constant reminder of what *could* happen, and somehow reassuring, relaying the thought that one could somehow avoid the worst. It would travel in my luggage for many months to come, remaining untouched.

Conclusion: locating security expertise

My field experiences and observations differ little from those of the hundreds of researchers who have written on 'dangerous fieldwork' (Lee, 1995), 'danger in the field' (Lee-Treweek and Linkoogle, 2000) or 'fieldwork under fire' (Nordstrom and Robben, 1995). This extensive body of often fairly navel-gazing literature draws similar conclusions concerning how researchers obtain and assess security knowledge and translate this knowledge into guidelines for action. It tends to emphasize the importance of profound immersion in the research context (Peritore, 1990) and of constructing a social network and maintaining relations with 'key informants' (Kovats-Bernat, 2002). Furthermore, it highlights how access to information and exposure to risks are shaped by researchers' and research collaborators' positionality, including their political position, race, and gender (Nash, 1976; Green et al, 1993).

It also offers dozens of practical guidelines for 'surviving fieldwork' (Howell, 1990), which has become something of a cottage industry. These guidelines include: reflexivity, flexibility, anticipating and imagining danger, not growing complacent about the dangers one faces and making efforts to 'constantly define and redefine risk and danger in light of actual experiences' (Sluka, 1995: 280).

What was specific to my situation, and may be comparable for those studying foreign interventions, is that the nature of my subject matter led me to first interact with foreign security 'professionals'. Contrary to what I had expected, their assessments of 'the security situation' were highly inaccurate—burdened rather than enriched by their professional background. They seemed to assess risks based on their own professionally shaped notions of 'safety', whether stemming from being used to bearing arms or being attuned to sexual violence. In addition, they appeared to read the security situation through inappropriate analytical lenses, grounded in particular ideas of what 'war' was about. Aside from being tinged by cultural and racial biases, their assessments were often heavily coloured by professionally imposed restrictions on their contacts and movements (cf. Higate and Henry, 2009). These observations left me disillusioned about the added value of sending foreign security 'experts' to war zones, whether to observe or stabilize security dynamics, reform security services or secure humanitarian operations.

Finding little security knowledge among foreign security 'experts', I shifted my orientation towards Congolese human rights defenders, journalists and key informants within the Congolese army. But I was only able to assess the information they provided by triangulating it with the stories and observations of the hundreds of other people I contacted for my research—including local authorities, a wide range of security agencies, and political and military armed group members. In the end, I concluded, security 'knowledge' was not the sole prerogative of a few designated people. It rather seemed an immense puzzle that had to be painstakingly put together from hundreds of pieces, with individual pieces often being initially misplaced, and some pieces never found. What is remarkable is that few of the people who most decidedly contributed to piecing the puzzle together explicitly asserted having 'security expertise'. Hence, that expertise seems to reside precisely where it is not claimed, implying we should perhaps not look for it where it is ostensibly offered.

Note

[1] All names in this chapter have been changed for security reasons.

References

Green, G., Barbour, R.S., Barnard, M. and Kitzinger, J. (1993) 'Who wears the trousers? Sexual harassment in research settings', *Women's Studies International Forum*, 16(6): 627–37.

Higate, P. and Henry, M. (2009) *Insecure Spaces: Peacekeeping, Power and Performance in Haiti, Kosovo and Liberia*, London and New York: Zed Books.

Howell, N. (1990) *Surviving Fieldwork: A Report of the Advisory Panel on Health and Safety in Fieldwork*, Washington, DC: American Anthropological Association.

Kalyvas, S.N. (2006) *The Logic of Violence in Civil War*, Cambridge: Cambridge University Press.

Kovats-Bernat, J.C. (2002) 'Negotiating dangerous fields: pragmatic strategies for fieldwork amid violence and terror', *American Anthropologist*, 104(1): 208–20.

Lee, R. (1995) 'Dangerous fieldwork', *Qualitative Research Methods Series*, 34, Thousand Oaks, CA: Sage.

Lee-Treweek, G. and Linkogle, S. (2000) *Danger in the Field: Risk and Ethics in Social Research*, London: Routledge.

Nash, J. (1976) 'Ethnology in a revolutionary setting', in M. Rynkiewich and J. Spradley (eds), *Ethics and Anthropology: Dilemmas in Fieldwork*, New York: Wiley and Sons, pp 148–66.

Nordstrom, C. and Robben, C.G.M. (1995) *Fieldwork under Fire. Contemporary Studies of Violence and Survival*, Berkeley: University of California Press.

Peritore, N.P. (1990) 'Reflections on dangerous fieldwork', *American Sociologist*, 21(4): 359–72.

Sluka, J. (1995) 'Reflections on managing danger in fieldwork: dangerous anthropology in Belfast', in C. Nordstrom and C.G.M. Robben (eds), *Fieldwork under Fire: Contemporary Studies of Violence and Survival*, Berkeley: University of California Press, pp 276–94.

Verweijen, J. (2015a) *The Ambiguity of Militarization. The Complex Interaction between the Congolese Armed Forces and Civilians in the Kivu Provinces, Eastern DR Congo*, Utrecht: Utrecht University, Faculty of Humanities.

Verweijen, J. (2015b) 'Coping with the Barbarian Syndrome: studying everyday civilian–military interaction from below in eastern DR Congo', in K. Nakray, M. Alston and K. Whittenbury (eds), *Social Science Research Ethics for a Globalizing World: Interdisciplinary and Cross-Cultural Perspectives*, New York: Routledge, pp 243–57.

Verweijen, J. (2017) 'Strange battlefield fellows: the diagonal interoperability between blue helmets and the Congolese army', *International Peacekeeping*, 24(3): 363–87.

10

Being Watched and Being Handled

Jesse Driscoll[1]

> There are many parallels between ... fieldwork and espionage. Both involve looking, listening, eavesdropping, taking notes, recording conversations, snapping photos, and establishing trusted confidants. We call it participant-observation; they call it spying.
> (Borneman and Masco, 2015: 781)

Protecting sources and confidentiality are of practical importance to certain kinds of data collection. This necessitates a number of different kinds of concerns which are properly, and usefully, addressed by institutional review board (IRB) reviews and thoughtfully considered in other chapters in this volume. It is obvious to most people that the safe collection of original data in post-conflict settings requires improvisation. Less obvious is that this improvisation sometimes has the feel of flaunting the inability of state security services to enforce the laws of their home state. This chapter departs from the vital conversation about subject confidentiality and rather takes up a somewhat more complex and difficult topic: the adversarial relationship that can, sometimes, evolve between a researcher and the indigenous security institutions of the state where research is conducted.

An adversarial strategic relationship between state security forces and academic researchers is not necessary and is not generally desirable. On the contrary: I can report from experience that there can be both personal and professional benefits to outright *collusion* with state security forces under certain circumstances.[2] For those who are appalled by this suggestion—because they already know the police are the bad guys—but plan to conduct fieldwork anyway, the epigraph by Borneman and Masco (2015) expresses the nub of the problem. There can be a real conflict of interest between activist researchers and conservative police officers working in authoritarian states. Since there may be no practical alternative to a passive permanent confrontation, in this chapter I model the strategic relationship between a researcher and a low-level agent embedded in a state security bureaucracy (police, domestic intelligence, and so on). Under some circumstances, each player prefers not to yield to the other, but both must also structure strategies to avoid the worst possible outcome that can occur when neither yields.

The model in this chapter is informed by the research for my first book, a multi-year study of state formation in Central Asia and the Caucasus (Driscoll, 2015b). The work involved collecting many not-for-attribution anecdotes, slowly sifting truth from the vapour of street stories, developing strategies to cultivate empathy with former combatants, and strategies that would allow me to signal that I was not employed by the American national security state. I did not convince everyone. Nor did I convince all members of a secondary, invisible audience for my research: various military, police and national security professionals patrolling the conflict zones where I collected my data. Many continue (in a cordial way) to question my motives. I still get some cold stares.

I have also gradually been made aware, in intervening years, that my activities were carefully monitored. I knew some of this at the time and, to be honest, it made me feel cool at first—like I was a character in a John le Carré novel. It did not stay cool for very long, however. Near the end of my time in Tajikistan someone put an empty syringe in my luggage at the airport as I left the country. I found it upon re-entry into the US. It was empty—but the message was clear. The incident permanently changed my relationship with that field site.

A game

Thomas Shelling (1965) compared crisis bargaining to a game of chicken. Two cars speed towards each other to see who swerves first. Most of the time at least one player swerves, but sometimes players both miscalculate the resolve of their opponent and a collision occurs. Schelling's observation that 'If you are .... invited to play chicken and say that you would rather not, you have just played' (Shelling, 1965: 118) may be relevant in the planning stages of fieldwork, in frank conversations between dissertation advisors and intrepid advisees. Some research projects are inherently riskier than others. What follows is an invitation to envision the fiery crash.

Scope conditions

Let us imagine a contest takes place in a weak state recovering from traumatic civil violence. The war is settled, but the emotional wounds are still bleeding. The economy of this post-war state is highly dependent on foreign charity and development assistance. The rule of law is weak. Civil liberties that are taken for granted in institutionalized democracies—specifically the expectation that telephone conversations and emails are private, and the expectation of freedom of speech—do not really exist. The laws of the state are vaguely written. Crimes like 'sedition', 'espionage', 'instigating ethnic violence' and 'insulting the president' can be invoked retroactively and punitively.

Academic research in these sorts of post-conflict settings often occurs, as a practical necessity, in cooperation with non-governmental organizations (NGOs). These NGOs are tasked with executing grants tied to development assistance, democracy promotion and post-conflict reconstruction. The NGOs conduct their business with indirect assistance from a social milieu that mixes embassy workers, academics and local affiliates. The game is structured to emphasize that some of these NGO–researcher collaborations result in research that could be interpreted in the shadow of the poorly written laws sketched in the previous paragraph.

The model is derived from my experience conducting research in small states whose governments perceive a need for Western charity and thus tolerate researchers. This entire stylization is fundamentally mis-specified for 'hard' authoritarian settings in which the state is *not* dependent on foreign charity. It is not clear what leverage anyone has over governments like Iran, the UAE or Uzbekistan, which is why research on certain topics does not much occur.

Actors

The first actor in the strategic contest is a bureaucrat, generically male, employed in the state security apparatus. The second actor is an academic researcher, generically female, preparing an academic manuscript about the weak state.

Some expository statements about the psychology of the academic researcher might be helpful. Let us presuppose that she imagines she thinks the work she is doing really matters. She may be a careerist, but also considers herself to be involved in a subtle long-term representational political project in her research site, the kind of actor that Ian Shapiro (2005: 179) valorizes as a 'roving ombudsman'. In her mind, she is volunteering time in her 20s and 30s, leveraging her privilege to stand in solidarity with powerless civilians living in badly governed parts of the globe, to uncover socially uncomfortable facts on behalf of people who cannot easily speak for themselves, to aid slow-moving processes of liberal social transformation, and so on. The basic strategic dynamics can apply to researchers who do not share this psychosocial profile, but this sketch is meant to invoke a sympathetic ideal type that is probably familiar to the reader.

The security bureaucrat monitors the academic's activities. He does not like what he sees at all. The experience of civil war has taught the bureaucrat that idealistic political projects can inadvertently get people hurt.

Their interests are, therefore, diametrically opposed. A good day for a security bureaucrat is a day in which his labour contributed directly to the squashing of a story that the academic would consider great data. A good day for the academic is a day in which a story that might expose elite corruption is promulgated globally on a platform that is not easily censored (ideally a peer-reviewed academic journal or blog whose servers are hosted in a different country). Both actors' values are opposed in a zero-sum way. One's gain really is the other's loss.

Strategy sets and joint strategy payoffs

To minimize notation and highlight essentials, assume that the psychological states are symmetric: Good days and bad days are exactly as (dis)satisfying for the academic as the security bureaucrat. It could easily be the case that a zealot on one side or the other of the game would have different underlying payoffs or different risk tolerances. The assumption of symmetry should be considered merely provisional (all major conclusions remain the same).

The game begins with an unexpected event. Something previously unknown about the regime, the elites or the political economy of the weak state is exposed by the momentum of events. It might be a financial scandal, the violent suppression of a prison riot or rural uprising or a political challenge that splits the loyalties of the family of the president. The academic faces a basic choice: 'Escalate' the process of investigation or 'Ignore' the event. Escalation entails gathering more data, conducting interviews, and perhaps beginning to indirectly assist local partners with indigenous activist journalism. Ignoring the event means just that: spending intellectual, financial and political resources on other projects and sending a signal to subordinates to do the same. Assume that the choice set for the security bureaucrat is to either 'Enforce' the law as written, launching an investigation with intent to prosecute perceived malfeasance, or 'Ignore' the researcher.

For this short chapter I analyze the game in a one-shot setting to emphasize the interaction is high-stakes, one-time only and not repeated (since each crisis is unique). The security bureaucrat is player one (payoffs listed first) and the activist academic is player two (payoffs listed second), but the two players act simultaneously (to emphasize that both players must commit to strategies without certain knowledge of what the other player is doing).

The simple scenario is the one in which the security bureaucrat 'Ignores' the activities of the activist academic while the academic 'Ignores' the action-causing event. Nothing happens. The status quo payoffs for (I,I) are (0,0).

What happens if the security bureaucrat 'Ignores' the activities of the activist academic, but the academic 'Escalates' the investigation into the details of the crisis? In the mind of the academic, she is doing what she came there to do. The story will come out faster, more credibly and with more intersubjectively-rendered 'truth' attached to the details than would have been possible if the academic had just stayed home in the ivory tower. This is, reciprocally, embarrassing for the security bureaucrat. It was his job to stop this sort of thing from happening. It is a source of shame when privileged transnationals flaunt their position as guests to write things that would be illegal if written by nationals. Payoffs for (I, E) are $(-\alpha,\alpha)$.

If the security bureaucrat 'Enforces' the law during a time when the activist academic chooses to 'Ignore' the political crisis, what is observed? The activist academic might get a sense that she is being watched. (She might be followed. The Internet might not work quite right. It might all be in her imagination, of course.) Some of her research assistants might report an unusual amount of interest in their activities. In time, after the academic decides not to pursue the story, the harassment fades. Within the bureaucracy, perhaps reports are written to superiors documenting the intimidation, with the implied claim that foreign troublemaking was deterred by their vigilance. The bureaucrat derives psychological satisfaction from a job well done. The academic pays some cost associated with being bullied. Payoffs for (E, I) are $(\alpha,-\alpha)$.

If the security bureaucrat 'Enforces' the law at the same time that the activist academic chooses to 'Escalate' the investigation, there is a direct clash of interests. The foreign-funded academic risks revocation of her privileged guest status. The security bureaucrat is being challenged on his institutional home turf and cannot easily back down.

What might happen? The academic's toolkit could involve a high-profile transnational media campaign, or perhaps just the subtler activation of informal networks that link embassies, universities and foreign capitals (Keck and Sikkink, 1998). This could spiral, however, because these activities can be read as evidence confirming of the theory that the activist academic was a spy or constructing a fifth-column network, all along. To show that the security agency has the upper hand, not just the academic's trusted research assistants but also the assistants' families may be targeted for reprisals. There is nothing the academic can do but wonder if it was all her fault. (And, from a certain point of view, it *was* her fault, since she could have, but did not, correctly anticipated that the security bureaucrat would choose to 'Enforce').

From the perspective of the low-level security bureaucrat the story is not over. Crimes like espionage and sedition can carry long prison sentences. The paperwork for a trial could go on and on. The security services of neighbouring countries and/or the great powers will gradually become involved. (More paperwork.) The academic may be forced to leave the country, but this does not end her ability to 'tell all' in book or media form years or even decades later. Aid programmes may be cut. Security assistance may even be threatened. The foreign presence in the capital city may shrink, lowering the total taxable income in society. And, once the crisis passes, someone will go looking for a scapegoat. Even if he is not fired, the paperwork for this incident will follow his whole career and, quite likely, define it. If he is fired, he has few transferrable skills. Even if none of this actually comes to pass, years of fear that it might come to pass is sufficient to make this a terrible outcome for the bureaucrat. Payoffs for (E, E) are $(-\gamma,-\gamma)$.

Most of the costs of confrontation are paid by people *other than* the faceless security bureaucrat or the academic activist. The extreme $-\gamma$ negative utility function is meant to capture the psychological harm caused to the academic (as she internalizes the costs of her failure) and the risk of contagion and collateral professional harm to the bureaucrat.

Analyzing the game

The preference ordering for both players is straightforward. The best outcome is to play E at the same time that the other player chooses I. The next best outcome is for both players to play I. Barring that, playing I while the other player plays E is better than the worst possible

Figure 10.1: Game Payoffs (Hawk-Dove)

	Security bureaucrat	
Academic activist	I	E
I	0,0	$-\alpha, \alpha = -2, 2$
E	$\alpha, -\alpha = 2, -2$	$-\gamma, -\gamma = -100, -100$

Source: Jesse Driscoll

outcome, which is both players playing E. Generically $\gamma \gg \alpha > 0$, but, for exposition, since most readers will find it easier to keep track of numbers rather than Greek letters, assume that the payoffs for (E, E) are (-100, -100), the payoffs for (I, I) are (0, 0), and the payoffs for (E, I) and (I, E) are (2, -2) and (-2, 2), respectively. This lends itself to a simple 2 x 2 payoff matrix in Figure 10.1.

Selecting a pure strategy equilibrium: coordination on focal points

There are two pure strategy Nash equilibria in a game of chicken: (E, I) and (I, E). If one player is committed to confrontation, the other player ought to back down. A head-on collision is costly to both players. If one player can infer that the other player plans to play 'Ignore', however, then they can increase their payoffs from 0 to α by playing E (Enforce or Escalate), so agreeing to mutually ignore (I, I) is not a Nash subgame perfect equilibrium. On the other hand, both choose Escalation or Enforcement knowing that it opens the door to the worst outcome ($-\gamma$).

Call the equilibrium (E, I), in which the security bureaucrat gets away with bullying the academic with a threat of prosecution, a 'Self-Censorship' equilibrium, which emphasizes the psychological costs paid by the activist. Call the other equilibrium (I, E), in which the academic gets away with publishing material that is damaging to the indigenous elite (because the security bureaucrat did not take the bait), the 'Symbolic Confrontation' equilibrium. The tools of game theory provide no insight whatsoever into which of the two equilibria actors will coordinate upon, however. A rule of thumb is that the equilibrium selection will favour the player who is more capable of setting the rules. When 'setting the rules' is unpacked in practice in informal or non-institutionalized settings, what often matters are signals of relative resolve.

Signalling resolve depends a great deal on the context in which a game of chicken is played. If the game being played is literally two cars speeding towards one another, a player might signal resolve by putting on a blindfold (so that he cannot see the other car and does not know when to swerve) or publicly disabling the steering mechanism on his car with a tire-iron so that swerving is impossible. In the context of military action, troops can burn bridges behind them to make retreat costly or impossible. The 'one-shot' nature of the game leaves out a great deal, here. We could enrich the setting by adding multiple opportunities for both players to update their strategies, in light of gradations of harassment or the tenacity of the researcher. The root problem is the social distance between the researcher and the state security service personnel, watching invisibly or from a distance and trying to decide if we are actually spies (see Driscoll and Schuster, 2017).

In this stylized setting, does the researcher or the security agent 'set the rules'? It depends on the research topic. Transnational norms provide visibility to certain topics and thereby can change the strategies of the security agent by establishing enforcement expectations. Consider the specific case of embassy aid programming, subcontracted through democracy promotion NGOs with clear operational mandates, as a form of signalling in this context. Large fixed costs are paid in advance by members of the transnational civil society to communicate *exactly* what narrow issue area they prioritize. Certain activists are 'part of the package' that comes with these aid projects. Setting up a local office with a permanent address, employing locals, paying taxes (and all sorts of bribes)—all of this sends a signal of resolve about how serious they are about the international norm that elections ought to be free and fair. A great deal of programme funding is devoted to monitoring and reporting on election day activities. With the electoral spectacle as a clear focal point, and the international community clearly engaged to provide symbolic support to domestic activists in the case of a close *and* fraudulent election, there is a great deal of 'Symbolic Confrontation' in the weeks before and after elections. As such, social scientists today have access to orders of magnitude of information about behaviours on election day than we did a few decades ago. So far, when social scientists have worked in solidarity with local activists—on election monitoring and on 'get out the vote' campaigns to help opposition candidates—it has been state security entities that have swerved.

On the other hand, in the absence of a focal transnational event like an election, the 'Self-Censorship' equilibrium may predominate. This is especially true when researchers are working in close proximity to the kinds of subaltern social actors that state security agents regularly surveil. Anything that a foreign researcher 'discovers' about social malcontents, criminal fraternities, radical political parties or drug users (or worse dealers) flaunts the inability of the government to treat social diseases. Resources that a security bureaucracy invests into passive surveillance of these populations can be easily repurposed to subtle forms of intimidation of the researcher (for example, conspicuously denying visa applications, forcing detailed financial audits, following up with interview subjects, and so on). All of this sends signals of intent to Enforce.

The upshot is that context matters. Partnerships with genuine area experts and local NGOs are vital for assessing the degree of political risk associated with different research topics in order to identify the mutually acceptable focal points for a 'symbolic confrontation' equilibrium. They have played this game in this setting before. They are also more attuned to the costs than a roving ombudsman can be. University networks (advisors, the IRB and the wider peer network) can provide a lot of advice and assistance to researchers as well. Scholars should be encouraged to learn the relevant local laws, acquire allies across the spectrum of relevant civil society actors and consult about best practices. In political science, we are increasingly incentivized to precommit to data analysis plans at various stages of the research, prospectus and grant-writing process. In the context of games of chicken, of course, all of this work must also be understood as a mechanism for locking-in one's commitment—for better or for worse.

A mixed-strategy equilibrium

What if the event forcing players to commit to either confrontational or 'go-along-to-get-along' strategies is a truly rare event without a clear precedent? The situation is much more dangerous. Elections, held at regular intervals, are at one end of the predictability/acceptability spectrum, and violent government responses to prison breaks by self-identified Islamic social reformers are at the other end. But what about a food riot in the home region of the president? The conspicuous disappearance of key members of the elite—or of a researcher? Clear evidence of fabricated data? Reports of military clashes along an ungoverned border?

One reason the unexpected is more dangerous is that if the event is genuinely unexpected, the focal point analogy may be different for the researcher than for the security service. The security bureaucracy may itself be adapting in response to the crisis (personnel reassignments, different management, different day-to-day accountability), but none of this would be transparent to even seasoned researchers. The 'normal rules of the game' for NGOs may yield misleading intuitions. Everyone might be improvising.

A personal anecdote may be useful here. I was living in Kyrgyzstan in 2005 when the Andijan events unfolded across the border in Uzbekistan. In brief, Uzbekistan's government put down an attempted prison break with great violence. For a few very uncomfortable days, however, it was really not clear what was happening. Would refugees who had fled to Kyrgyzstan spread the contagion of ethnic fear across the volatile Ferghana Valley? Was the war in Afghanistan creeping north? I recall asking my new colleagues in the NGO milieu these kinds of questions. None of us really had any idea. I recall distinctly three things: (1) the feeling of vulnerability when the Internet stopped working correctly; (2) understanding that if I chose to 'double down' on the investigation of the Andijan events, it would make it very difficult for me to do other things; and (3) understanding that being 'on site' for an unexpected event like this was truly once-in-a-lifetime and exactly what I was there for. By *not* publishing my thoughts on Andijan, I did feel like a coward for a short time ($-\alpha$), but I kept this impulse in check. I made a calculated assessment to 'Ignore.' It was not a mathematical calculation, not exactly, but it was a logical decision denuded of impulsive and emotional distractions. I decided that if I got too close to this particular event it would erode my ability to do any work in the region at all. By staying silent I maintained a freedom to manoeuvre for three more years, ultimately allowing me to conduct the research that gradually produced my first book.

What this anecdote captures, I hope, is an application of the other solution concept relevant to analysis: a mixed-strategy equilibrium, in which each plays a strategy calibrated to make the other player indifferent between the two choices in her strategy set. One player's mixed strategy must be a probability distribution that makes the other player willing to literally flip an unweighted coin; the other player does the same. The payoffs in Figure 10.1, which are symmetric, suggest a mixed-strategy equilibrium in which each player would 'Ignore' 49 times out of 50, and 'Escalates/Enforces' one time in 50. If both players implement this mixed strategy, more than 19 times out of 20 the response to an unexpected crisis will be for both the activist and the security bureaucrat to ignore it. About 2 per cent of the time either the activist or the bureaucrat will play E while the other ignores. A small percentage of the time the strategies collide.

The vast majority of the time in the mixed-strategy equilibrium, the result will be (I, I) because both players are worried about (E, E). In more than 95 per cent of unexpected events, therefore, in this stylization nothing would happen. Both players have adapted by choosing strategies designed to exploit the other side's desire to avoid an embarrassing and confrontational outcome. Notice also that the expected utility for both players in playing this sort of game according to a mixed-strategy-equilibrium, however, is negative. The game of chicken with the payoffs defined in this stylization has a resemblance to a game of Russian roulette using a modified gun with many chambers. Most of the time nothing happens, but there are *certain* to be high costs if the game is played over and over indefinitely.

Conclusion

A career police officer, and very good friend, responded to an early draft of this chapter with the following pointed observation: "Is there not a deeper problem of politicization of the role of research by accepting crusading in the guise of academic inquiry? Maybe gently suggesting … that as scholars they actually *aren't* roving ombudsman on personal missions?"

My friend has a point. Researchers working in post-conflict settings should sensitize themselves to the fact that the self-censorship equilibrium (E, I) is normatively justifiable and, perhaps, as my friend suggests, on balance desirable—even if it stings ($-\alpha$). In a post-conflict research setting, bringing state capacity to bear in order to shape the information space through juridical and disciplinary modes of censorship—such as tempering the content of radical sermons delivered from the pulpit or prohibiting subversive political ideas from being distributed in school curricula—is a time-tested component of maintaining social order (Hobbes, 1651). Conducting fully open research on another country's civil war may run afoul of social taboos designed to keep certain uncomfortable truths out of the public sphere. This offends liberal sensibilities about the value of free speech and academic inquiry. I will only suggest, gently, that if a researcher is engaging in knowledge production that would violate strong local taboos (or laws), if the researcher were local, it may be worth reflecting on why those taboos exist.

The solution is also not quite as simple as my friend wants to make it, however. Few mechanisms exist to discipline students, or advisors, who imagine they have 'a right to treat' and are unapologetic about their desire to cause change in a field site that they have adopted as a cause. Many academic departments hire and promote based on signals of activist political attributes. Junior scholars are told they have to publish or perish, which can contribute to a host of motivated misperceptions and make it hard to assess risks (see further, Driscoll, 2015a).

We do owe it to our subjects to try to think very hard about risks before green-lighting fieldwork in dangerous places. There may be personal costs that follow the researcher long-term that 20-somethings are poorly prepared to judge.[3] Taking these costs seriously should be part of making a decision to do certain research in certain places. If you think the work is worth these risks, you are an adult—but you should not be caught flat-footed. Be prepared. Also consider that the costs of something going terribly wrong will not be borne just by us, but also by our affiliates who cannot flee the jurisdiction with a one-way ticket out of the country.

Finally, embedded in this chapter's simplified model is a humanizing assumption. The activist is not confronting a faceless bureaucracy. She is rather confronting a real person, like my friend, doing his job. This person probably resides near the bottom of a bureaucratic totem pole. This person is probably trying to support a family on his meagre government salary. He is not perfect, but, if he is like my friend, he is motivated by a personal code of honour. If he could speak, he would be able to explain (with great eloquence) why he resents our privilege, as researchers representing the Western academy, to come and go as we choose. So, to the extent that you can, consider making friends with, or at least being sympathetic to, this compromised social actor. Regular social interactions with your minders and handlers is a compromise to pure confrontational ethics, but it provides opportunities to defuse the game. These people are our doppelgangers. If we had been born into their societies, we might well be doing their jobs. If all of this seems a bridge too far, at least make an effort to make friends at your embassy—especially among the kinds of people that might have pull with the security services of the host state. You never know when you might really, really need those kinds of friends.

Notes

[1] Note: Some material is adapted from *Doing Global Fieldwork: A Social Scientist's Guide to Mixed-Method Research in Difficult Places*, forthcoming from Columbia University Press.

² Weighing these benefits (against quite different psychic costs) would require a different model speaking to an entirely different set of moral quandaries, which I will address elsewhere.

³ Type the words 'Matthew Hedges UAE' or 'Xiyue Wang Iran' into Google, if you are not certain what I mean; see also Russo and Strazzari, and Heathershaw and Mullojonov, in this volume.

References

Borneman, J and Masco, J. (2015) 'Anthropology and the security state', *American Anthropologist*, 117(4): 781–5.

Driscoll, J. (2015a) 'Prison states and games of chicken', in S. Desposato (ed.), *Ethics and Experiments: Problems and Solutions for Social Scientists and Policy Professionals*, New York and London: Routledge, pp 81–96.

Driscoll, J. (2015b) *Warlords and Coalition Politics in Post-Soviet States*, New York: Cambridge University Press.

Driscoll, J and Schuster, C. (2017) 'Spies like us,' *Ethnography*, 19(3): 411–30.

Hobbes, T. (1651) *Leviathan* (1981 reprint), London: Penguin Classics.

Keck, M. and Sikkink, K. (1998) *Activists Beyond Borders*, Ithaca, NY: Cornell University Press.

Schelling, T. (1965) *Arms and Influence*, New Haven, CT: Yale University Press.

Shapiro, I. (2005) *The Flight from Reality in the Human Sciences*, Princeton, NJ: Princeton University Press.

PART III

Distance and Closeness

In the violent and closed contexts for fieldwork-based research discussed in this book, shaped additionally by an international intervention of some form, questions of distance and closeness between researchers and researched arise in different forms. Contributions to this part of the book highlight the different nuances and constant negotiations around cultural distance and closeness, the insider–outsider binary, and different (performances of) identities in the field; they explore distances researchers create themselves through their own interventions into a specific context, by means of over-research of some people and issues at the cost of a lack of attention to other people and issues; and they discuss the challenges of doing intervention-related fieldwork in situations in which direct access to the field is restrained, be it due to security concerns or because the authorities of the host countries control foreigners' access to (parts of) their territory, thereby creating a physical distance from the field. The research underpinning the chapters took place in the Yemeni capital Sana'a in a situation of deteriorating security, among over- und under-researched groups in post-war Bosnia and Herzegovina, as embedded research with the UN mission in Darfur (Sudan), and in a collaboration between a Northern and a Burmese team on an arts-based research in Myanmar's Kachin and Rakhine states.

11

Positioning in an Insecure Field: Reflections on Negotiating Identity

Maria-Louise Clausen

This chapter reflects on different aspects of identity in relation to fieldwork and interviews in Sana'a, the capital of Yemen, in 2013 and 2014. In 2011–12, the Yemeni rose in peaceful protests that eventually destabilized Yemen to the point where civil war seemed not just possible but imminent. In this context, the Gulf Cooperation Council (GCC)—spearheaded by Saudi Arabia—and the United Nations intervened, formulated a deal that forced the president of 33 years, Ali Abdullah Saleh, to step down in return for immunity. Yet, whereas the deal temporarily helped Yemen avoid full-blown civil war, the economy as well as the security situation kept deteriorating in 2013–14. In September 2014, the Houthis, a group that has a long history of marginalization and armed resistance against the central state, took control of Sana'a, assisted by the former president Saleh.

The crumbling political transition and a violent takeover of the capital by an armed militia formed an important backdrop to my interviews with politicians, tribal leaders, activists, analysts and civil servants who all had stakes in the political transition. The gradual collapse of security also meant that most internationals left Yemen and those who remained had limited possibilities of individual movement. However, I was a doctoral student without formal links to any international organization operating inside Yemen, so I had fewer constraints. Instead, I relied on personal contacts, built through previous visits to Yemen, for risk assessments, practical advice and access to key informants. This strategy of relying on a personal network had practical consequences, for example related to accommodation and transportation, but it also affected which meetings I was able to schedule as well as how I was seen by interviewees and, consequently, the data I was able to access.

Ethnographic researchers are encouraged to reflect upon how their identity influences which questions are asked and how the answers are interpreted. The notion that knowledge is positional assumes that the researcher's descriptive characteristics such as gender and ethnicity as well as ascribed aspects of the researcher's identity based on appearance or behaviour play a role in framing the research and its outcomes (Godbole, 2014; Rinita and Lunn, 2014: 96). This entails being aware of how the individual researcher influences the context under study and how the researcher's biases affect the research (Warden, 2013: 154). However, research outcomes are not just about how the researcher interprets the research situation. The assumptions and perceptions made by the interviewee about the researcher also affect data. This form of reflexivity and attention to the socially constructed and negotiated self in the research situation unveils the contextual and relational nature of knowledge production.

This chapter focuses on three key themes that shaped my fieldwork and the data I was able to collect in Yemen in the context of an internationally supported transition and a deteriorating security situation. The first section focuses on how to balance security concerns and being a white female in a highly conservative Islamic context. The second section looks specifically at the interview situation and how power was negotiated based on different aspects of my own and my interviewees' identity. The final section discusses how the inside/outside distinction was negotiated and subject to various perceptions during research encounters. The conclusion reflects on how the initial decision to enter an insecure field as an independent academic without institutional ties to an international organization shaped these three issues.

Negotiating visible aspects of identity

Descriptive characteristics such as gender and ethnicity are more obvious than ascribed aspects of the interviewer's or interviewee's identity. However, this does not mean that their meaning is not negotiated in the field. In this section, I discuss how gender was part of pre-interview conversations between me and the interviewees and generally influenced access to interviews in Yemen.

Yemen is a conservative Muslim society where unrelated men and women have limited interaction. However, as a Western female one is rarely excluded based solely on gender (Yadav, 2018). This includes access to qat chews, social gatherings which are political sites that see elite actors forming alliances and laying the foundations for political decisions.[1] Qat chews are overwhelmingly gender segregated, yet Western women are routinely accepted into this all-male universe.[2] Jillian Schwedler (2006), based on fieldwork in Yemen and Jordan, refers to Western females as a third gender. Whereas all researchers experience limitations of access, some difficulties are greater for women than for men, for example in gaining access to conservative religious environments, but the point is that the room for manoeuvre for Western females is much larger than for local women. Hence, whereas access to the field is largely determined by the same factors for women and men such as contacts, knowledge of the subject and social skills, being female *can* be an advantage in Muslim societies as it allows you to enter private settings where unrelated men are not welcome. This was very evident during my fieldwork in Yemen.

Whereas being a Western female generally did not seem to hinder access to research participants, it did raise some gender-specific issues related to security. During previous visits to Yemen, I had moved around quite freely and felt relatively secure, especially since crime rates were low and social norms largely prevented unwanted (male) attention. Yet, in 2013 and 2014 the security situation had deteriorated and there was an increased number of assassinations and terrorist attacks as well as a general increase in violent incidents which made me feel more insecure. One practical implication was that I began to consider wearing the *niqab* to be able to move around more unnoticed.[3] This would have been in accordance with security advice and general practice among foreigners in 2013 and 2014. However, I did not want to wear a *niqab* during interviews as I felt that would position me as a 'woman' more than a researcher, in addition to inhibiting rapport with interviewees. I was also unsure of how it would be conceived if I began interviews by removing clothes, although it would likely have been unproblematic as interviewees would understand why I did so and possibly have seen other Western women do the same. In the end, my personal inclination against wearing the *niqab* prevailed, but I did wear an *abaya*, a black dress, over my ordinary clothes and veil to cover my hair.

These choices would often be part of the pre-interview small-talk that would revolve around security and, repeatedly, the fact that I am tall and therefore unable to hide in plain sight even if wearing the *niqab*. I sought to steer these discussions away from my gender and, instead, used my height to carve out a more gender-neutral space. In one interview, the male interviewee jokingly said that if I wanted to conceal myself to minimize the security threat associated with being a foreigner in Yemen, it would make more sense that I wore the male Yemeni attire instead of the *niqab*. The comment played with gender norms and underlined my foreignness, but it made me feel accepted and I saw it as verification of my position as a third gender. Another aspect of these pre-interview conversations that focused on my clothes, means of transportation and housing arrangement was how the questions simultaneously showed the interviewees' genuine concern for me and underlined Yemeni values of hospitality and generosity towards strangers, but also marked my status as a foreigner in need of protection. In this sense, it created an opportunity for the interviewee to exert authority over me as it underlined my ineptitude in navigating Yemeni society without help. Again, this would most likely have played out differently had I been male, but the key issue was my foreignness, not my gender.

Although difficult to substantiate with hard proof, there seemed to be a small difference in how the interviewees would approach me depending on their gender. The fact that I was a young, female interviewer can have made it less likely that male interviewees felt the need to actively assert their power over me, instead activating norms of protection. This was expressed through offers to drive me home or, in several instances, leading to invitations to visit their families. These personal interactions provided an opportunity for more informal conversations and a broader introduction to living and working through a political transition. I received fewer invitations by women to visit them in their private homes, although it did happen. In fact, whereas the ethnographic literature often presents non-Western women as subordinate to the white researcher, I found that the female interviewees were more actively seeking to control the interview situation and upholding a professional interviewer–interviewee relationship. For example, at the beginning of one interview with a politically astute female Yemeni, I asked if she could outline the main topics that had been discussed in a working group she had been part of during the transitional process. This type of broad question had been a good opener in other interviews but, in this instance, she told me, in a very firm tone of voice, that I could not ask questions like that. It was too unspecific. She went on to tell me that I should have read up on the main topics of the working group, so I could ask her more specific questions. This illustrates how researchers cannot always depend on interviewees to uphold the division of labour implied in an interview. In this case, the interviewee, who was afterwards very friendly and ready to share her thoughts, began the interview by making me feel as if the interview was an examination, where I had showed up unprepared.

Positionality and negotiations of power

Although a key question in constructing interviews must be, to quote Aberbach and Rockman (2002: 673), 'What do I want to learn?', it is not enough to the think about the wording or order of questions when preparing for interviews. One aspect of this arises from the recognition that the interview situation is a social interaction between an interviewer and an interviewee. The tendency to describe the interview situation as one where the interviewer is somehow able to extract some objective truth from the interviewee, if only the interview is properly designed, leaves the interviewee deprived of agency and exaggerates the ability of the interviewer to control the situation and their interlocutor. It is also an approach to fieldwork and interviews that tends to portray the researcher as the one in the position of relative power (Smith, 2006). However, in my experience this is not straightforward as every interview saw a negotiation and mutual positioning, which was influenced by social categories such as gender and age but also by the broader context of the interview situation (see also Bjørkhaug, and Göransson, in this volume).

In this case, the broader context was the ongoing UN-supported transitional process. Thus, to the extent that the interviewees interacted with young(ish) Western females in Yemen, they were associated with international organizations or part of diplomatic missions. Consequently, it is likely that my presence was interpreted through the prism of the intervention, that is, that I was subject to an evaluative positioning (Roberts, 2001: 2–3). Importantly, positionality is not just something the researcher controls, but also concerns how the interviewee positions the researcher. Moreover, the way the researcher constructs herself might not correspond with how interviewees perceive and positions the researcher (Thapar-Björkert and Henry, 2004). Instead, positionality is a dynamic process where the researcher underlines different aspects of her identity, which interact with the interviewees' perceptions and understandings. Hence, the interaction between the interviewee and interviewer does not take place in a vacuum.

In a context defined by political turmoil and rumours such as the Yemeni in 2013–14, it is not neutral to be seen in deep conversation with a foreign female. There are a few cafés in Yemen's capital that are considered safe for foreigners and these are mainly used by the Yemeni liberal elite. Whereas, to quote Marieke Brandt who has worked extensively on the Houthis in Yemen, 'in Yemen's highly politicized and conflict-prone environment, the mere physical presence of a foreign researcher can already be compromising' (Brandt, 2017: 508), these cafés provide an environment where interviewees are unlikely to have their safety compromised by being seen with a foreigner. Moreover, these cafés are guarded and private, so they can provide a setting for meetings where social conventions are less strict. In addition to the practical aspect of meeting in these cafes, I did in some cases sense that the interviewee viewed the opportunity to be seen with me as a way of undergirding an image of themselves as integrated with the international community. This was especially the case for young activists who had spearheaded the protests in 2011 against former president Saleh, but found it increasingly difficult to exchange their role in the 2011 uprising for political clout in the subsequent political transition. Whereas these are speculations on my part, it reflects that I had a growing awareness of how I could not assume to be fully aware of the perceptions and assumptions held by the interviewees.

Although I met many Yemeni who welcomed support from the international community, there was a widespread feeling that the international community writ large knew little of Yemen, but still acted as if they were experts. As one very politically well-connected activist formulated it in 2014: "You know, Maria, the problem, many of them [representatives from the international community], they come here for one day, they think they know Yemen, and they go back, and they say we have to do this, and this and this."[4] In this context, it was not enough that I referred to myself as an academic or a researcher, as this would not distinguish me from these so-called experts. Instead, I had to think of strategies that would position me as a researcher with a *real* interest in getting to know Yemen. These strategies were not devised at my desk before entering the field, but were gradually refined during fieldwork as the same questions kept reappearing. First, during pre-interview small-talk, where I would always be asked how I found Yemen, I would phrase my response in a way that showed that I had a long-time interest in Yemen, for example by comparing the situation in 2013–14 to my first visit to Yemen in 2005. I would then underline that this long-term interest in Yemen had made me more aware of all the complexities of Yemeni politics. Generally, this introduction was well received as it positioned me as someone with knowledge of Yemen but at the same time payed homage to the interviewees' superior knowledge. In one interview, the interviewee specifically related this to his experience contributing to a World Bank report, where, when he received the first draft, it had contained a reference to an Asian country. He told this story to prove that these reports were primarily copied and pasted from one country to the next. The fact that I had repeatedly visited Yemen and sought to stay for longer periods of time, while at the same time showing a willingness to seek to understand the specific Yemeni context instead of making Yemen fit my preconceived notions, was appreciated.

The second factor was less deliberate. As the fieldwork was part of my doctoral research, I was travelling on a budget, which meant owning only one slightly too small *abaya*, as I would have had to have one tailor-made to fit. In addition to being underdressed, my limited budget meant not having access to a private driver or staying in one of the expensive hotels that usually hosts foreigners, instead opting to live in a private house in Sana'a's old city. On a side note, this accommodation also felt safer. During fieldwork I became increasingly aware of how choices that for me were not meant to communicate anything, to the interviewees were still part of how I was positioned in the field. For example, arriving by taxi distanced me from other international actors who were only allowed to leave their compounds in armoured cars with professional drivers. It was seen as a very concrete example of my resolve to get to know Yemen. Moreover, as I was pursuing doctoral research, I was considered a student. Consequently, it was obvious that many of those I spoke to believed that they surpassed me in power and wealth. As a result, I spent most of my field work feeling like the 'obscure academic, who poses, so far as [the elites] are concerned, absolutely no threat' (Schoenberger quoted in Boucher, 2017: 100).[5] This was expounded by a general feeling of insecurity that was difficult to escape as violent incidents happened on a nearly daily basis, and my mundane struggles with electricity cuts and limited water supply, in addition to the substantial pressure to perform academically. My understanding of how the interviewees perceived me was thus shaped by the lack of control that I felt.

Arguably, gaining access to the field and relevant interviewees is one of the most challenging aspects of ethnographic data collection (Warden, 2013: 152). I did not have a fixer but instead relied on a mixture of previous contacts, snowballing and random meetings where people would hear about my research and then volunteer help. This process is gratifying as it, in a sense, forces you to build relationships in the field, but it also meant that I was constantly reminded of how dependent I was on the help of near strangers. However, although I felt relatively devoid of power, this was not necessarily the way the interviewees saw me. The most obvious indication of this was how my interview request, once I had someone on the phone, would almost always be granted even before I could explain the purpose of the research. Speaking English and saying that I was a researcher was enough. And, at the very least, as mentioned by Rose (quoted in Warden, 2013: 155), there is power inherent in the production of knowledge of others. If news of Yemen reaches an international audience, it is mainly through the lenses of Western researchers and journalists. Many I spoke to were acutely aware of this fact and consequently thanked me for my interest in Yemen.

Negotiating identity—finding your place in the field

Power relationships are highly complex and context-dependent, as they reflect personal and professional characteristics of both the interviewer and the interviewee. In the interview situation, both interviewer and interviewee can draw on and be positioned according to a multiplicity of different social categories. Consequently, interviews are not just about what the interviewer wants, but also about the social context of the interviewee and their reasons for talking to the researcher. This makes it difficult to suggest a uniform approach, but the researcher should be aware of how the interviewee might place her within a specific category regardless of whether this reflects her own self-identification. During my interviews, I have felt that interviewees have spoken to me like to an ignorant child, a should be (or could be) activist, a friend, a distinguished academic and things in-between. In consequence, I have responded by playing up different parts of my identity to achieve rapport but also, and this has been a recurring challenge for me, to find ways of managing to live and remain sane while being under substantial pressure to produce an academic output.

Although it is increasingly recognized that the 'unobtrusive ethnographer' is an illusion, the idea of being able to detach the researcher from the research subject remains an ideal for many political scientists (Rinita and Lunn, 2014:. 96). The goal is to carry out objective research, meaning that the researcher can generate knowledge from outside the research setting without herself affecting the research outcomes (Schwartz-Shea and Yanow, 2012: 95). However, it is not clear how the researcher presence can be neutralized. Consequently, instead of denying that the researcher affects the research setting, the goal should be more openness on the potential impact of the researcher's visible identity and how the researcher chooses to underscore or downplay specific characteristics while in the field and in between interviews where the researcher might interact in more informal ways with people who contribute to the research.

One important discussion has been whether the researcher operates as an 'insider' or an 'outsider' within the research context and how that affects data (Roberts, 2001: 1). In the Yemeni context, I would best be categorized as a pure outsider as I am not a member of any group, nor do I have strong personal links to any group (Augustin, 2018). However, the distinction between being an insider or an outsider can operate on different levels, even simultaneously. During my first round of data collection for my PhD, I interviewed an academic who was involved in the political transition. We departed on good terms, so during the second round of data collection a year later I called him again, and he immediately agreed to meet. On the day, I was frustrated with the PhD and he immediately not only sensed my frustration but related it to his own PhD experience. Although on most parameters we were very different, we shared an experience of writing a PhD and doing fieldwork in a setting where we were outsiders. Thus, in the specific case, the struggles of doing a PhD created a small space where a shared experience took precedence over other potential categorizations.

The distinction between insider and outsider is fluid and one will often be both. As already discussed, I was clearly an outsider to Yemen, but would be associated with a specific group of outsiders, the so-called international community in Yemen, who were heavily involved in the transition. This assumed linkage most likely helped me gain access but might have influenced the data I was able to collect. Importantly, this was not a positioning that I chose nor was able to escape. Even if the interviewees recognised that I was not formally employed by the UN or similar, then the international community in Yemen is very small, so interviewees could assume, and in part rightly so, that I would informally meet and share insights with representatives of the international community. Hence, although I saw myself as lacking power and was not a part of an international agency or organization while in Yemen, it is perfectly possible that my interviewees perceived me differently. This underlines that interviewees are subjects with agency, history and their own ways of making sense of the interview and the presence of a researcher (Godbole, 2014: 85–6).

In the early stage of my research in Yemen, I did fieldwork within an organization where, following advice, I sought to first interview a key gatekeeper in the organization to show respect and avoid obstruction. However, the person twice stood me up, repeatedly made me deeply uncomfortable and then, the day before I was to leave, insisted on carrying out an interview in an open office environment where he was speaking more to the gathered crowd than me. I became annoyed as I felt he was disrespecting my time and it must have shone through. The next evening when I was saying my final goodbyes, a woman from the organization handed me a set of jewellery that he had instructed her to buy for me, as he was afraid he had insulted me. I was and remain convinced that it was not just about my sensibilities but because he feared that I would turn the organization's external funders against him. This presented me with an awkward dilemma. My first inclination was to turn the jewellery down, but I did not want to create a conflict. My key concern was that my actions might create problems for those in the organization who had (informally) vouched for me. I asked the woman who had bought the jewellery how to respond, and she was very clear that I had to accept the jewellery and at least send the giver a text message to thank him. This led to, for me at least, an awkward exchange of text messages that did, however, successfully diffuse any potential conflict. In addition to demonstrate how I was not able or, to be honest, willing to conceal my personal emotions towards the interviewee, it taught me an important lesson about how I, as the outsider, am positioned by interviewees. In this sense, for me, the situation has become both an example of my lack of control in the field, of the power that I do potentially possess or am perceived to possess, and finally of how my actions may not just reflect on me but also people who have in some way vouched for me during the fieldwork. As a researcher I can leave, but my actions can impact the lives of those who stay.

Conclusion

This chapter has discussed three key themes that shaped the data I was able to collect in the context of the collapsing political transition in Yemen. It has focused on the issue of positionality that has often been neglected in political science due to the ideal of researcher objectivity. However, as this chapter illustrates, there are numerous challenges to negotiating prescriptive and ascriptive characteristics in the interaction between interviewer and interviewee that all affect the data. This chapter has specifically discussed how the context of an international intervention in a collapsing political transition meant that I, as an outsider to Yemen, was inscribed in the nexus between the local and the international. The insecurity of the field both indirectly, for example through the absence of a larger research environment, and directly as my obvious foreignness made me particularly exposed, influenced discussions and research choices. I chose to approach the field as a complete outsider, but whereas my non-Yemeni background was never questioned, my relationship to the so-called international community in Yemen was more ambiguous. The reality is that we as researchers cannot fully control how research participants perceive us, but the more we know the context and allow ourselves to engage with respondents, the more we will be aware of both our own assumptions and those of the interviewees.

Finally, it is important to accept that doing fieldwork, especially in conflict-prone settings during periods of political turmoil means compromising and finding workable solutions on the go. This requires some flexibility and, in my opinion, willingness to listen to and comply with advice from trusted locals, especially if these have somehow become associated with the research. I depended on people in the field, and not just for information related to my research but for basic things such as how to get from A to B or how to do my laundry. My personal security was an important aspect of this, again underlining how a neat separation between the professional and the personal is not possible. Looking back, the initial decision to trust personal relationships more than fences to keep me safe was perhaps the most defining decision for the data I collected for my PhD.

Notes

[1] The elite category is used for people who hold positions of political power or professional prestige (Boucher, 2017: 100).
[2] See Wedeen (2008) for an account of the qat chew. Qat is a mild narcotic stimulant.
[3] The *niqab* is a black piece of cloth that covers the face so that only the eyes are visible.
[4] Interview, activist working with international donors, Sana'a, 2014.
[5] See also Caretta and Jokinen (2017) for a discussion that nuances perceptions about the privilege of postgraduate (female) students in the field.

References

Aberbach, J.D. and Rockman, B.A. (2002) 'Conducting and coding elite interviews', *PS: Political Science and Politics*, 35(4): 673–6.

Augustin, A.A. (2018) 'Rumours, fears and solidarity in fieldwork in times of political turmoil on the verge of war in Southern Yemen', *Contemporary Social Science*, 13(3–4): 444–56.

Boucher, A. (2017) 'Power in elite interviewing: lessons from feminist studies for political science', *Women's Studies International Forum*, 62: 99–106.

Brandt, M. (2017) 'Delocalization of fieldwork and (re)construction of place: doing ethnography in wartime Yemen', *International Journal of Middle East Studies*, 49(3): 506–10.

Caretta, M.A. and Jokinen, J.C. (2017) 'Conflating privilege and vulnerability: a reflexive analysis of emotions and positionality in postgraduate fieldwork', *The Professional Geographer*, 69(2): 275–83.

Godbole, G. (2014) 'Revealing and concealing: ethical dilemmas of manoeuvring identity in the field. Experiences from researching the relationship between land and rural women in western India', in J. Lunn (ed.), *Fieldwork in the Global South: Ethical Challenges and Dilemmas*, London: Routledge, pp 85–95.

Rinita, D. and Lunn, J. (2014) 'First impressions count: the ethics of choosing to be a "native" or a "foreign" researcher', in J. Lunn (ed.), *Fieldwork in the Global South: Ethical Challenges and Dilemmas*, London: Routledge, pp 96–108.

Roberts, J. (2001) 'Dialogue, positionality and the legal framing of ethnographic research', *Sociological Research Online*, 5(4): 1–14.

Schwartz-Shea, P. and Yanow, D. (2012) *Interpretive Research Design: Concepts and Processes*, New York: Routledge.

Schwedler, J. (2006) 'The third gender: western female researchers in the Middle East', *PS: Political Science and Politics*, 39(3): 425–8.

Smith, K.E. (2006) 'Problematising power relations in "elite" interviews', *Geoforum*, 37(4): 643–53.

Thapar-Björkert, S. and Henry, M. (2004) 'Reassessing the research relationship: location, position and power in fieldwork accounts', *International Journal of Social Research Methodology*, 7(5): 363–81.

Warden, T. (2013) 'Feet of clay: confronting emotional challenges in ethnographic experience', *Journal of Organizational Ethnography*, 2(2): 150–72.

Wedeen, L. (2008) *Peripheral Visions. Publics, Power and Performance in Yemen*. Chicago, IL: The University of Chicago Press.

Yadav, S.P. (2018) 'Ethnography is an option. Learning to learn in/though practice', in J.A. Clark and F. Cavatorta (eds), *Political Science Research in the Middle East and North Africa: Methodological and Ethical Challenges*, New York: Oxford University Press, pp 165–73.

12

A Different Form of Intervention? Revisiting the Role of Researchers in Post-war Contexts

Daniela Lai

"You know the story how many researchers we have had in this country, and how useless most of that is/was for activists and organizations. Don't take it personally, but that is the fact."[1] I did not take it personally: by the time a participant told me this as part of his reply to my interview request, I had heard similar views from numerous other participants. I was in the process of planning a seven-day follow-up research trip to Sarajevo, Bosnia and Herzegovina (BiH), after I had already spent about six months conducting interviews and observation in various Bosnian cities earlier that year.

The purpose of that trip was to carry out more interviews with members of the civil society sector in Sarajevo, which was under-represented in my research sample, but probably over-represented in research about post-war BiH. This specific interviewee, a long-time NGO activist, had met with dozens of researchers like me over the years and was quite straightforward that he was reluctant to keep giving up his time for research that not only would not make an impact, but that he would not even come to see and read. I ended up meeting this interviewee, keeping in touch and sending him my research results, but that is not the key point of this story. The point is that his feelings were common among members of NGOs in Sarajevo, who felt that the city had been used as a kind of 'training ground' for researchers, who often disappeared once their fieldwork was over.

In this chapter, I reflect on the role of researchers in BiH and post-conflict societies in general and discuss in what sense their presence in the country could constitute another form of (mostly international) 'intervention'. Based on fieldwork experience in BiH during my doctoral studies, when I stayed in the country for a combined period of about nine months between 2014 and 2016, the chapter examines the features that associate the practices of international researchers to those of the international interventions whose effects we set out to study. On the one hand, this is evidenced by the concentration of research on Sarajevo-based NGOs and activists, which is leading to a renegotiation of the relationship between researchers and Bosnian participants. On the other hand, research as intervention can also mirror some of the problems of the international intervention itself: as researchers—similarly to international organizations—were concentrating in Sarajevo, other problems of the post-war transition, occurring in other cities that remained outside of the spotlight, were at risk of being overlooked.

The research context

The reflections on fieldwork presented in this chapter matured over the course of a few years, during which I was visiting BiH frequently and for extended periods of time. I was carrying out research on the socio-economic dimension of transitional justice, studying experiences of socio-economic violence during war; the resulting socio-economic justice claims; and instances of social mobilization connected to them. Joining ongoing debates over whether (and how) transitional justice programmes should address socio-economic issues (Arbour, 2007; Laplante, 2008; Sharp, 2012, 2014), my project focused on the case of BiH for two key reasons. First, while transitional justice in the former Yugoslavia has been the subject of a vast literature, socio-economic issues have been remarkably absent from it. BiH is not one of the more 'recent' post-conflict cases that frequently appear in current debates on socio-economic issues in transitional justice, such as Nepal, Peru or Colombia (Carranza, 2008; Kaleck, 2013; Robins, 2011). Second, the Bosnian War has been commonly framed as an 'ethnic' conflict featuring widespread ethnically motivated crimes against civilians. These narratives of the war justified the establishment of transitional justice mechanisms such as the International Criminal Tribunal for the former Yugoslavia (ICTY) and domestic war crimes courts and trials. With all their limitations, war crimes trials took on the important task of establishing individual criminal accountability for war crimes, genocide and crimes against humanity. Given the widespread assumption, reinforced by the post-war justice focus on war crimes trials, that the Bosnian War was all about ethnicity, I set out to show how socio-economic violence played a crucial role in people's experiences of war, and that it led to the formulation of socio-economic justice claims. To do this, I also researched the international intervention in BiH, as international actors are usually involved in addressing justice claims in post-war contexts, and thus contribute to delimiting the boundaries of post-war justice processes. In practice, given the reliance on war crimes trials as a tool for dealing with the past, this resulted in the marginalization of post-war justice claims of a socio-economic nature. Other aspects of the 'international intervention', such as economic reforms that privatized firms and reduced the role of the state in the economy and the social sector, posed further obstacles for conflict-affected communities to push forward their socio-economic claims. By the end of this project, I had carried out about 80 interviews, some with international officials, but most of them in smaller cities, such as Prijedor (northwestern BiH) and Zenica (central BiH). I also carried out interviews and observation with activists around the country as well as observation of protests and meetings.

This background to my research is relevant for two main reasons. First, it helps problematize the role (and the actual meaning) of the 'international intervention', addressed in the following section, which sets the basis for the discussion of research as a form of intervention. Second, it contextualizes the subsequent reflections, revolving around the contradictions and tensions generated by my attempts at getting close to conflict-affected communities, while simultaneously being a credible interlocutor for international organizations, and doing so against the background of decades of international research that had left their mark on the country.

Researchers and the 'international intervention'

While often preferred to 'international community', the term 'international intervention' itself is quite broad, encompassing military and civilian, governmental and non-governmental actors (for example, Autesserre, 2014; Bliesemann de Guevara and Kühn, 2009; Jansen, 2006; Nettelfield and Wagner, 2014; Sabaratnam, 2017). In BiH, international involvement began during the war with UN peace-keeping missions and the military intervention by NATO that brought the conflict to an end. It was the peace agreement, however, that requested the presence of an impressively wide range of actors: from the establishment of an international authority overseeing the state- and peacebuilding process (the Office of the High Representative), to the NATO peace enforcement missions, to the ICTY, the Organization for Security and Cooperation in Europe (OSCE), and International Financial Institutions such as the IMF (International Monetary Fund) establishing BiH's new central banking and currency systems.[2]

In relation to my research, doing fieldwork in an 'intervention context' had multiple meanings. First, the context of the intervention were the communities affected by conflict that I was researching, specifically Prijedor and Zenica, and the groups that took part in social mobilization across the country from 2013–14, which I compared and contrasted to NGO activism on justice issues, more commonly supported by international donors in Sarajevo. Supposedly the 'target' of interventions, post-conflict cities like Zenica and Prijedor were rather removed from the day-to-day work of international officials mostly based in the Bosnian capital. Second, doing fieldwork in an 'intervention context' referred to my research on and with those international actors who defined post-war justice processes in BiH and how socioeconomic justice issues were dealt with. This included both officials working on transitional justice (as commonly understood in terms of war crimes trials, truth, search for missing persons, and so on), and those working on social and economic reforms or programmes, from UN agencies such as the United Nations Development Programme (UNDP) to the World Bank and IMF.

Most importantly, it was only once I set foot in Sarajevo to begin my research (and before moving to Zenica and Prijedor), that I came to terms with the fact that researchers carrying out fieldwork in BiH were part of the intervention context itself. Researchers were not simply there as observers of the work of international organizations or of civil society engagement with justice processes. Our presence was part of an intervention that was producing specific and discernible effects on the ground. As a critical researcher, I was aware that fieldwork entails different kinds of research interventions into the local context and the lives of participants (Lai and Roccu, 2019). However, the fact that intervention as a methodological tool can be embraced by the critical scholar (rather than rejected in favour of taking a 'neutral' or 'objective' stance) should not prevent us from questioning the ethical and practical challenges it entails, and which derive especially from the cumulative presence of a high number of researchers over the course of a few decades during the post-war transition.

Among local research participants and activists, the presence of foreigners—or 'expats'—is often associated with both international organizations and researchers. This is hardly surprising if we consider that, in many post-conflict countries, foreign researchers have personal connections to people who work with international organizations, even if their research does not focus on them directly. These relationships form through common friends, by hanging out in the same cafés or restaurants (which often cater explicitly to internationals), or by living in the same neighbourhoods or buildings. Moreover, researchers from Western universities have privileged access to post-conflict countries, having the institutional and economic resources that allow them to travel and spend time away doing fieldwork, and this also shapes local perceptions. Overall, researchers can become part of the international intervention because they are often indistinguishable from officials working at the UN, US or EU delegations—despite the differences in their work and everyday interactions.

Too close? Doing research in an over-exploited site

While the securitization of research makes it increasingly difficult to travel to conflict-affected areas (Fisher, 2017), travelling to a post-war country like BiH, easy to reach from European universities and with good levels of security, is relatively easy. Thanks to this, and because getting practical experience of fieldwork is considered an important part of research training, a high number of students and more experienced researchers have visited BiH, and especially Sarajevo, over the past couple of decades.[3] From the point of view of NGOs and activists who are often our interlocutors on the ground, this has somewhat saturated Sarajevo as a field of research, and led many to question our motives and contributions to understanding BiH—similarly to what is done with reference to international organizations in the country.

While looking at the challenges of working in over-researched contexts through the comments of local activists, the reflections presented here are not meant as an accusation or criticism of their attitudes, and it must be noted that most researchers have very positive experiences in BiH, and Sarajevo in particular. In fact, the aim of this chapter is to turn the critique and analysis towards ourselves as researchers, to understand how our presence in the field changes or affects the very context we set out to study. In the case of my research, while NGOs in Sarajevo were not the main focus of my work, I was conducting interviews with them to explore how their engagement with justice issues differed from more informal and grassroots activism that we had witnessed in the 2014 protests (Arsenijević, 2014; Lai, 2016; Štiks and Horvat, 2014). While I felt I had a certain degree of credibility in front of some NGO activists, either due to research or personal connections or because of my prolonged presence in the country and my (far from perfect) language skills, this did not exempt me from having to address questions related to the legitimacy of my presence or to the usefulness of my work for Bosnian activists or citizens. It was not easy to hear interlocutors question the relevance of a PhD project that was costing me so much effort. In that situation, however, I thought that the best thing I could do was not to take the comments personally and instead ask the interviewees to explain their frustration, which would help me (and possibly other researchers) commit to better practices.

Based on my interview findings, one of the ways in which the presence of researchers has affected Sarajevo is the amount of time and effort that local activists have put into giving interviews and assisting scholars during their projects. The most popular NGOs often complain that during busy times they feel overwhelmed by interview requests. One activist commented: "We cannot employ one person just to respond to requests and do interviews."[4] Another commented that whenever a new request arrives they usually say, "Here they come to test us again."[5] This 'experimental' reference is not only indicative of how NGOs perceive the attitude of the research community as exploitative, but also lays bare the artificiality of research endeavours that benefit from these unequal dynamics. While many activists believe that research is needed, they also accept that—given all the work that has been done so far—people get tired of meeting researchers just to repeat the same things over and over,[6] especially when their energy and time would be better spent in activities with a more direct societal impact, including protests and meetings with citizens.[7]

Activists sometimes doubted the usefulness of all this work: "There is some sort of hyper-production, and I don't see any use in that."[8] Others questioned the ethics of researchers who arrived and said, "I am a researcher, and I need six women victims of rape, or five veterans."[9] In general, activists are wary of researchers' attempts at contacting war victims directly, given that many might not have the necessary training to deal with such a sensitive situation. On the other hand, worryingly, many NGOs claim they had never seen research results of projects they took part in, despite the fact that they might have been potentially useful for their work. One of my interviewees thought this was very unfair, given that researchers "get their PhDs" (or publications) out of the research process,[10] while they do not get anything except—perhaps—a bit of visibility.

This has led to the renegotiation of relationships between researchers and local interlocutors. Some NGOs have started rejecting interview requests or selecting researchers whose projects are more developed, interesting or useful. One organization reported turning down requests from researchers who do not come with a recommendation from people they know or trust.[11] Organizations have also started asking explicitly for something back before agreeing to interviews. In most cases, NGOs and activists have asked that I send them copies of my PhD thesis when completed. In the case described at the beginning of the chapter, a participant's email response to an interview request pointed out that since I had been to BiH for some time, I was probably aware of how many researchers came to the country and how most of this work had been useless for activists. Therefore, the activist asked for something in return and agreed to be interviewed in exchange for either promoting the Facebook page of the organization he works for or writing a short article for their website. I agreed and chose the latter option, and decided to write a short piece on the ethical issues involved in doing research in BiH (see Mreža Mira, 2016).

This shift in attitudes potentially modifies power relations between interviewer and interviewee, but more reflection is needed into how this might occur and what its impact might be not only for Bosnian activists, but also for different groups of researchers at different stages of their career, or coming from more or less prestigious institutions, from the Global North or South. This may help Bosnian activists establish themselves as interlocutors on a more level ground and offer opportunities for more meaningful collaboration with international researchers who work on issues that are directly relevant to their organization. In fact, filtering or rejecting interview requests or the adoption of a more strategic approach to interactions with researchers may be understood as coping mechanisms on the part of NGO activists. From my point of view as a researcher, this entailed abandoning preconceived assumptions about the relationships between Bosnians and internationals. While in methods training courses we are usually encouraged to consider power relations in terms of the 'vulnerability' of participants, a reflection on the exploitative nature of fieldwork here seemed more urgent.

Non-intervention contexts? The peripheries of research interventions

Another way in which the presence of researchers mirrors the international intervention is the lack of engagement with the specific situation of smaller Bosnian cities and towns. The international intervention, both in its policy and academic forms, has always had a privileged outlook on Sarajevo, due to the sizeable presence of internationals. While the international intervention in BiH has been far-reaching and comprehensive, and the effects of such intervention are clearly visible everywhere in BiH, Bosnian cities other than Sarajevo have remained quite peripheral in some respects. As a result, some aspects of BiH's post-war transition are thoroughly researched, while there is a lack of academic and policy knowledge about other issues that are very close to the interests of many Bosnian citizens.

International organizations have their Bosnian headquarters in Sarajevo, and few have field offices in smaller cities (for example, EU Delegation, UNDP, and OSCE regional offices in Banja Luka). Some international organizations have been scaling down their presence in BiH, a process that is most visible outside of the capital. The OSCE, for instance, used to have up to 15 field offices, which are now reduced to eight (some only staffed part-time).[12] Smaller cities are visited less frequently and less observed.[13] International researchers tend to reproduce this bias by making Sarajevo their main base while conducting fieldwork in BiH. This is understandable, as travelling in Bosnia can be difficult, especially during the winter months. Buses often break down, train connections are rare and unreliable. The lack of services and reduced opportunities for socialization make living in smaller urban centres or villages much less appealing.[14] As a result, the direct observation of the politics, society and economics of peripheral regions of BiH is much rarer, on the part of international officials and researchers alike. From a methodological perspective, this risks producing knowledge that is usually purported as being on 'Bosnia and Herzegovina', while actually being based on work conducted in a few thoroughly researched regions or cities. It also downplays the variety of trajectories in political, social and economic change that Bosnian cities have undergone from socialist Yugoslavia, through the war, and throughout the post-war transition. Under these conditions, research interventions risk reproducing images and narratives (of the war, transitional justice and peacebuilding processes) that are partial, distorted and less significant than we are led to believe.

If international organizations working in Bosnia are usually far removed from the everyday life of people in smaller cities and towns, so does academic research often steer away from them. As International Relations (IR) scholars, we are encouraged to study the operation of international interventions before we are drawn to pushing the boundaries of research towards issues that are marginal, obscured or whose relevance is contested. This process of making certain parts of a post-war country such as BiH doubly 'peripheral' (for policy and research) results in a lack of knowledge about certain people and places. Here I give one example of the kind of stories that have gone untold and places that remained marginal, both in research practices and as a target of the work of international organizations.

The example relates to the marginalization of Zenica, a city whose development during the Yugoslav era was linked to the presence of a steel mill employing up to 20,000 people. During the war, the steel mill operated at much reduced capacity and was partially shut, until it was privatized and sold to Mittal Steel (now ArcelorMittal) in 2004. The post-war story of the city is also interwoven with the plant. On the one hand, the war and subsequent privatization entailed the reduction of the steel mill workforce to less than one tenth of pre-war numbers. Workers lost their jobs, often in questionable circumstances, or were forced to retire with minimal pensions. The high levels of unemployment and low levels of activity in Zenica are a direct consequence of this. On the other hand, the functioning and huge steel mill complex lies at the edge of Zenica's city centre, spitting out smoke and creating a reddish haze around the lowest part of the city. Air pollution is dangerously high, and doctors and environmental organizations have campaigned for years for proper monitoring systems to be installed. None of Zenica's two most pressing problems—unemployment due to deindustrialization and pollution—have been at the centre of international organizations' work in post-war BiH. The first is usually considered a necessary by-product of the transition, while air pollution has simply not received much attention. According to my participants, for a long time the situation in Zenica has been overlooked by researchers, who have rarely written about the steel mill, the city's declining working-class identity or its environmental issues, let alone lived in Zenica itself. In my research, recovering the experiences of wartime violence and post-war injustice in Zenica serves to counterbalance the tendency in analyses of Bosnian history and politics to focus on ethnicity as a key explanatory variable for the Bosnian War and the problems of its transition, and to show the possibilities for solidarity and resistance that exist even in places that remain distant from official post-war justice initiatives.

One last element should be highlighted regarding the role of researchers and their distance or closeness to the research context. When I set out to do fieldwork, although my research questions and theoretical frameworks were far from developed, I was determined to put the experiences of communities affected by conflict and post-war intervention at the centre of my project. The more I conducted research in places like Zenica, the more my research questions and methodology reflected this concern with the 'socio-economic dimension' of wartime violence and post-war justice. The relevance of these questions for participants from Prijedor and Zenica seemed understood: they extensively talked about material destruction, social marginalization and exploitation during the war, and how these constituted an important dimension of wartime violence and were entrenched in the transition period. Once back in Sarajevo, I carried out a set of interviews with international officials, with whom I had to make considerable effort to explain the topic of my research, in the end resorting to presenting the topic from different angles depending on the interlocutors' job role and expertise ('conventional' transitional justice issues or social and economic reforms). More than posing a challenge for me, however, this highlighted a problem for international organizations, which keep missing the connection between dealing with the consequences of wartime violence and socio-economic issues that was, instead, very clear to local communities (cf. de Soto and del Castillo, 1994, 2016, on siloed expertise in international organizations). While being another consequence of the uneven geographies of international intervention in Bosnia, this also constitutes a warning for researchers who must remain able to interact and communicate across spaces and language registers. On paper, communication with international officials should have been easier, as I spoke English with them and sat in a formal interview setting. And yet, conveying my research questions and interests felt easier with people from Zenica and Prijedor, with whom I spoke my imperfect Bosnian and carried out impromptu interviews in places that were sometimes noisy, crowded and hot. I was clearly marked as an outsider (as I was), sometimes patronized, as young women often are, but always offered serious engagement with my research questions. Despite the challenges it may have generated, locating the study of wartime violence and post-war justice among conflict-affected communities enabled me to challenge conventions and assumptions on the meaning of justice in post-conflict societies in ways that I would have not otherwise been able to do.

Conclusion

In this chapter I have drawn attention to the role of researchers in intervention contexts, arguing that it can be configured as a form of intervention. This is because, first, the prolonged presence of researchers in post-conflict settings can make local interlocutors feel overwhelmed and sometimes exploited, as I observed in Sarajevo. Second, the work of researchers also tends to mirror some of the pitfalls of the intervention of international organizations, which tend to be out of touch with some of the local realities in the post-war country. This casts places such as Zenica, where I was carrying out part of my research, as peripheral both with respect to the internationally led post-war transition and with respect to academic knowledge about BiH.

Three suggestions can be abstracted from my specific experience. First, I recommend avoiding walking into the field with established assumptions on the relationship between 'local' participants and researchers. When I arrived in Sarajevo, I thought it would be harder to interview the head of mission of the IMF than local NGOs, and I was certainly wrong. In this, I think the way researchers are trained too often still reflects a worldview where 'local' participants in a post-war country are seen as inherently 'vulnerable' or in need, rather than as individuals and groups with agency and resources. As such, they are often expected to welcome researchers' attempts to interact with them, rather than holding critical opinions of our work. On the other hand, we tend to see powerful international actors as less accessible, when they may actually have an interest in using research interviews to present specific narratives about their work and the local context in which they operate (see also Kostić, in this volume). Reflecting on the nature of vulnerability and avoiding harm is undoubtedly necessary, but this should not be done through Western-centric frameworks.

Second, doing research that involves local communities as well as large international institutions will always entail a struggle for critical researchers to position themselves in the research context and during fieldwork. The closer I got to citizens of cities like Zenica, to understand their experience of post-war transition, the more distant I was from the international financial institutions that were producing policies affecting those citizens. While I am not claiming I have been fully successful in this, I ultimately believe there is no definitive solution other than being reflexive of your positionality, continuously questioning your vantage point and assumptions (see also Clausen, in this volume).

Lastly, I encourage researchers not to lose sight of the social and political purpose of their work. As discussed in this chapter, establishing relationships with participants became difficult at times. In such cases, the strongest motivating force for continuing the research was my belief in the relevance of socio-economic violence in war and socio-economic justice claims for the everyday life of conflict-affected communities.

Notes

1. Activist's response to interview request, November 2015.
2. General Framework Agreement for Peace in Bosnia and Herzegovina, www.ohr.int/?page_id=1252.
3. Many researchers proceed to conduct research with less-represented groups outside the capital, but virtually all those who visit BiH will get in touch with well-known Sarajevo-based NGOs, contributing to the feeling of saturation.
4. Interview, NGO activist (1), Sarajevo, November 2015.
5. Interview, NGO activist (2), Sarajevo, November 2015.
6. Interview, NGO activists (3) and (4), Sarajevo, September 2015.
7. Interview, grassroots activist involved in the 2014 protests, Sarajevo, June 2015.
8. Interview, NGO activist (1).
9. Interview, NGO activist (2).
10. Interview, NGO activist (2).
11. Interview, NGO activist (5), Sarajevo, September 2015.
12. Interview, OSCE official, Sarajevo, May 2015.
13. Also: interview, NGO activist (6), Sarajevo, November 2015.
14. Language barriers may pose a further obstacle to conducting research in peripheral regions where participants are less likely to speak English.

References

Arbour, L. (2007) 'Economic and social justice for societies in transition', *NYU Journal of Law and Politics*, 40(1): 1–28.

Arsenijević, D. (2014) 'Protests and plenum: the struggle for the commons', in D. Arsenijević (ed.), *Unbribable Bosnia and Herzegovina: The Fight for the Commons*, Baden-Baden: Nomos, pp 45–50.

Autesserre, S. (2014) *Peaceland: Conflict Resolution and the Everyday Politics of International Intervention*, Cambridge: Cambridge University Press.

Bliesemann de Guevara, B. and Kühn, F. (2009) '"The international community"–rhetoric or reality? Tracing a seemingly well-known apparition', *S&F Sicherheit und Frieden*, 27(2): 73–9.

Carranza, R. (2008) 'Plunder and pain: should transitional justice engage with corruption and economic crimes?' *The International Journal of Transitional Justice*, 2(3): 310–30.

de Soto, A. and del Castillo, G. (1994) 'Obstacles to peacebuilding', *Foreign Policy*, 94 (spring): 69–83.

de Soto, A. and del Castillo, G. (2016) 'Obstacles to peacebuilding revisited', *Global Governance: A Review of Multilateral and International Organisations*, 22(2): 209–27.

Fisher, J. (2017) 'Reproducing remoteness? States, internationals and the co-constitution of aid "bunkerization" in the East African periphery', *Journal of Intervention and Statebuilding*, 11(1): 98–119.

Jansen, S. (2006) 'The privatisation of home and hope: return, reforms and the foreign intervention in Bosnia and Herzegovina', *Dialectical Anthropology*, 30(3/4): 177–99.

Kaleck, W. (2013) 'International criminal law and transnational businesses: cases from Argentina and Colombia', in S. Michalowski (ed.), *Corporate Accountability in the Context of Transitional Justice*, London: Routledge, pp 174–88.

Lai, D. (2016) 'Transitional justice and its discontents: socioeconomic justice in Bosnia and Herzegovina and the limits of international intervention', *Journal of Intervention and Statebuilding*, 10(3): 361–81.

Lai, D. and Roccu, R. (2019) 'Case study research and critical IR: the case for the extended case methodology', *International Relations*, 33(1): 67–87.

Laplante, L.J. (2008) 'Transitional justice and peace building: diagnosing and addressing the socioeconomic roots of violence through a human rights framework', *International Journal of Transitional Justice*, 2(3): 331–55.

Mreža Mira (2016) 'Some reflections on doing research in Bosnia and Herzegovina', 13 April, www.mreza-mira.net/vijesti/clanci/reflections-research-bosnia-herzegovina/.

Nettelfield, L.J. and Wagner, S. (2014) *Srebrenica in the Aftermath of Genocide*, Cambridge: Cambridge University Press.

Robins, S. (2011) 'Towards victim-centred transitional justice: understanding the needs of families of the disappeared in postconflict Nepal', *International Journal of Transitional Justice*, 5(1): 75–98.

Sabaratnam, M. (2017) *Decolonising Intervention: International Statebuilding in Mozambique*, London: Rowman & Littlefield.

Sharp, D.N. (2012) 'Addressing economic violence in times of transition: toward a positive-peace paradigm for transitional justice', *Fordham International Law Journal*, 35(3): 780–814.

Sharp, D.N. (ed.) (2014) *Justice and Economic Violence in Transition*, New York: Springer.

Štiks, I. and Horvat, S. (2014) 'The new Balkan revolts: from protests to plenums, and beyond', in D. Arsenijević (ed.), *Unbribable Bosnia and Herzegovina: The Fight for the Commons*, Baden-Baden: Nomos, pp 83–8.

13

The Road to Darfur: Ethical and Practical Challenges of Embedded Research in Areas of Open Conflict

Mateja Peter

Knowledge on conflict-affected areas and modes of intervention is becoming increasingly important for scholarship and policy. Yet how we generate that knowledge is most often, purposely or not, hidden from the reader. In our attempt to produce scientifically valid scholarship accepted by the broader discipline of international relations (IR), we sanitize our work by eschewing ethical considerations. Ethical considerations, I would argue, are even more central when researching conflict-affected areas and vulnerable populations, or as Elizabeth Dauphinee (2010: 808) writes, '[t]he ethics of responsible scholarship are significant in terms of how we question, how we adjudicate between answers, and how we situate ourselves as writers, witnesses and participants'. While critical scholars have long acknowledged the normative nature of scholarly research, reflexivity is often wanting. In peace and conflict studies, we are good at exploring challenging and problematic practices of other interveners (Duffield, 2010; Higate and Henry, 2009), forgetting that we are often subject to the same practices ourselves (Peter and Strazzari, 2017).

In this chapter, I reflect on my own experiences of doing embedded research in Darfur, Sudan. I do so to, first, illustrate how practical considerations of accessing sites of conflict are entangled with ethical considerations for scholarly work and for interventions themselves, and, second, to highlight how a combination of practical and ethical constraints impacts what we can say about places we study. While I had previously conducted embedded research—most notably in Bosnia and Herzegovina after the war—the two-week research visit to Darfur in November 2014 was different. This was an open conflict and, in my research, I was entirely reliant on our host infrastructure. The trip was ridden with practical and ethical challenges specifically related to conducting fieldwork in areas of open conflict, which I focus on here. To substantiate my argument, I first briefly outline what I understand as embedded research and how this practice is used as a method in peace and conflict studies. I then provide a narrative of my fieldwork in Darfur, laying out the context and practical considerations, before discussing ethical challenges of such research. Here I briefly address how the combination of practical and ethical challenges limited what I could say about the conflict and my host. In the conclusion, I point to some broader implications for scholarship and interventions.

Embedded research in conflict and intervention research

Embedded research involves university- or research institute-based individuals or teams (embedded researchers) conducting work on a previously agreed agenda within a host institution, which might itself be the subject of the study. This practice describes a mutually beneficial relationship between academics and their host institutions, entailing a certain *quid pro quo* not always made clear to wider audiences. The researcher is provided with greater access to the host institution, with benefits for collecting data and potentially also research funding. When it comes to conflict areas, there is also the mere question of access to the geographical area of research. To conduct fieldwork in places like Darfur, Mali or Iraq, researchers may need to travel with international or local security forces and live within their host compounds, for both practical reasons and to satisfy their own institutional requirements (see also Russo and Strazzari, in this volume). For the host institution, the arrangement provides 'a bridge to academia and academic knowledge, networks and critical approaches to developing organizational policies and practices' (McGinty and Salokangas, 2014: 3). Embedded research is in many ways akin to embedded journalism, whose ethical considerations are much more widely researched (Fahmy and Johnson, 2012; Maguire, 2017) and reported on (Ignatius, 2010). In both cases, researchers or journalists are attached to a host institution gaining access to exciting and topical stories of interest in a mediated way. In regions of open conflict, the host institution is typically an armed actor, compounding concerns about informed consent, confidentiality, choice of focus and abuse of findings.

The severity of potential problems with embedded research were brought to the attention of wider publics with the controversy surrounding the US Army's Human Terrain System Project in Iraq and Afghanistan, where social scientists and linguists were embedded in army units to conduct research that fed into military plans. While there was an outright disciplinary rejection of such practices (CEAUSSIC, 2009), fieldwork in conflict regions does not always involve clear choices about how to relate one's work to other actors in the field. Many important scholarly works in peace and conflict studies benefited from their authors having inside access and/or conducting consultancy work for the organizations they were writing about (for example, Autesserre, 2014; Campbell, 2018; McMullin, 2013; Smirl, 2015). With dwindling research funding across the higher education sector, some find a way to finance their fieldwork this way. The extent and nature of a researcher's relationship with host institutions, however, is often not explicitly acknowledged. Even more scarce are serious reflections on how this relationship influenced the knowledge production itself.

Embedded research is an increasingly utilized way of researching conflict and intervention today. It is a method that needs to be understood both in its narrow meaning, but also a broader one. Embedded research as a method is first and foremost a technique for gathering and analyzing bits of data (Jackson, 2011: 25), but it also acts as 'a device', meaning that it is performative, not merely an extraction of information but 'part of a process of continuous production and reproduction of relations, an endless process of bringing worlds into being' (Aradau and Huysmans, 2014: 603). The choice of a specific method is knowledge-producing and has stakes both for relations of power within scholarship and those in the wider worlds. Addressing the ethics of their choice and implications this has on our understandings of conflicts and interventions is thus of crucial importance.

How does one get to Darfur?[1]

To address why Darfur is a great study for thinking about the ethics and effects of embedded research, it is important to first lay out the background of the conflict and why embedded research was the only option for travel to the region. Here, I discuss two interrelated processes: restrictions imposed by external actors (host state, host institution) and restrictions put on by my own research institute (ethical approval and risk assessment procedures). These two sets of restrictions feed into each other, narrowing the choice of methods available to a 21st-century scholar wishing to conduct grounded research in places like Darfur.

The Darfur region in western Sudan has been embroiled in decades-long violent conflict due to a complex set of postcolonial dynamics. The current cycle of violence started in 2003 because of political and economic marginalization of the predominantly African pastoralist population in Darfur by the Arab central authorities in Khartoum. The dissatisfied rebel groups started attacking government forces and, in response, the Sudanese armed forces and government-supported militias (the most notorious being the Janjaweed) targeted the civilian population of Darfur, who were seen as supporting the rebellion. The brutality of this war led to what the UN has called one of the world's worst humanitarian crises (for more see Flint and de Waal, 2009; Mamdani, 2010). More than 2.7 million people have been displaced since the beginning of the conflict, most of them living in squalid camps around major towns of Darfur and in the neighbouring Chad (Sudan Tribune, 2018).

Travel to Darfur is notoriously difficult, not just due to security concerns, but also as access to the region is heavily restricted by the Khartoum authorities, a practice not unusual for many regimes. These legal restrictions have much to do with Sudan's relationship with the international community. From the beginning of the conflict, Sudan firmly resisted UN involvement, seeing it as a Western imperial ploy. A ceasefire was initially brokered by African mediators and monitored by a small African Union (AU) peace-support mission, known as AMIS (the African Union Mission in Sudan). Once the ceasefire broke down and attacks on civilians escalated, the UN Security Council sought greater involvement and Darfur famously became the first case, where the Council invoked the then newly emerged norm of responsibility to protect (Gifkins, 2016). To obtain Sudan's consent for a peace-keeping mission, a compromise UN-AU hybrid operation in Darfur (UNAMID) was established in 2007. UNAMID became one of the largest peacekeeping operations in UN history. The already tenuous relationship with the international community deteriorated further, when in 2009 the International Criminal Court (ICC) issued an arrest warrant for Sudanese President al-Bashir for war crimes and crimes against humanity. Several international agencies were expelled from the country and the region, with further restrictions on travel introduced in subsequent years (Pflanz, 2009).

Obtaining Darfur travel permits is (almost) impossible for Western travellers, and my interlocutors at UNAMID confirmed that even some of their staff failed to obtain the necessary paperwork from Khartoum authorities. Unless one was willing to cross the border between Chad and Sudan and be escorted by local militias—which would not only be dangerous, but also a breach of Sudanese law and therefore against all ethical and risk-management procedures—the only way to gain access to the region was to go through an international organization. When such an opportunity presented itself, I embraced it. My fieldwork was organized around an existing relationship between a network of research institutes in Africa and Europe, and UNAMID. In return for the invitation and facilitation of travel permits, we undertook to prepare an independent study on the police component of the mission, with my own research examining broader questions of protection of civilians. The team consisted of five researchers: two of us had an academic focus, the others were working on policy and training inputs.

Not only are there legal restrictions on travelling to Darfur, but logistically getting to the region is no less complicated. The Darfur travel permits are not normal visa stamps, they are issued in Arabic, making it difficult to board flights to Sudan itself. All of us had complications, with one team member getting stuck at an airport, only joining us after an additional intervention to the airline company was made by the UN. At the Khartoum airport, the UN personnel had to vouch for our presence in the country. Once in Sudan, the only flights to or near Darfur are UN flights, for which additional permissions are required. It quickly became clear that embedded research was the only viable option to conduct any research in the region.

However, even if constraints coming from local authorities and logistical difficulties were not as stark as in the case of Darfur, working for a European institution, with its own set of regulations, would have limited my options for fieldwork. Most Western universities and research institutes today implement strict ethical and risk assessment procedures. Being the only member of the team working for a Western institution (I worked for a Norwegian institute, while all other team members were employed by African institutes), my institutional pre-travel approval was far more elaborate. Given that there was only a fortnight between receiving an invitation and leaving for Sudan due to evolving security concerns, I was even fortunate that my institution had extensive experience with similar research and had developed a relatively flexible approval process. Had I been employed in a different environment, for example a UK university (see also Heathershaw and Mullojonov, in this volume), where such applications must proceed through committees, I might well never have made it to Darfur.

Despite the relative flexibility of my home institution, the approval process was not only difficult but also restrictive of my choices. For years, Darfur has been designated as a complete no-go zone. The UK Foreign and Commonwealth Office (2018), for example, advises against all travel to the region, labelling Darfur a 'red zone'. As a result, I was subject to an additional level of risk assessment, having to fill out a detailed risk assessment form regarding possible evacuation plans, medical facilities, and so on. Many of the mandatory security precautions (nearby hospital, maintaining daily communication with my designated home contact) could not be put in place, requiring two laborious risk-assessment meetings before my travel was approved. For my institution to give me a green light, I had to agree to several risk reduction conditions: my Darfur travel was to be arranged and secured by UN peacekeepers; while in Darfur, I was to conduct research primarily within the compound where I was to live; and an armed UN security escort would be provided whenever I left the compound. These conditions mirrored the requirements the UN had put on us, but the point here is that even without UN restrictions, my choices would have been constrained. Compounded with ethical requirements put on researchers (do not break any local laws!), even without any external limitations, embedded research becomes the only available method for research in places like Darfur.

Ethical challenges and hidden effects of embedded research

Researchers in peace and conflict studies quickly learn how to practically put together fieldwork, even at a short notice. After a couple of missed opportunities at the start of one's career, we learn to reach out to our networks, refine our research focus and questions, liaise with our host institution/interviewees, and put together safety and ethical packages. When the invitation to conduct research in Darfur came with a two-week notice, the wheels started turning automatically. These preparations were laborious and stressful, but the entire process can also be oddly comforting. Every single (administrative) hurdle crossed brings you closer to the subject of your study. Thinking through ethical considerations at a short notice is much tougher. While ethical approval processes put in place by Western universities force researchers to address the most rudimentary concerns, they are in many ways box-ticking exercises and much remains unresolved until your feet hit the ground.

Embedded research, where a researcher is heavily reliant on a host institution, one that does not share her scholarly/ethical sensibilities, means that ethical trappings and uncertainties multiply. I was anticipating many of the problems we encountered, but the magnitude of these still came as a shock. With a relatively short visit and the chance of a repeated trip almost non-existent, finding creative solutions on the spot became vital. My frustrations over not coming up with these remedies sooner were often high, as making up missed opportunities was proving impossible in the type of scenario we were in. Even more heart-breaking was the on-the-ground realization that I needed to give up on some lines of inquiry, as pursuing them would compromise my interviewees, me, or my data. The concerns where our host's priorities/ethical standards and my own scholarly priorities/standards clashed most obviously were: choice of focus and approach to research, informed consent, and confidentiality.

Choice of focus and approach to research

I came to Darfur convinced that the overlap between the study for our host and my own research interests was extensive and I would have no problem implementing both simultaneously. The UNAMID police component, which we were to write a report on, has protection of civilians—an interest of mine—as one of its core tasks. It is also arguably doing the most on-the-groundwork in this area. Our host institution was also very helpful in advance. The people we discussed meeting were key people involved in civilian protection, we were going to have access to international police officers who engage in the day-to-day work with the local population, and the mission agreed to provide us with a security escort so we could do limited interviews with the internally displaced population and local police outside the compound. In addition, the Police Commissioner's endorsement of the study and the fact that she provided us with an administrative assistant (host contact) to help with the scheduling, meant that we had the practical support needed. Before leaving, I expected that the five of us—with our different priorities—would be the biggest problem when it came to focus and approach in interviews, a problem that in the end proved not only to be negligible, but a research solution.

From the moment we arrived at the mission headquarters in El Fasher, it was clear we were operating with different expectations from our hosts. Knowing that we only had a short time and that we wanted to visit two sites, our host contact packed our agenda with meetings. Having the police commissioner's support somewhat unexpectedly proved to be a double-edged sword. While it was indisputably easier to arrange both initial and additional interviews, several senior people, whose work was only tangentially related to either the UNAMID study or my own interests, were keen to speak to us. As people were generous with their time and our contact put us on their schedules, we felt obliged to take these meetings, even though we were pressed for time—not least as it was clear to us that meeting with us impacted their daily routines and the actual work of the mission. Arranging for interviews with representatives of other international organizations, who also live in the UN–AU compound and could provide invaluable outside views on the work of the mission, proved an almost impossible task. For whatever reason, our host contact did not manage to arrange a single interview outside the mission in El Fasher, and it was only through a random encounter in the canteen that I managed to talk to a representative of another international organization informally. It was on our two-day site visit to another UNAMID compound in Nyala, where we were directly liaising with the sector commander, that we managed to arrange some interviews with other international actors. We further remedied some of the gaps in our research by taking additional meetings with other actors upon our return to Khartoum. Choosing who your interlocutors are can be difficult in embedded research and in time-sensitive settings that influences your research trajectory.

The scholarly approach to research can also be substantially different from research that a host institution normally undertakes, making it crucial to discuss how to reconcile the two formats. While we discussed our plans and expectations in advance, problems were inevitable. The UN and its peacekeeping missions are highly accustomed to evaluation studies, internal reviews, and benchmarking procedures. They are also used to arranging visits for high-level politicians seeking 'authentic insights' on conflict zones (Bliesemann de Guevara, 2017). Our host contact therefore prepared our schedule in ways they were used to, arranging our meetings closely together and asking our interlocutors to provide us with an overview of their work. This led to one highly awkward situation on our first day, where our interviewee was still in the middle of their presentation, we had not asked any questions, and our host contact was already urging us to leave for the next meeting at the other side of the compound.

Over the next few days we further tweaked our schedule in discussion with our host contact, but ended up still needing to find workaround solutions. I arranged a couple of follow-up interviews when time was running short, and often a smaller group would sacrifice the in-depth discussion and go meet our next interlocutor. Having a team of researchers worked to our advantage. However, while these all seem obvious and easy fixes from afar, in Darfur they were a major hassle. Not only were we dealing with the sensibilities of our interviewees and host organization, but we were completely reliant on their infrastructure. The compound in El Fasher is a massive complex in the middle of the desert making travel on foot in over 40 degrees Celsius only feasible over short distances. Splitting up or arranging side meetings required additional logistics. When this was unavailable, I resigned myself to an understanding that in-depth quality-focused interviews were not always possible and that I was doing good enough research.

Informed consent

Informed consent is one of the founding principles of research ethics. The purpose of this principle is for human participants to enter research voluntarily with full information about what it means for them to take part. Each participant should also be free to withdraw from the study at any time. As part of the process, the researcher is supposed to provide information on the study and how the data will be treated. As a second step, the interviewee should reflect on the information provided and be given reasonable time to decide whether to participate or not. While written consent is the preferred choice in most research, in conflict studies oral consent is often needed. In situations such as Darfur, where authorities heavily restrict travel and information, both me as a researcher and participants in the study could be put at risk by existence of a paper record.

When doing embedded research, a lot of requirements around informed consent become difficult to fully satisfy. The most easily observable practical challenge grew from the incredible time constraints we experienced during our interviews. Our host contact did not entirely understand why we were asking for longer appointments and at the same time 'wasting time' explaining what the project for the mission was about, what we were researching in addition to that, and why we were allowing our interlocutors to think about the research and ask follow-up questions. This is not how UN studies are done usually. I felt that going through this process was even more important for my work, as the study we were conducting for UNAMID was endorsed by the police commissioner, who asked her subordinates to help with our research. We were therefore dealing with a fundamental question of whether participants under her command would even feel comfortable withdrawing their consent. Explaining to interlocutors that they are under no obligation to answer specific queries, even if their overall participation was requested by their superior, as well as reading their (dis)comfort with a line of questioning is key to preserving ethical standards of informed consent in embedded research.

Confidentiality

Questions of confidentiality go together with informed consent and become even more visible with embedded research. Given the security situation, we—as a team—agreed that nothing in our research would be attributable to any single person, our notes would be anonymized, and that nothing was to be recorded. Maintaining confidentiality in our outputs and ensuring that our interlocutors were protected from local authorities was the easy part. The bigger problem revolved around the question of how we could ensure that our interlocutors felt comfortable that the raw data they were providing us was kept confidential from our host institution. Very early on we needed to have an awkward conversation requesting that our host contact, who we were heavily indebted to for all the logistical arrangements, wait for us outside the room so our interlocutors would not fear that conversations were being directly reported to the police commissioner.

More difficult was trying to determine what to do with group interviews. While focus groups and group interviews are a useful and heavily utilized method in conflict studies, several of our small groups contained clear hierarchies. For example, we would meet with a head of a division and their analysts, or a commander of a national police unit and their police officers. The lower ranking personnel were often instructed in the room to tell us about this or that. It was questionable how comfortable an analyst or a police officer would feel providing compromising opinions or contradicting their superior while they were in the room. To remedy concerns around such research both me and the other scholar ended up conducting quite a lot of informal interviews with lower-ranking personnel over lunches and dinners. Perversely, we were fortunate that the isolation of living in a compound environment meant that most people were more than willing to spend their free time with us as newcomers.

The most troubling questions of confidentiality, and ones that made me realize that some lines of inquiry would not be feasible, concerned our conversations with the internally displaced population (IDP). Because of the security concerns, we were aware that any travel to

IDP camps would need to be secured by heavily armed UNAMID forces. But upon arriving at the camp, we were informed that their own security protocols require that armed escort is present in the room when accompanying international civilian personnel. We therefore had no options but to conduct interviews under their watchful eye, which made both us and undoubtedly our interlocutors highly uncomfortable. Due to some logistical issues, we also ended up having to rely on a male translator when having a focus group discussion with local IDP women, common targets of gender-based violence. As a result, I abandoned my planned line of inquiry on the spot having to rely on broader questions about the security situation and perceived threats. My frustrations with this situation were high, especially as given the quickly changing security situation and the high demand for armed escorts, repeat meetings with the internally displaced population could not happen. It was this experience that highlighted how modifying arrangements on the spot can become impossible.

The hidden effects

The collective effect of having to reconcile practical and ethical constraints on my findings is difficult to assess. Perhaps the clearest one was that my ambition as to what I could say about Darfur and the international intervention there was quickly scaled back. Before the trip, I had hoped to be able to provide some nuance as to how the population of Darfur, both the IDP and the institutions of the state, perceived the work of the peacekeeping mission. In theory, I had all the building blocks for such observations having conducted two focus group discussions with IDPs (one with male and one with female leaders), interviews with local community policing volunteers, as well as with a police chief in El Fasher and representatives of the Ministry of Interior in Khartoum. Serious articles have been written with much less. But as our fieldwork was so heavily mediated, with UNAMID armed personnel present in all our meetings and in the case of the female focus group us having to rely on a male translator, my ability to provide deep nuance of local perceptions was limited. Hints, stories and complaints had to be taken with a hefty grain of salt and often I had a feeling that it was not me, as a researcher, but the UN, as my host, that was the intended audience. In embedded research, the two can be difficult to separate, especially when dealing with vulnerable populations (see also Bjørkhaug, in this volume).

The report we prepared for UNAMID (Caparini et al, 2015) and its section on protection of civilians therefore mostly relied on observations of other civilian staff working with the local population, and our analysis of priorities in UNAMID's concrete activities and programmes. In terms of my academic knowledge, this trip added less nuance to my research on local perceptions of UN missions than hoped for. Instead, it heavily shaped my understanding of protection of civilians and responsibility to protect as activities that frame human security through statebuilding, something that is now influencing my writing. It was also a valuable form of participant observation allowing me to reflect on internal UN practices and the dynamics between UN peacekeeping missions and host populations.

Reconciling two worlds and reflexivity

Embedded research is an exercise in reconciling two worlds, that of a researcher and of their host. It therefore carries its own specific trappings around approaches to interviews, informed consent and confidentiality. In conflict and intervention studies, where our research sometimes takes us to war zones, such method might not be a choice but a necessity. But it is exactly this danger that makes embedded research more ethically complex, fast adaptations more crucial, and any mistake more consequential for both personal security and our research. Scholars might therefore have to reconcile themselves with good enough research. My experience was highly telling of the differences between scholarly and practitioner knowledge production. The disparities between my approach to research and an approach that an internal evaluation team would take were subtle reminders of why even good enough scholarly work was needed in understanding contemporary interventions. The report we prepared for the mission, while couched in policy terms, was at the time a rare grounded research done by outsiders questioning the appropriateness and the implementation of the UN's mandate in Darfur.

But gaining access to people and places that few can experience first-hand needs to involve a high level of reflexivity. As stated in the introduction, our research makes us not just writers, but also witnesses and participants in conflict dynamics affecting vulnerable populations. It is therefore crucial to constantly evaluate not just how our data might be compromised and what we can and cannot say based on our research, but also how we are intervening into relations of power. And with embedded research, where a researcher is heavily reliant on and indebted to one actor—most often an actor that already enjoys power in the conflict dynamics—reflecting on how we relate our findings and critiques of our host is central for ethical research.

Note

[1] This case study was first developed in a co-authored article (Peter and Strazzari, 2017) and is expanded upon here to address ethical considerations in more detail.

References

Aradau, C. and Huysmans, J. (2014) 'Critical methods in international relations: the politics of techniques, devices and acts', *European Journal of International Relations*, 20(3): 596–619.

Autesserre, S. (2014) *Peaceland: Conflict Resolution and the Everyday Politics of International Intervention*, Cambridge: Cambridge University Press.

Bliesemann de Guevara, B. (2017) 'Intervention theatre: performance, authenticity and expert knowledge in politicians' travel to post-/conflict spaces', *Journal of Intervention and Statebuilding*, 11(1): 58–80.

Campbell, S. (2018) *Global Governance and Local Peace: Accountability and Performance in International Peacebuilding*, Cambridge: Cambridge University Press.

Caparini, M., Aubyn, F., Davies, O., Dessu, M. and Peter, M. (2015) 'The role of the police in the African Union–United Nations Hybrid Mission in Darfur (UNAMID)', *ISS Monograph* 190, Pretoria: Institute for Security Studies, April.

CEAUSSIC (2009) 'AAA Commission on the engagement of anthropology with the US security and intelligence communities: Final report on the Army's Human Terrain System proof of concept program', submitted to the Executive Board of the American Anthropological Association, 14 October.

Dauphinee, E. (2010) 'The ethics of autoethnography', *Review of International Studies*, 36(3): 799–818.

Duffield, M. (2010) 'Risk-management and the fortified aid compound: everyday life in post-interventionary society', *Journal of Intervention and Statebuilding*, 4(4): 453–74.

Fahmy, S. and Johnson, T.J. (2012) 'Invasion vs occupation: a hierarchy-of-influences analysis of how embeds assess influences and performance in covering the Iraq War', *International Communication Gazette*, 74(1): 23–42.

Flint, J. and de Waal, A. (2009) *Darfur: A New History of a Long War*, London: Zed Books.

Gifkins, J. (2016) 'R2P in the UN Security Council: Darfur, Libya and beyond', *Cooperation and Conflict*, 51(2): 148–65.

Higate, P. and Henry, M. (2009) *Insecure Spaces: Peacekeeping, Power and Performance in Haiti, Kosovo and Liberia*, London: Zed Books.

Ignatius, D. (2010) 'The dangers of embedded journalism, in war and politics', *The Washington Post*, 2 May.

Jackson, P.T. (2011) *The Conduct of Inquiry in International Relations: Philosophy of Science and its Implications for the Study of World Politics*, London: Routledge.

Maguire, M. (2017) 'Embedding journalists shape Iraq news story', *Newspaper Research Journal*, 38(1): 8–18.

Mamdani, M. (2010) *Saviors and Survivors: Darfur, Politics, and the War on Terror*, New York: Random House.

McGinty, R. and Salokangas, M. (2014) 'Introduction: "embedded research" as an approach into academia for emerging researchers', *Management in Education*, 28(1): 3–5.

McMullin, J. (2013) *Ex-Combatants and the Post-Conflict State: Challenges of Reintegration*, London: Palgrave MacMillan.

Peter, M. and Strazzari, F. (2017) 'Securitisation of research: fieldwork under new restrictions in Darfur and Mali', *Third World Quarterly*, 38(7): 1531–50.

Pflanz, M. (2009) 'Sudan expels Oxfam and Médecins Sans Frontières from Darfur over war crimes threat to Omar al-Bashir', *The Telegraph*, 4 March.

Smirl, L. (2015) *Spaces of Aid: How Cars, Compounds and Hotels Shape Humanitarianism*, London: Zed Books.

Sudan Tribune (2018) 'S. Darfur begins to transform IDPs camps into permanent residential areas', 12 February.

UK Foreign and Commonwealth Office (2018) 'Foreign travel advice: Sudan', www.gov.uk/foreign-travel-advice/sudan.

14

Interpretation by Proxy? Interpretive Fieldwork with Local Associates in Areas of Restricted Research Access

Katarina Kušić[1]

This chapter discusses collaborative interpretivist research on conflict as it unfolded in the project *Raising Silent Voices: Harnessing Local Conflict Knowledge for Communities' Protection from Violence in Myanmar*. The project was produced in cooperation of a team of researchers from the Global North, research associates from Myanmar and an international non-governmental organization (INGO), Nonviolent Peaceforce (NP).[2] Specifically, based on my interviews with the research team members from the Global North and South, this chapter will highlight a paradox central to 'interpretative research by proxy': that even when research tries not to impose and hierarchize research relationships between North and South, it may end up creating problems by not providing those same structures.

NP is an INGO that provides direct physical protection to civilians in conflict zones, working with unarmed, civilian-to-civilian strategies. In Myanmar, NP's conflict assessment, programme planning and implementation are heavily constrained by Myanmar authorities' travel restrictions preventing the INGO from working directly with communities in conflict zones. In conversations with the Northern research team NP staff voiced concerns that their work in Myanmar was missing something crucial about the conflict dynamics, because instead of living in the communities they sought to protect from violent conflict, they mainly held short-term trainings for local civil society organizations (CSOs) in major accessible towns, which did not allow for much interaction with or learning from CSO volunteers. Against this background, *Raising Silent Voices* sought for creative ways NP could access communities' experiential conflict knowledge without being present in conflict-affected communities. Additionally, the three Northern researchers who applied for the project funding hoped to use experiential knowledge to overcome limits of mainstream conflict analyses and produce different insights into Myanmar's conflict dynamics.[3]

Upon arrival in Myanmar, the researchers were faced with the same access issues NP faced: travel restrictions for foreigners, funding limits and time constraints meant that the team could not easily conduct research in the regions experiencing conflict. Hence, a twofold question emerged: what could local experiences tell about conflict, and how might these experiences be accessed? Berit, one of the three original researchers, summarized the core problem in my interview with her as: "There is something important to be learned from local experiences of conflict, but how can we find out what that something is, if we are not allowed to actually work in the communities?" To address this question, the team employed three Myanmar research associates who conducted fieldwork by facilitating art-based workshops in two conflict zones: Kachin and Rakhine states. The generated data was translated and shared with the original research team.

In the context of this specific project, the decision to work with Burmese researchers did not just mean that people other than the original team would be collecting quantitative or qualitative survey data or conducting predesigned interviews. Rather, it was *qualitative–interpretive* sensibilities that were to be transmitted by proxy. The four core premises of interpretive research are a focus on meaning and its polysemy, an analysis wherein concepts emerge from context, an abductive logic of inquiry, and reflexivity (Kurowska and Bliesemann de Guevara, 2020). Interpretivism is interested in the worlds of meaning through which individuals make sense of their life and its political, social, economic and so on context. Yet while interpretivist research is usually not practised 'by proxy', in this case local associates were going to implement the project's interpretivist epistemology during data generation. Together with the feminist sensitivity that additionally inspired the project design, this approach manifested on two levels: in giving ownership of the project to local associates, and in the arts-based method that the local associates would practice with research participants (Julian et al, 2019).

The project responds to two particular issues in peace and conflict literatures. First, it addresses the growing difficulties of access in conflict and post-conflict areas. The problems of 'bunkerization' first associated with practitioners (Duffield 2010, 2013; Fisher, 2017) are increasingly common in research communities with shrinking funding opportunities, growing security concerns and ever-more restrictive travel regimes (Bliesemann de Guevara and Kostić, 2017; Perera, 2017a, 2017b; Russo and Strazzari, and Peter, in this volume). Second, the involvement of a Myanmar team addresses a particular paradox in the 'local turn' of intervention scholarship—namely that after years of studying 'the local', this scholarship still almost exclusively relies on researchers from the Global North traveling to collect data (Dzuverovic, 2018; Richmond and Mac Ginty, 2015). The choice to work through a Myanmar-based, ethnically diverse team thus in a way provides the 'next step' in the efforts to include local knowledge in analyzing conflicts.

This chapter is based on interviews with all the researchers involved (but not the participants in the workshops nor representatives of NP) that I conducted in the autumn of 2018—a year after the workshops in Myanmar took place, but before first outputs were produced. The interviews allowed me to pry open different understandings and experiences of the people involved. Perhaps expectedly, the researchers from the Global North saw and experienced the project quite differently from the Myanmar researchers. However, speaking to the team in Myanmar also showed me the different understanding within the 'local team'—how they experienced the project was not only different during its design and implementation, but has also led to different paths upon its completion.

While space prevents further reflection on my 'meta' access to the project experiences, I interpret the interviews as a discussion of the challenges that emerge when ideas about emancipatory research methodologies travel from academics' desks to the real world of a place like Myanmar. Even though everyone agreed that the research collaboration was successful, the issues highlighted stem from the fact that the research was imagined as doing interpretation by proxy. The removal of structure and predefined research questions, and the freedom given to local associates—the strengths of interpretivist and feminist epistemologies and methodologies—proved difficult to practically implement. The result is paradoxical: research that tries not to impose and hierarchize relationships ends up creating anxieties by not providing those same structures.

The chapter proceeds in four sections. I first discuss how 'interpretation by proxy' emerged as an approach that responded to both the feminist epistemologies underwriting the project and the practical limitations of access. The later sections follow the project as it unfolded to discuss how issues of design, implementation and output production were differently understood by various people. The conclusions offer some lessons learned that might help future projects that seek to interpret by proxy.

Accessing experiential/local knowledge

Besides practical restrictions of access, time and money that led to hiring local researchers, there was a strong epistemological grounding of this research design. Following a broadly feminist and dialogical orientation, the Northern researchers wanted to help a *different* kind of knowledge to emerge. This was knowledge not mediated by NGOs and country experts or by Eurocentric concepts and methodologies, as the original team were "worried about reproducing the old dynamics by coming in and saying directly what we need" (Interview, Rachel).

The question of *how* to access this different type of knowledge was pursued differently at various stages of the project: first, by seeking an entry point into the field through artists and activists in Yangon; second, by the involvement of local researchers who developed and implemented the project methodology; and third, in the methodology itself that relied on drawing as a tool for accessing local knowledge and narratives in conflict areas (Bliesemann et al, forthcoming; Julian et al, 2019).

The local team consisted of three researchers: S., R., and B.[4] S. is an entrepreneur in Yangon who also actively participates in broadly defined civil society and peace activism. R. and B. are an activist/artist couple who were contacted by S. during the explorative phase of fieldwork. While they were first contacted as artists and asked for initial input, their interest and expertise soon led them to become key actors in developing and implementing the project methodology. Another added value of the local team was the fact that they had family roots in different parts of the country, thus increasing the ethnic diversity within the team itself and facilitating more meaningful access into states within Myanmar.

The project proceeded through partnership: the workshops were designed jointly by both teams, and were then implemented by S., B. and R. who had the administrative capacities, language proficiencies, and on-the-ground presence to travel to the different regions and facilitate the workshops. The methodology broadly drew on Berit's previous experience in (metaphor-centred) drawing as a method for accessing experiential knowledge (Gameiro et al, 2018). R., B. and S.'s input changed initial plans: the idea of six two-day workshops in Mon and Karen states turned into two three-day workshops in Kachin and Rakhine, respectively.

While the idea of giving autonomy to the local research team motivated the project, the relationship between the foreign team and the local team cannot be understood outside of power dynamics and structural hierarchies in which it unfolded.[5] Not only was Myanmar a British colony until 1948, but it is still a recipient of overseas development aid. The terms of project funding further complicated efforts at horizontal organizing: while the foreign team was 'salaried' in the project, the local team was not known during the application period and thus contracted for 'services' such as translation, interpretation and workshop facilitation. Moreover, the ethics and safety procedures of the funding body and the researchers' home universities did not include the local research team: they were neither 'the researchers' identified in the original funding application, nor were they 'participants' in the workshops (Bliesemann de Guevara et al, forthcoming). These tensions between horizontal aspirations and structural hierarchies in which the relationships unfolded provide the background for issues that emerged during the workshops' design and implementation, and the production and evaluation of project outputs.

Designing the workshop between research and art

Diverse understandings of 'what matters' emerged from different experiences and priorities people brought to the project. While the foreign team was driven by desire to access knowledge unmediated by imposed categories and techniques, local researchers brought in sensitivities to art and graphic design. For R., drawing is a skill to be learned, and the better learned the better it can express what people want to communicate. Moreover, because R. and B. had experience in working with international agencies, especially in refugee camps, they were used to providing pedagogical workshops in which they were not there only to listen, but also to teach.

Accordingly, R. facilitated the first workshop with an emphasis on drawing skills. For the foreign team, however, drawing as a data-generation method arose from the assumption that drawing is not a skill, that everyone is able to do it regardless of language proficiency, and that it does not matter how the resulting image looks, as long as it allows participants to capture something that language cannot. R., however, had a different vision:

> In Myanmar, we don't get any art or drawing experience in education. This is why we also needed more time: more time to explain basic art, how you can draw, how you can

use colour to express feelings ... This is because it is a different context in Myanmar, so this is necessary. It was also different for us [R. and B.] because when we worked with IDPs previously, they were younger people and children. With them, it's much easier to work with art, they are more active. It's harder with adults. (Interview, R.)

R.'s explanation captures some of the benefits of working with local researchers: they know details like the structure of education, and they take this context into consideration. The problem arises when the logical next step—teaching people how to draw—is not the main goal of the project.

More than just a different emphasis, that is drawing as a prompt for people's stories versus drawing as a skill, the original researchers also expressed a fear that their methodology that allowed local researchers to take ownership of the research process would actually impinge on the interpretivist premises of the methodology itself. For example, in the first workshop in Kachin, the participants were asked to draw "what makes them proud of being Kachin", instead of just asking what 'being Kachin' meant to them. This difference seemed small to R., B. and S. who were not experienced in interpretivist epistemologies and critiques of research design. However, the original research team saw the question's structure as imposing precisely the frames the methodology sought to avoid.

The only way these questions could be addressed was through online communication: the original research team was available through Skype, WhatsApp and Facebook. But even with instant communication, the tension between letting go and enjoying the local input that the project epistemology argued for, and the needs of keeping research 'under control', were undeniable. This anxiety was differently handled within the original team: while some were happy to let the local team take the rein and excited about the different type of knowledge this might generate, others were concerned about the requirements of their funding: how to justify participant selection, methods and outcomes in the language of Western academia, when they were done without any reference to it? Ellen captured the dilemma well when she said that "problems mostly arose because R., B. and S. took it as their project and did what they wanted". This, however, "is a strength and a weakness: weakness because we didn't get what we wanted, imagined, but strength because this was the local input that we were looking for" (Interview, Ellen).

Implementing a research design with a feminist sensitivity

While the original team grappled with the tensions between a methodology that allows local researchers to design and implement their own methodology, and the lack of control that this approach leads to, they were also amazed by the results. First reports from the workshops showed that project had managed to "challenge the researcher-researched relation". Importantly, this success also showed that "it is not necessary for [foreign researchers] *to define what needs to be done*, people have the capacity to see and do this" (Interview, Rachel; my emphasis).

The local researchers, however, were faced with the practical problems of 'defining what needs to be done'. The project ownership that the foreign team saw as working against the usual power dynamics of Northern research in the Global South was more complicated among the local team—empowerment also had a practical side that needed to be navigated.

In talking with the local team, it soon became clear that besides building their relationship with the original researchers, the relationship between S., R. and B. also needed attention. While R. and B. were used to working together and were in fact already married when the project started, this was their first time working with S., who they had met only through the project. S. told me: "The most difficult thing was building trust in the beginning. I had full trust in Ellen, Rachel and Berit, but I did not know R. and B. at all—I had no idea about how they like things done, what they are thinking, and what they want" (Interview, S.) .R. and B. expressed similar feelings:

> The biggest challenge was working with S. She was in charge of all the logistics and participants for both workshops. We knew each other, but we were not really partners. We didn't take time to be honest with each other, to share opinions and break the ice. This caused some misunderstandings and created problems. A part of the problem is that we were not given the details of the task, there were no clear details of responsibilities, and then misunderstandings happen. (Interview, B.)

> We also had a lack of trust—we did not trust each other's abilities. For example, during the workshop I was explaining about drawing, and others would assume that my explanation is not understood by the participants. (Interview, R.)

What the foreign researchers perceived as giving freedom turned into a lack of direction for the local team. The absence of clearly delineated roles proved to be a problem for the local researchers to navigate. For example, S. thought that she was solely in charge of administrative issues like hiring venues and organizing participants, but B. and R. were also soon involved. Here, differences of opinion and visions emerged without a clear system of dealing with them—a system that was avoided precisely to give ownership to local associates.

Another dimension of logistical problems emerged around budgeting. Having had negative experiences with foreign researchers in the past, B. and R. were eloquent about wanting to be recognized for their contributions. This concern came to the fore on the last day before the first workshop when B. and R. raised the point of payment, which had not yet been clarified. While R. and B. were wary of participation in projects where their work would remain unacknowledged and monetarily ignored, the foreign researchers arrived with experiences of being cast as 'rich foreigners' (see Poopuu and Bliesemann de Guevara, 2017: 22–3).

Here, we again see how particular experiences shape relationships, but in S.'s explanation this was also a matter of structure: in her account, the problem arose not only because the people in the two teams did not yet trust each other, nor because the relationship was fraught with colonial legacy. On the contrary, she saw the problem in the fact that neither the original team nor R. and B. specified their needs and requests early on. The foreign team never asked R. and B. how much they would need to be paid. When asked by S., they were vague saying that they would do it for free for people without money, while they would charge for people who have funds. After no one moved in any direction, S. created a budget on her own and thus overstepped the role and responsibilities R. and B. understood her to have. B. captured the tensions when she summarized: "Rachel, Ellen, and Berit gave us a lot of freedom, and this can be good, but it can also be bad" (Interview, B.). S. provided more detail:

> R. and B. expected these things [the budget and administrative responsibilities] to be sorted out in the beginning. I think it would have been better if this basic structure was put in place in the beginning to avoid confusion and make the roles clear. In the end, I asked them to discuss the payment directly and be paid directly, as opposed to through me: this also gives R. and B. some feeling of respect and value. … I wanted to keep my role separate, but R. and

B. wanted to be involved. It would be better to decide on these things in the beginning and ask and be explicit about the budget. (Interview, S.)

Here, lack of trust not only relates to the asymmetries of foreign and local researchers—a relationship well analyzed in critiques of extractive methods (Smith, 2012)—but the lack of trust within the local team itself. And while it is easy to prescribe time as crucial for building these relationships, all three local researchers agreed that a structure, imposed by the foreign research team and thus in direct confrontation with the sensitivities of the project, might have actually helped. S. told me: "Overall, the [foreign] researcher team were great. They are different from the people who come and just collect data, they have a good attitude, and they are good at working with people. But they could make things easier by having a brief plan about administration: so that everyone knows what their jobs and responsibilities are." The desire for clarification did not relate only to the division of responsibilities. When asked how a project using a similar methodology could be improved, B. was clear: "I think the one thing that has to be made clear is *what do we actually want to get from this research*? I did not understand what they wanted! I would prefer them to give me a topic, or a framework of a topic—it's the professors who should do this because this is their research!" (Interview, B.; my emphasis). The strength of the methodology was supposedly precisely in that they did not know what exactly they wanted to get from this research. Instead of coming in with (Eurocentric) predefined questions, they wanted to give agency to people in the field and allow them to find their own puzzles. This iterative or inductive research design is usually juxtaposed with rigid prescriptions of qualitative–positivist methods (Schwartz-Shea and Yanow, 2012: 26–38), but here it was actually in conflict with the needs and preferences of local researchers and their daily work. While the open-ended design might find new insights, it also pushes local researchers into roles that they themselves do not see fit. An openness that was meant to be liberating ended up burdening the local team.

Navigating outputs: what is research for?

The practical issues of methodology and responsibility allocation point to larger questions of what it means to do research more generally, and with an interpretivist epistemology or local partners specifically. In talking about how the difficulties that arose during the workshops could be ameliorated, Berit had two practical suggestions: more training with R. and B. to give them more direction and a better understanding of what it means to practice an interpretivist methodology, and cooperating with gender studies/conflict researchers "who already speak 'our' language" (Interview, Berit).[6] When reading the draft of this chapter, B. clarified that the major problem for her was precisely the lack of training in research methods—after going through a week-long course in basic research methodology, she now understands that the problems they faced were due to "the freedom to implement/design a methodology" without having "proper knowledge" in research.

And while one can see how this would make the project smoother, it is also noticeable that the 'training' might be actually introducing/imposing precisely those categories that an interpretivist research design wanted to avoid in the first place. Even if those frames are now interpretivist instead of positivist, they are nevertheless 'brought in', if not 'imposed'. Choosing to work with already 'trained' researchers, or training new ones, might mean continuing talking with the voices that fit comfortably with our existing ideas of what knowledge is and how it should be produced.

The fact that S., R. and B. are not trained social scientists was crucial for co-producing a different kind of knowledge that is not filtered through frames of international academia or expert language. In this co-production, local associates had goals that transcended research itself: B., for example, was faced with pain and suffering in stories that she was previously unfamiliar with despite the national belonging she shared with workshop participants. In reflecting on the workshops, she wished for healing expertise that would enable her to ameliorate some of the suffering and help participants deal with their traumas. R. similarly envisioned a very different type of improvement: one-to-one workshops that would give attention, time, space and privacy to individuals telling their personal stories (Interview, R. and B.).

These sentiments were shared by the original researchers. In trying to explain why she was not too concerned about research outputs running late because of delays in translations, Rachel told me that "the project's impact and value lie in the process itself", and the data regarding the complexity of the conflict that they gathered was a completely "different level" of contribution. (Interview, Rachel).[7]

While it is difficult to imagine an academia that does not require outputs, demands for them come from other people as well. One of the things that all local associates referred to were previous negative experiences of foreign researchers coming, extracting data and then disappearing forever (see also Lai, in this volume). There is a clear expectation among the local team that this will not happen in this case, that results will be shared. In our conversation, S. summarized this most clearly when she said, "I cannot have any opinions yet because I still haven't read anything of the work that came out of it. Only once I read, I can have opinions" (Interview, S.). R. echoed similar thoughts:

> Using the metaphor is very interesting, more interesting than talking about things. However, what I am really interested in is seeing how the professors will analyze this, how they will structure it—not only in terms of graphic design, but actually how they will tell the stories. I really want to hear how they will place the order of the conflict—how they are going to reflect on it. (Interview, R.)

Here, questions revolve around the individual visions of what a 'different level' of contribution might be. R.'s desires for more individual work, B.'s emerging interest in research methods, and the emphasis on the interpretation that the foreign team will provide relate to radically different expectations of the same project.

Conclusions

The whole research team evaluated the project as a success. The foreign team were happy to challenge entrenched power dynamics in conflict research and excited by the new insights. The Myanmar team was introduced to research methodologies and discovered new themes and tools with which to build onto their existing work. Yet, when I asked about giving advice to researchers wanting to develop similar methodologies in future, they all recognized the possibility of 'doing better' and offered advice. The major paradox of the research process—that the absence of a structure meant to empower the local team ended up creating more anxieties—seems unavoidable in interpretive research. However, paying attention to relationships and expectations might help the process.

When it comes to relationships, it is crucial to recognize that building relationships starts before assembling the team. All original researchers reflected on the importance of 'preliminary investigations'—time in which you are not pursuing a specific question or goal, but getting to know the place, the people and the issues you are interested in. However, this chapter showed that the relationship between local and foreign researchers is not the only one that needs attention; the local team also requires energy to be built.

This type of research also requires noticing and accommodating unforeseen expectations. The fact that the local team wanted structure whose absence was the defining feature of the project is perhaps the best illustration of the problems that differing expectations can bring. Moreover, unforeseen expectations can also relate to more fundamental questions about what the purpose of the project is and how that purpose can be pursued.

With these lessons, it is important to remember the project's twofold methodological intervention. First, it responds to the growing constraints of conducting fieldwork in conflict areas. And second, it recognizes the problematic ways in which knowledge itself is produced and tries to practise an interpretivist/feminist epistemology to challenge power relations and Western frames of conflict and intervention knowledge. The reflections provided in this chapter show the potential of such research to question both who is supposed to do research and what its goals should be, but they also highlight the practical problems that this emerging agenda of interpretation by proxy entails.

Notes

[1] I would like to thank the editors and reviewers for their comments, and all the researchers for taking the time to provide interviews and comments on the draft of the chapter.
[2] See www.nonviolentpeaceforce.org/what-we-do/2014-09-19-15-18-31/myanmar.
[3] See further https://gtr.ukri.org/projects?ref=AH%2FN008464%2F1.
[4] The names of the foreign team are widely available online, so I chose to use their first names: Rachel, Ellen, and Berit. I anonymize the local team to protect their privacy and safety.
[5] For a more detailed reflection on the hierarchies that shaped the project, see Bliesemann de Guevara et al (forthcoming). This paragraph draws more on that piece than on the interviews I conducted. For example, even though the foreign researchers all reflected on the colonial heritage of the UK in Myanmar, the local researchers did not mention it to me. However, the local researchers talked about their previous experiences of predatory researchers that are the consequence of the same structural inequality (see later in this chapter).
[6] When reading a draft of this chapter, different members of the foreign team reflected that by 'training' they did not mean a one-directional transmission of knowledge, but more time to discuss and come to a common understanding of what is important and how to proceed. I, however, leave the formulation of 'training' because these discussions would nevertheless include translating, if not 'explaining' the epistemological critiques that the project was founded on to the local team, thus making them, indeed, a bit more 'like us'.
[7] Berit, by contrast, reflected: "Why does academia need to do this type of project, if furthering our knowledge about a problem is not what the foremost goal is? ... For me, positive impact on participants is a welcome by-product of the methods chosen, not a goal in itself."

References

Bliesemann de Guevara, B., Furnari, E. and Julian, R. (forthcoming) 'Researching with "local" associates: power, trust and data in an interpretive project on communities' conflict knowledge in Myanmar', *Civil Wars*.

Bliesemann de Guevara, B. and Kostić, R. (2017) 'Knowledge production in/about conflict and intervention: finding "facts", telling "truth"', *Journal of Intervention and Statebuilding*, 11(1): 1–20.

Duffield, M. (2010) 'Risk-management and the fortified aid compound: everyday life in post-interventionary society', *Journal of Intervention and Statebuilding*, 4(4): 453–74.

Duffield, M. (2012) 'Challenging environments: danger, resilience and the aid industry', *Security Dialogue*, 43(5): 475–92.

Dzuverovic, N. (2018) 'Why local voices matter. Participation of local researchers in the liberal peace debate', *Peacebuilding*, 6(2) 111–26.

Fisher J. (2017) 'Reproducing remoteness? States, internationals and the co-constitution of aid "bunkerization" in the East African periphery', *Journal of Intervention and Statebuilding*, 11(1): 98–119.

Gameiro, S., Bliesemann de Guevara, B., El Refaie, E. and Payson, A. (2018) 'DrawingOut—an innovative drawing workshop method to support the generation and dissemination of research findings', *PLoS ONE*, 13(9): e0203197.

Julian, R., Bliesemann de Guevara, B. and Redhead, R. (2019) 'From expert to experiential knowledge: exploring the inclusion of local experiences in understanding violence in conflict', *Peacebuilding*, 7(2): 210–25.

Kurowska, X. and Bliesemann de Guevara, B. (2020) 'Interpretive approaches in Political Science and International Relations', in L. Curini and R.J. Franzese (eds), *The SAGE Handbook of Research Methods in Political Science and IR*, London: SAGE.

Perera, S. (2017a) 'Bermuda triangulation: embracing the messiness of researching in conflict', *Journal of Intervention and Statebuilding*, 11(1): 42–57.

Perera, S. (2017b) 'To boldly know: knowledge, peacekeeping and remote data gathering in conflict-affected states', *International Peacekeeping*, 24(5): 803–22.

Poopuu, B. and Bliesemann de Guevara, B. (2017) 'Reflections on researching war and peace from below: insights from Burma and Syria', paper presented at the EISA Paneuropean Conference on International Relations, Barcelona, 13–16 September 2017.

Richmond, O.P. and Mac Ginty, R. (2015) 'Where now for the critique of the liberal peace?' *Cooperation and Conflict*, 50(2): 171–89.

Schwartz-Shea, P. and Yanow, D. (2012) *Interpretive Research Design: Concepts and Processes*, New York: Routledge.

Smith, L.T. (2012) *Decolonizing Methodologies: Research and Indigenous Peoples* (2nd edn), London and New York: Zed Books.

PART IV

Sex and Sensitivity

Research on wartime and intervention-related sexual violence has become an important subfield of conflict and intervention studies, which in addition to the other challenges discussed in this book needs a specific research sensitivity as it often takes place among particularly marginalized or vulnerable research participants. The contributions to this part of the book critically discuss issues such as victimhood and agency, critiquing parts of the stereotyping in the current women-and-war discourse without losing sight of the human suffering that sexual violence affects, and also accounting for fragile masculinities and the precarious lives of young men (combatants and non-combatants). The authors address questions of how to manage research among sex workers and people who occasionally use sex as a transactional field of body politics, and how to deal with actions and issues such as sexual exploitation and abuse, which may be hard to accept but still need to be dealt with, while treating those involved with a clear sense of humanity. The research underpinning the chapters was carried out among sex workers who are part of the wider peacekeeping economies in Liberia, Haiti and the DR Congo, with rebel armies in Burundi, South Africa and Uganda, among different peacekeeping missions around the globe including Cambodia, Timor-Leste, the Central African Republic, Haiti and Kosovo, and in a refugee camp in Uganda.

15

Sex Workers and Sugar Babies: Empathetic Engagement with Vulnerable Sources

Kathleen M. Jennings

It was getting dark in Goma in the eastern Democratic Republic of the Congo (DRC). I was sitting with Bennett Shabani, my field assistant/fixer/translator, planning out the next day's meetings. My PhD project on peacekeeping economies—the formal and informal economies that grow up around peacekeeping missions, and that enable missions, and peacekeepers, to function—in the DRC and Liberia involved interviewing a diverse range of sources, from peacekeeping leadership and rank and file, to expatriate businesspeople and local elites, to people working, mostly informally, in the services and establishments catering to peacekeepers. I had talked to drivers, domestic workers, private security guards, student leaders, waitresses, restaurant owners, property managers, street market sellers, hotel managers and local employees of the UN mission and international nongovernmental organizations (NGOs), in an attempt to understand how peacekeepers and peacekeeping—as practice, politics and as a locus and driver of gendered socio-economic activity—interact with, implicate and are affected by local women, men and communities. Most of the previous day was spent with a group of young women who supported themselves, in whole or part, through relationships with UN peacekeepers or rich Congolese men, but did not consider themselves (nor were generally considered by others) as sex workers. In Liberia, women in similar situations are referred to as 'sugar babies'; in Goma, according to Oldenburg (2015: 323), a term in circulation is *fille maline* ('smart girl'). Getting in with the sugar babies was largely coincidence. Bennett had an acquaintance who had been dating a MONUSCO guy. She agreed to meet with me, and her story rang so true—the small details about MONUSCO (the United Nations Organisation Stabilisation Mission in the DR Congo), including the specifics of how much of the peacekeepers' monthly allowance was paid out in DRC for local spending and when—that I accepted her invitation to meet other girlfriends of her acquaintance. The afternoon with the girlfriends was fun and well spent, adding to my store of details, nuances and observations about transactions, interactions and life in the 'peace-kept' city (Jennings and Bøås, 2015).

But still, nagging at me was the fact that I had not yet on this trip interviewed any 'real' sex workers, in the narrow sense of women[1] who transact sex for money (or other compensation), independent or outside of the confines of an ongoing relationship, where compensation is owed at the time that services are rendered. Bennett and I discussed the issue several times and were at a loss on how to proceed. There was no interest group or NGO that we were aware of that represented sex workers' interests or could act as a gatekeeper to them. Previously in Liberia, I used the services of an enterprising ex-combatant known to a colleague, who offered 'workshop facilitation' to researchers and whose mode of operation was a bit too reminiscent of a pimp's (making me the john). I got my interviews—of varying believability, though even the less credible informants[2] were useful in adding information or confirming certain details sourced elsewhere—but the process left a bad aftertaste. For his part, Bennett's wide web of professional connections did not extend to the sex work milieu. Not one to be stymied, however, he suggested a drive, and eventually we pulled up outside a ramshackle gated compound. "There's always UN cars here", Bennett said by way of explanation (although there were not any at the moment). We got out, exchanged greetings with the guard at the gate, and Bennett disappeared to go find the establishment's boss. "Huh", I remember thinking to myself, "I'm in a brothel".

After a protracted negotiation with the madam—handled by Bennett—we established ourselves in an unused bedroom with six women willing to talk to us, with the understanding that I would not use their real names and that they would come and go as needed. A further negotiation ensued regarding compensation, ending in the agreement that I would buy drinks and food for the women. A man was dispatched to bring dinner and beers, and the focus group was set. Approximately two hours later we exited again, after a conversation that was, by turns, intense, sad, challenging, goofy and exhausting. Bennett got us in the door and we got the material.

This story is typical of how I have done fieldwork in the conflict-affected countries of Liberia (Monrovia), Haiti (primarily Port-au-Prince) and the DRC (Goma and Kinshasa). Persistence, luck, dedicated and able field assistants and, when all else fails, a willingness to turn up uninvited on people's doorsteps—whether at brothels or UN mission compounds—have been a common thread. But there are a couple of points worth highlighting, because they get at issues particularly salient in interviewing sex workers, girlfriends and, to some degree, other hard-to-reach, marginalized or vulnerable groups in intervention sites.

The first point relates to access. Without Bennett—a local man—the focus group never would have happened. Alone, I would have felt too insecure to make such a bold approach, nor (I suspect) would I have gotten the same reception from the madam. Differing circumstances aside, this point holds true in my interviews with sex workers in Monrovia, as noted earlier, and later in Kinshasa. At the same time, I am equally certain that, once access was gained, the rapport and exchanges I had with the women would not have been replicable by Bennett or any other man. While my focus group and interviews in Goma and Kinshasa (but not Monrovia) were mediated by a male translator, there was no question who shaped and drove the discussion: myself and the women, in dialogue. It seems essentialist to claim that I could connect with, and get information from, other women that a man could not. After all, I had less in common with these women than with Bennett; in some ways, he had more in common with them. But in my limited experience, it has been the case that there are inflections, assumptions, points of connection, moments of testing each other out and give and take that are shaped as much by who I am—a cis straight white woman academic—as by who they are, where gender is inseparable from the whole. This is less about essentialism and more about the contingency of knowledge production. In this kind of fieldwork, no two interviewers will ever get the exact same answers. This owes to circumstance and to a multitude of other factors, including the experiences and axes of identity of both interviewer and interviewee (see also Clausen, in this volume).

The second point has to do with what happened before Bennett got us in the door. Because before stepping foot in the brothel or spending the afternoon with the sugar babies, the preparation and the groundwork was already in place. Some of this groundwork was done at my office in Oslo—chiefly reading academic sources on sex work and sex tourism (especially from African authors and contexts), sexual exploitation and abuse (SEA) in peacekeeping, gender and militarism, and other related literatures. Some was done in the long discussions and strategizing between Bennet and myself, resulting in a running, constantly revised idea of what I needed and wanted to know, and how he/we could best facilitate it. Interviews with other sources also laid important groundwork, allowing me to obtain a working knowledge of how the sex market in Goma functioned (prices, venues, different categories of johns)—knowledge critical for quickly gauging the credibility of my interviewees, but also for establishing my own credibility in their eyes. Finally, from my own previous field experiences and from trial and error, I had a feel for productive lines of enquiry and a tested opening question. The point is that, while knowledge production is indeed contingent, it is neither arbitrary nor (mostly) accidental. Preparation is essential, and this is especially so when undertaking such a sensitive endeavour as interviewing sex workers and other vulnerable groups.

In this chapter, I draw on my experiences in Liberia and the DRC to highlight some common challenges posed by intervention fieldwork, specifically where fieldwork is conducted with typically marginalized (possibly criminalized) and stigmatized groups such as sex workers and sugar babies. I focus on both ethical and practical aspects—in so far as these are separable—as well as some analytical considerations in the writing up of research. I start by arguing that researchers have an ethical obligation to interrogate themselves and their motives when deciding to interview women and men in vulnerable or stigmatized groups. I further make the case for empathetic but critical engagement that respects the source's agency and avoids assumptions of victimhood, while being attentive to the violence, fear, trauma and insecurity that are present in, and shape, their lives and stories. I then briefly turn to some challenging practical issues related to this type of fieldwork, including questions of access and compensation. Finally, I conclude with a call for critical self-reflection and humility in our analysis and claims, accordant with the contingency, intersubjectivity and circumstance shaping our knowledge production.

Know your 'why'

Writing on the challenges of conducting research on sexual violence in conflict, Boesten and Henry (2018: 570) argue that seeking firsthand accounts of 'victim-survivors' of conflict-related sexual violence (CRSV) can be problematic. They pay particular attention to the phenomena of over-research and research fatigue among populations, exacerbated by the fact that '[d]isclosure of experiences with sexual violence can have devastating effects in the everyday lives of survivors, in spaces where researchers may not enter, or after they have left' (Boesten and Henry 2018: 570). Accordingly,

> researchers need to be encouraged to think carefully about research questions, and what the varied answers might contribute to a field of understanding. ... one sees that the same research questions are asked over and over again by different people seeking to understand particular phenomena, not to increase overall understanding of that phenomena, but rather as a shortcut to increasing individual knowledge on a subject. (Boesten and Henry, 2018: 582)

Boesten and Henry's advice is salient not least because it contrasts with the prevailing feeling among many researchers that they always have to have *more* interviews, data, focus groups and information about anything that tangentially touches their research question. This quest for 'more' is productive. But it can also lead to an insufficiently discriminate approach that, in the worst case, disregards the wellbeing of sources. Researchers must not treat sources as vessels from which they can endlessly extract (the same) knowledge. Especially with vulnerable, marginalized and/or stigmatized groups, researchers' obligation is to ensure that the people they interview and the questions they ask are actually necessary to their project—and that their project itself brings new knowledge to the table.

This is not an easy ask. In my peacekeeping economies project, I was—and remain—convinced that first-hand testimony of sex workers and sugar babies was important to understanding the diverse and multifarious impacts of peacekeeping missions and how local residents negotiate the political economies they spawn. As noted earlier, I also used other sources of information to learn about the functioning of the sex industries in Goma, Kinshasa and Monrovia. If I had not been able to access sex workers and girlfriends for interviews, these second-hand sources could have sufficed to cover the strictly economic aspects of sex transactions. At the same time, I felt that talking to sex workers and girlfriends would bring new and valuable information, perspectives and insights to my understanding of international–local interactions in peacekeeping sites beyond the narrow economic facets—the very focus of my PhD. This was not least because (at the time of my fieldworks in 2011–12) I found little in the peacekeeping literature that represented these perspectives, despite an increasing volume of work on sexual and gender-based violence in conflict and on SEA in peacekeeping.

Conversely, in an earlier project on peacekeeping SEA in Liberia and Haiti, I did not seek the testimonies of victim-survivors. In that project, I examined how the zero-tolerance policy (ZTP) against SEA was implemented in the two missions and how uniformed and civilian peacekeepers experienced the ZTP. During my fieldworks, I talked to local NGO representatives to hear their perceptions of peacekeeper SEA and, more generally, how peacekeepers interacted with local communities, especially local women. Using these connections, I could have facilitated interviews with victim-survivors of SEA. But I purposely did not, because that would have been a distraction from my research question. My focus then centred not on victims' stories, but rather on how UN missions dealt with (or did not) the ZTP. This narrow focus was in turn a reaction to an even earlier project focused on ex-combatants in Monrovia, in which I experienced some incidents in the field that I found ethically challenging and emotionally ill-equipped to deal with (Jennings 2020). I thus designed the project in a way that enabled me to sidestep the emotional and ethical issues involved in interviewing victim-survivors, without sacrificing substance or integrity. Then in the intervening four years between the SEA fieldworks and my PhD fieldworks, I learned from experienced colleagues and read up on qualitative methodologies, especially feminist methodologies (Ackerly, Stern and True, 2006; Klotz and Prakash, 2008), to improve my understanding of how to do such interviews sensitively, empathetically, but also critically.

Victims, agency and 'critical empathy'

There is no one right way to conduct interviews, or to guarantee that they are done sensitively, empathetically and critically. What works for one person may provoke a completely different reaction in another. Thus, what follows is not a how-to guide, but rather reflections on notions of victimhood, agency, empathy and what it means to be critical. These concepts are anything but abstract when doing fieldwork with/on sex workers and other vulnerable groups.

First, I want to draw attention to my persistent slippage in usage: sex workers (itself a controversial designation), sugar babies, victim-survivors, girlfriends, vulnerable/marginalized/stigmatized/criminalized groups. Some of the slippage is due to the terms used in other work, as in the earlier reference to Boesten and Henry (2018). But this slippage is also illustrative of the complexity of the experiences and situations of women (and men) in conflict-affected communities. It is important to acknowledge this to avoid setting up or reinforcing an implicit binary between 'victims' and 'agents', actors and those who are (violently) acted upon. The sex workers I interviewed were both agents and victimized. Most had been subject to violence by their customers, including assault (some, allegedly, by peacekeeper clients); most claimed to have been robbed or cheated at least once; some claimed to have been pressured or coerced to have unprotected sex or anal sex; and all were vulnerable to arrest and mistreatment by their own police forces.

Common to my informants was also a downplaying of these dangers: they were almost uniformly talked about as part of the job. With one exception, painful stories were minimized. But this is also intrinsically connected to the questions I asked and how I asked them. I approached my interviews (and in the Goma case, focus group) with sex workers the same way I approached my interviews with all my other sources: I asked them to tell me about their job. One opening I found particularly successful was to ask sources to talk me through the process of getting ready for a night out: what time do they start getting ready; how do they spend their day before then; how long do they spend on their hair, makeup, nails, clothes; roughly how much money do they spend on their look per month (salon visits, clothes and accessories); who looks after their kids when they are working; how long does it take to get from home to the venue; what transport do they use; how much does transport cost; which venue do they start out at; does this change according to the day of the week; do they have understandings with the bartender or staff at one or more venues; what sort of understandings; and so on, all before even getting to questions related to categories of johns, price ranges, the security measures they take, and specific experiences with clients, especially peacekeepers or other internationals. I found that this back-and-forth on the details of their everyday (work) life prompted immediate engagement, establishing a tone of openness and frankness even while our dialogue delved into more sensitive topics. My perception remains that my sex worker sources—like my other sources—appreciated being treated as agents and as equals, possessing valuable knowledge and experience.

That said, focusing on the details related to the *work* of selling sex, rather than primarily on the lived *experience* of being a sex worker, is arguably problematic in that it accepts (or does not actively contest) the exploitation and violence that are central elements of sex work. For me, that critical work came later. My questions were thus chiefly information-seeking rather than interrogatory (in the sense of being framed so as to interrogate the structures and power relations that the sex workers negotiate). They were intended to elicit details, experiences, and stories of the sources' stigmatized, criminalized, marginalized—but also visible and relatively well-remunerated—work. Had I chosen another approach, the responses I got would likely have been different. This does not mean my sources were lying to me or omitting relevant information. But had I started with questions honing in on exploitation and violence—their worst experience, the extent to which they experience stigma, the number of times they have been cheated, robbed, or beaten up, the physical and emotional toll the work takes—then it is likely that the dangers that my sources downplayed would have taken greater precedence.

Thus, while automatically treating all sex workers as victims risks undermining their agency, the opposite risk applies to my approach. It is possible that my sources responded to my lead by understating their own insecurity and victimhood; that I essentially overstated their agency, thus minimizing their vulnerability and constraints. Of the nearly 20 sex workers I interviewed, only one became visibly upset and emotional in discussing her experiences. At the time, her reaction surprised me, because it was so atypical of my other interviews. Upon reflection, I realized that the only surprising thing about it was that it had, in fact, been atypical. Thus, we circle back to the starting point: there is no one 'right' way to interview people, and it is hard to know while you are doing it if you should be doing it another way. Knowing your 'why' is necessary but insufficient. You have to also be guided by your own judgment, convictions, experience, and respect for your sources in order to navigate intervention fieldwork.

This gets to my final point, on being critical and critical empathy. Being critical applies both to your own actions and to the information you get from your sources. The former refers to what I just wrote: maintaining a reflexive, intentional relationship with your own conduct, questions, investment in the interview, how you are pushing or leading things in specific directions, and how this might affect the information you receive. By the latter, I mean that it is important not to suspend critical judgment based on who your source is. As noted earlier in the Liberia case, I found that a couple of sources were trying to pass off their experiences as something else: specifically, they were fronting that they worked the international sex market rather than the local market. In this, they were likely following the (implicit or explicit) instructions of the ex-combatant gatekeeper who facilitated the interviews, and who knew I was interested in talking to sex workers with international clientele. Given that compensation was being offered for the interviews, as I detail later, they may have feared missing out on the money if their story did not fit what (they thought) I wanted. I was able to figure out the ruse using standard verification methods: their answers were significantly out of line with what I had heard from other informants. Rather than stop the interviews, I reoriented my questions towards finding out about the local sex market. There is no contradiction between treating your sources with respect and understanding, while treating the information they give you with the same critical attention you give all other data sources.

Indeed, this is at the heart of what I call 'critical empathy'. I use this term loosely to designate, not theory or methodology development, but practice and approach. It means listening to and empathizing with sources; engaging in dialogue, not least by opening yourself up to questions and challenges; and asking informed and difficult questions, while being alert to cues to back off, change tack or stop entirely; but not taking everything at face value or extracting painful or graphic stories just for the sake of eliciting horror. Sometimes these stories come out, regardless of your intent. In these cases, it is important to listen, comfort and minimize harm. Researchers are not therapists; we do not usually have the training or competence to deal with (re)traumatization among sources, which reiterates the importance of making deliberate choices about who and how you interview. My experience with harm minimization has thus been haphazard and undertaken in a context where a traumatic experience emerged unforeseen and organically in the interview process. It included ensuring that the source was not left alone after the interview; informing about the formal reporting processes available, and offering to accompany and assist in reporting to the relevant authorities; and asking again at the end of the interview for consent to use the material, allowing for a genuinely informed decision as to whether the source wanted her story (re)told.

Gatekeepers, compensation and security

Interviewing sex workers, girlfriends and other hard-to-reach groups also entails a number of practical considerations, which often have ethical and analytical implications. Three in particular have to do with gatekeepers, compensation and security.

'Gatekeepers' refers to individuals, groups or organizations that regulate or restrict access to sources. A typical example is an NGO working with particular communities and able to facilitate interviews with community members; this is the model I would have used in Haiti had I sought out interviews with SEA victim-survivors. My interviews with sex workers were also facilitated but, as I noted earlier, the way this worked in practice in Monrovia (and to a lesser degree, Kinshasa) had parallels with pimping as much as gatekeeping. In these instances, the gatekeepers' interests were very much on the surface: it was a service-for-fee dynamic. In Monrovia, I was actually presented a receipt for workshop facilitation services from our go-between; in Kinshasa, my fixer used a 'friend of a friend of a friend' as facilitator, with an unspoken understanding that he should be compensated for his time. The fees were not particularly large, but nor were they token (between US $20 and $50). In other cases, gatekeepers' interests are less obvious—but that does not mean they do not exist, nor are they irrelevant to the information you access and the analysis that follows (Crowhurst and Kennedy-Macfoy, 2013). Again, there is no single right answer for how to negotiate gatekeepers in doing intervention fieldwork. Researchers must weigh the importance of the sources, whether there are other means of gaining access, the ethical implications, and their knowledge of the gatekeeper's trustworthiness and motivations—and they must be willing to walk away if the terms are too unfavourable.

This in turn entails acceptance of the less-than-ideal circumstances that are the reality of intervention fieldwork. I find there is particular squeamishness around compensation of informants or gatekeepers. Full disclosure: all of my sex worker and girlfriend sources were compensated, either in money, in-kind (meals and drinks) or both. The compensation was agreed beforehand and all sources were compensated equally within field sites. Where cash was paid, the standard agreement was US $20, usually with a drink also paid by me (we met always in cafés or bars). The women in the brothel in Goma and all the girlfriends I interviewed did not get cash; instead, I paid for their food and drinks. Ideally, paying compensation would not be necessary to gain access to informants. Intervention fieldwork does not exist in the realm of the ideal. That said, none of my other informants in any of the field sites were paid in cash, although—given that many of my interviews took place outside office settings, often after working hours—it was not uncommon that I would pay for drinks and (very occasionally) meals. In the case of the sex workers and girlfriends, I accepted these arrangements as fair compensation for the women's time and a necessary cost of doing business: in the 'market of intervention' (Oldenburg, 2015), information is another commodity to be transacted and exchanged. The decision to compensate my sex worker sources did not dictate the approach I took to the interviews, namely my focus on sex work as *work*. In a way, by keeping things on a professional footing, it actually complemented this approach. This underscores that, where compensation is an issue, it is important to consider how this might affect your sources. If they think you are paying for a horror story, might they feel compelled to produce one? This dynamic can also exist independent of compensation, but it is particularly pertinent where payment is made (see also Bøås, in this volume).

A final point relates to security. With the exception of the gate-crash in Goma, I let the sex workers (via the facilitator) pick where and when the interviews would take place, because it was important that they felt as secure and comfortable as possible in the interview setting. But I also listened to and trusted my local assistants and their perception of the risks—not risks to the sex workers, but to them and me. Without going into extensive detail, I only stress that it is crucial that all parties—sources, researcher and local assistants—respect the others' boundaries and take common-sense measures to protect their own security in the interview situation (see also Göransson, Clausen, Verweijen, and Bøås, in this volume).

Conclusions

What all of this points to is that there is no one 'right' way to do intervention fieldwork. Fieldwork, especially in conflict-affected environments, requires compromise and willingness to accept less-than-perfect. It entails ethical, emotional, analytical, logistical and physical challenges. Especially when involving marginalized or vulnerable sources, it should also occasion an ethics of care for these sources and an ethic of (self) care for the researcher herself.

These challenges do not disappear once the writing begins. While judgments and compromises in the field are often rushed, even instinctual, those made in analysis should be more considered. This entails a degree of humility and honesty about the claims you can make. This is especially so where difficulties related to access or time mean that, as in my fieldworks, some of the most vulnerable sources—children, male or transgender sex workers, survival and street sex workers—are not included. I cannot know what kind of stories they would tell, but I tried to allow space for those stories to (co)exist in my analysis. By this, I mean that I made efforts to challenge and disrupt my own understandings and narratives of sex workers' lives and experiences, especially when the shaping and (re)telling of them made them seem smooth or facile—what Eriksson Baaz, Gray and Stern (2018: 539) refer to as 'being attentive to—and suspicious of—our feelings of comfort and ease'. Acknowledging the partiality of your knowledge is not discrediting. It can open up new paths for you and other researchers to explore—but only if it *is* acknowledged.

Finally, Eriksson Baaz, Gray and Stern (2018) remind us of the particular challenges attendant to normative research in which the researcher herself is deeply politically and ethically invested. Writing in relation to sexual and gender-based violence (SGBV), they argue that doing this work demands of the researcher '(self-) critical discussions' about our 'desire to produce certain kinds of useful knowledge that may improve women's situations', in order to 'better recognize the ways in which our various positions and desires shape how we make sense of such violence' (Eriksson Baaz, Gray and Stern, 2018: 523). This is uncomfortable, dislocating work. But to approach a credible, compelling representation of life in/under intervention, it is also necessary.

Notes

[1] Sex workers are not exclusively women. Men, girls and boys, not to mention trans-men and trans-women, also sell sex. In the DRC and Liberia, however, where homosexuality remains largely taboo and hidden, and where militarized peacekeeping missions introduce a gender imbalance in the international presence, the dominant mode of sex work is female sex worker–male customer. I therefore focused primarily on getting interviews with women sex workers.

[2] 'Less credible' here does not imply that the women were not sex workers. What was more questionable was whether they served primarily an international (and/or elite local) clientele, or the more down-market 'average' local clientele. I was mostly interested in the former group, and accordingly some of the sources started out by asserting that they worked the international market, even though basic questioning exposed this as a front.

References

Ackerly, B.A., Stern, M. and True, J. (eds) (2006) *Feminist Methodologies for International Relations*, Cambridge: Cambridge University Press.

Boesten, J. and Henry, M. (2018) 'Between fatigue and silence: the challenges of conducting research on sexual violence in conflict', *Social Politics*, 25(4): 568–88.

Crowhurst, I. and Kennedy-Macfoy, M. (2013) 'Troubling gatekeepers: methodological considerations for social research', *International Journal of Social Research Methodology*, 16(6): 457–62.

Eriksson Baaz, M., Gray, H. and Stern, M. (2018) 'What can we/do we want to know? Reflections from researching SGBV in military settings', *Social Politics*, 25(4): 521–44.

Jennings, K. (2020) 'Gendered challenges to fieldwork in conflict-affected areas', in R. Mac Ginty, B. Vogel and R. Brett (eds), *Companion to Conducting Field Research in Peace and Conflict Studies*, London: Palgrave.

Jennings, K. and Bøås, M. (2015) 'Transactions and interactions: everyday life in the peacekeeping economy', *Journal of Intervention and Statebuilding*, 9(3): 281–95.

Oldenburg, S. (2015) 'The politics of love and intimacy in Goma, Eastern DR Congo: perspectives on the market of intervention as contact zone', *Journal of Intervention and Statebuilding*, 9(3): 316–33.

Plotz, A. and Prakash, D. (eds) (2008) *Qualitative Methods in International Relations: A Pluralist Guide*, Basingstoke: Palgrave Macmillan.

16

Lifting the Burden? The Ethical Implications of Studying Exemplary, Not Pathological, Wartime Sexual Conduct

Angela Muvumba Sellström

Armed men in civil wars commit widespread and extreme rape. This is the public perception of wartime sexual violence.[1] These atrocities have occurred in Iraq and Syria, the eastern Democratic Republic of the Congo (DRC), Sudan's Darfur, the new South Sudan and in the Central African Republic. Thus, attention by policymakers and the media has increased. However, international advocates (and to a lesser extent scholarly communities) have fetishized the most grotesque types of violence such as slavery and abduction, gang rape and brutal rapes (Meger, 2016) without explaining patterns of variation in sexual misdeeds. They have also obfuscated lessons of restraint and sexual discipline in the conduct of war. After all, not all men rape and not all men in conflict commit sexual violence.

Indeed, a recent turn in research has begun to problematize the image of warzones as sites of perpetual sexual predation. Scholars have shown that not all armed actors allow rape; that abuses, including rape, can be organized by women; that men are also victimized; that perpetrator groups commit a diverse array of acts; and further, that sexual violence is not always a 'weapon of war' (Cohen, 2013; Cohen and Nordås, 2014; Dolan, 2016; Eriksson Baaz and Stern, 2013; Gutiérrez Saní and Wood, 2014; Hoover Green, 2018, 2017, 2016; Hultman and Muvumba Sellström, 2018; Kirby, 2012; Lieby, 2009; Muvumba Sellström, 2015a, 2015b; Sivakumaran, 2007; Wood, 2018, 2014, 2009,

2006). Still, most research addresses pathological wartime sexual conduct, not the control that is associated with punishing perpetrators by some conflict actors. What about the non-cases, where militaries and armed movements have stigmatized sexual predation and established effective practices to discipline their fighters?

My research has brought me into fieldwork and encounters with non-state armed groups in Burundi, South Africa and Uganda that established sexual discipline among their commanders and foot-soldiers. Since 2011, I have conducted field research on the Palipehutu-FNL (Forces Nationales de Libération) in Burundi (1980–2008); and, beginning in 2017, Uganda's National Resistance Army/Movement (NRA/M) (1981–86) and the African National Congress's armed wing uMkhonto weSizwe (MK) (1961–90/91). My explorations entail long semi-structured interviews and structured focus groups with leaders and commanders, serving members of militaries as well as ex-combatants. My empirical focus is on the normative work these groups carry out: their practices of prohibition and punishment and gender and sexuality norms and preferences. My main findings thus far suggest that prevention of wartime sexual violence is possible and a part of the history of each of these actors, albeit imperfectly. The research I conduct tells a story of altruistic armed groups, with leaders that demonstrate a concern for the welfare of others.

My results present an ethical dilemma. I often worry about lifting the burden of accountability from the shoulders of the political and military leaders that might benefit from this view of their respective organizations. While they have been exemplars of good conduct, these movements may have committed other harms against vulnerable groups that fall outside the boundaries of my research. Furthermore, not all incidents would have been reported and not all sexual violence was stopped. This means that there are survivors whose stories are not part of my results, and who may feel that this positive story silences their suffering. Finally, the ways and means of each armed group's practices may not always align with my own feminist norms. They may have anchored their normative work within a gendered framework of men as protectors of women, undermining female sexual autonomy.

This chapter addresses the ethical risks of lifting the burden. Researchers should weigh and consider the *potential* moral dilemmas that such research and fieldwork poses. The chapter begins with a brief introduction to my research. Then, I discuss how the armed groups may be viewed as a consequence of my research; whether or not new evidence about control over certain types of sexual violence will silence some survivors of other types of abuses; and if such research promotes a male-centred story of the 'protector' at the expense of female sexual autonomy. The chapter concludes with two priorities for mitigation: sustaining complexity and acknowledging uncertainty.

The set-up: my research on the prevention of wartime sexual violence

My reflections arise from conducting field research in Burundi, South Africa and Uganda. Mainly I consider ethical implications that emerged from my semi-structured interviews and focus groups in Burundi between 2011 and 2013, with ex-combatants of Palipehutu-FNL and other armed groups from the civil war of 1994–2008. The chapter also considers fieldwork in Uganda in 2017 and 2018, where I have interviewed military commanders of the NRA and present-day senior officers in the Ugandan People's Defence Forces (UPDF) and have mainly focused on the civil war years of 1981–86. I first carried out fieldwork in Uganda 18 years ago and was born and partly raised in that country. I maintain a wide network of interlocutors and have close relatives within the NRA/UPDF, but also outside of government and within the political opposition. The chapter also reflects upon preliminary work in South Africa, where I have interacted with a group of high-ranking former female leaders and combatants. I lived in South Africa for five years and know politicians and civil society representatives from a wide array of political backgrounds. Thus, while I write this contribution from the perspective of a researcher coming from the West, from 'outside', I am not entirely that. This is worth noting, although it is not the focus here.

In this chapter, I employ the term 'wartime sexual violence' or refer to a specific type of act or harm such as 'rape'. Wartime sexual violence is defined as rape, sexual torture, abuse, forced prostitution or acts of a sexual nature, based upon armed force or the threat of violence by a representative of a party to an armed conflict. Armed conflicts are contested incompatibilities whereupon one or more party uses organized armed force to advance their position, with at least 25 deaths in a year. This definition arises from classifications of armed conflict and one-sided violence by the Uppsala Conflict Data Programme (UCDP) (UCDP, 2019). Non-state armed groups are the focus, and I define them as formally organized groups that are party to a conflict. The definition includes rebel armies or insurgents, armed liberation movements and religious or ethnic separatists and nationalists. Some have strong and robust training, indoctrination and punishment against rape and other abuses. Others, despite having similar codes of conduct, will still allow the socialization of sexual predation within the ranks. While this variation exists, we lack systematic understanding of this phenomena.

The research area

Contemporary research has tried to untangle the causes of sexual violence during the conduct of war. The sub-field of empirical civil war research has provided a number of interpretations, including in terms of institutional characteristics, the principal–agent problem and combat socialization (Checkel, 2017; Cohen, 2017; Hoover Green, 2018, 2017, 2016; Wood, 2018, 2014, 2009, 2006). Such research includes cross-national and case study examination of the institutional conditions that contribute to sexual brutality by armed groups. Hoover Green (2018, 2017, 2016) explains the principal–agent problem as the 'commander's dilemma', whereby leaders have to find ways to control the violent behaviours of their fighters. The turn toward disciplinary practices against sexual coercion is linked to these insights, as scholars begin considering how socialization also creates norms and preferences (Checkel, 2017). Thus, the commander's dilemma is not simply central to unlocking how and why groups permit rape. Theorizing the process of adoption of rules through socially embedded values is increasingly viewed as central to interpreting norm adherence and restraint (ICRC, 2018).

My research design

My research fits into this stream of scholarship. The design is based on case study research methodology and the unit of analysis is the armed group. In this work, the outcome of interest is the stigmatization of sexual predation as an approximation of the prevention of wartime sexual violence. The main aim is to isolate the necessary and sufficient causal factor(s). Palipehutu-FNL, the NRA and the ANC-MK have all demonstrated low levels of reported wartime rape against civilians. They share a discernible, documented pattern of stigmatization of sexual predation. My intention is to identify any common causal mechanism contributing to this outcome.

I seek to gather insights about the institutional practices of these actors in order to ascertain their methods for indoctrination, training and punishment. Then, I am interested in more ambiguous and dynamic concepts such as perceptions of gender and sexuality or gendered political relationships and 'intimacies' within an armed group and between it and the civilian population. Data collection for my research is aimed at individuals credibly knowledgeable about each armed group's disciplinary practices and record of wartime sexual violence. Questions are semi-structured for the interviews, but the same (in order, content and sequence) for all the focus groups, assuring comparability and reliability. I rely on purposeful snowball sampling in order to identify interlocutors for interviews, or to invite participants to focus groups.

My ethical terrain differs from the majority of research on wartime sexual violence. As I focus on *cases of prevention* and the *unit of analysis is the armed group*, not the individual, I have managed to bypass the dilemma of contributing to the 'over-researching' of survivors of sexual violence and risking their retraumatization and appropriation (Boesten and Henry, 2018), although I have carried out a few interviews with them. The object of study in my research is not 'the perpetrator' or 'perpetrators' either, but rather those that have chosen to set up and enforce prohibitions and preferences against this violence.

Gaining access to respondents

My first entry-point was Burundi. I sought contacts for respondents in the ex-combatant community from local partners, foremost a civil society association established by ex-combatants from the civil war of 1994–2008, based in Bujumbura. The association had a weak internet presence, but I found it through an online search for veteran groups and demobilization, disarmament and reintegration (DDR) programmes. The association was established and managed by young men; all had been conscripts of rebel groups or the national defence forces. Beginning from my second visit to Burundi, they provided entry into a wider landscape of former fighters. They brought me into contact with other fighters, former commanders, current military personnel and even the head of one of the rebel groups. They gave me advice, organized meeting spaces, offered translation and interpretation and helped secure further interviews and meetings. These young men were not particularly influential or powerful, but they were smart, determined and, above all, resourceful.

What explains this level of cooperation? The ex-combatant association leadership felt it was important to address gender issues. They shared many of my views and objectives. Frequently, they expressed respect for my expertise and professional interest in the study. I furthermore came to feel that some of the members of the association—those I spent the most time with—also valued me as an adopted 'elder sister'. We talked about their personal lives, and mine. I expressed my admiration and respect, which was genuine. I was proud of their progress, of their attendance at university, or of falling in love and marrying, or their becoming fathers. Further, returning again and again to Burundi and keeping in touch made a difference. I reported back on my research results, recommended other researchers and visitors to the organization (including a future student) and have since written references for future job prospects. Reflecting back, I often felt as though these interlocutors were not simply facilitating my research but contributing to it. I treated them with respect and dignity, recognizing them as knowledgeable and worthy companions in my research.

In Uganda (and, to a lesser extent, in South Africa) I found that asking for contacts for fieldwork clashed with the practices of kinship and life-long friendship. Even in relationships unshaped by conflict in developed countries, affinities of love and high regard require drawing lines around narratives around the past. People stay within certain lines in order to protect one another from difficult memories, from shadows and wrongs of the past. Asking for help for research about armed conflicts can be difficult for such relationships. Using my personal networks in order to gain access to respondents meant asking them to think about, and engage with, the past when they may have not wanted to. Getting them to request meetings on my behalf could become personal and costly for them and they would spend their own individual currency, their own influence. This was problematic and felt transgressive at times, and I was clashing with the comforting bounds of the familial. Sometimes a contact from a relative was helpful, other times it was less so. Indeed, access to research contacts in places where I have lived before, and in my own native country, has been more tenuous than in Burundi. For instance, I have the impression that busy, elite-level individuals sometimes perceived me as an inconsequential insider, and it was easy to cancel meetings or delay interviews.

It became more productive to use formal channels. After several visits to Uganda I was able to meet officially with the Chief of Defence Forces, whose office vetted my research credentials, including my university affiliation and research plan. Once I presented myself formally, getting access to NRA/UPDF members became much easier and more systematic. Without conditions, the Office of the Joint Chief of Staff recommended potential respondents. I expressly clarified that I would interview people beyond these recommendations, and I have been able to use snowball sampling to find other contacts. I have enjoyed the interaction with the military, since it is a highly organized institution. Once vetted and approved, certain frictions lessened and it was more likely that others suggest other individuals that I may interview. Hopefully, a similar process will evolve in South Africa, although

I can already foresee that former female combatants and women's equality activists may play a greater role, as these types of individuals had positions of influence within the armed and political movements there. I also maintain cooperation with several South African scholars. People within these sectors are sympathetic to my research and have generously offered assistance in gaining access to respondents.

The main ethical risks

Despite the novelty of my research focus, there are clear ethical risks with this research. There is a danger that findings about the stigmatization of sexual predation will conceal or elide other experiences and realities. It becomes easy to cast an armed group as altruistic, and all other groups that order or tolerate this violence as barbaric. A new binary emerges of good guys in opposition to bad guys; protectors or predators.

Expunging culpability for other harms

The work I do focuses on actors that have invested in disciplinary practices against wartime sexual violence. Some, however, carried out other forms of atrocity. In 2004, for instance, Palipehutu-FNL infamously attacked a transit centre in Gatumba, resulting in over 150 fatalities of so-called Tutsi Banyamulenge refugees from the DRC. The Gatumba massacre is well-known. It is striking particularly if we recall that the 1994 Rwandan genocide, between similar ethnically identified groups, included widespread sexual violence committed by Hutu militia groups known as Interahamwe against tens of thousands of Tutsi women. Palipehutu-FNL and Interahamwe each aimed to defeat their respective Tutsi minorities. And yet, when it came to sexual violence, one allowed wartime rape and the other stopped short of these abuses. The fact that Palipehutu-FNL refrained from sexual violence is often unknown outside of Burundi, or under-theorized. My work strives to understand it. And yet, I run the risk of revising the representation of the rebel group and obscuring the other horrors it carried out. I admire its vision of exemplary sexual conduct. But I must take care not to expunge its culpability for other harms done to civilians that its leaders ordered or tolerated.

Silencing (some) survivors

Second, studying prevention may silence (some) survivors. Despite stigmatizing sexual predation, it is unlikely that an actor stopped all violence unvaryingly. There may be survivors of other forms of sexual coercion or unreported rape who may suffer because this research eclipses their individual experiences. In the armed resistance against South Africa's apartheid government, the ANC's armed wing MK's military code specifically cited rape as a punishable offence (ANC, 1996). There are no widespread allegations against MK fighters for wartime sexual violence against civilians. However, in 1996, former MK commander Teddy Williams (Wellington Sejake) testified before the South African Truth and Reconciliation Commission (TRC). He stated that he and others witnessed female members of the armed wing experiencing sexual abuse by their comrades in the group's military camp in Quibaxe, Angola (SAPA, 1996). Joe Modise, the ANC army commander between 1965 and 1984 admitted to the TRC that there had been a pattern of abuse by some MK members. However, he underscored that the ANC's political leadership punished perpetrators and reinstated accountability (SAPA, 1997).

In my encounters in the field, I run the risk of missing some forms of sexual violence: that which may be a variant from my study's focus, or that which was unreported. Survivors of some sexual violence from within the armed group may have been reluctant to come forward in the past. I have met with a few of these women or read their accounts in other contexts. In some instances, they are wives and daughters of commanders, and the abuse they experienced is intimate and domestic. Or they are former comrades who report gender-based discrimination and harassment that stopped short of rape. These are stories of inequality and exclusion. Or they are about transactional sex. In one example, I was told that sexual violence was uncommon since the armed group was fighting on behalf of the people, but that other harmful sexual conduct was apparent because in war "everything has a price".

Rewarding protection, not recognition of women's sexual autonomy

Third, an armed group might formulate progressive views on rights, citizenship and equality, but its prohibitions against rape may not legitimize women's sexual rights and, instead, undermine female sexual autonomy. In the 1980s, Uganda's NRA launched a rebellion with a handful of weapons and very few men. It defined itself as a people's army and depended heavily on support from the country's peasant population. The rebellion is believed to have had little to no record of sexual violence. The NRA code of conduct asserted that rape was punishable by death. Over 30 years later, former NRA members have recited to me an expression of their code against rape, which they learned: "Any woman is a wife or a daughter of somebody, somewhere".

Do such catchphrases represent the promotion of masculinities that patronize women as in need of male protection? Notions of female dependency may not stop at sexual autonomy but foreshadow other social processes. Male protection could correlate with patterns of transactional sex, which could arise from unequal distribution of material, social and political capital across the genders. At the same time, the participants in my study articulate a value-laden critique of sexual predation. Women seemed to appreciate serving in the NRA, and in the other groups such as Palipehutu-FNL and the ANC-MK, in contrast with other actors in each respective conflict. The idea that males will protect them was not always viewed negatively and, in some instances, it may have been a small step toward a more emancipatory, egalitarian framing of their agency.

Mitigating the ethical risks

My task as a researcher is to weigh the ethical risks associated with this line of research, and to mitigate the moral dilemmas ahead. Two key priorities are useful. First, situating this research as part of the overall pattern of wartime sexual violence, and not its entirety, in essence *sustaining complexity* (Eriksson Baaz et al, 2018; Eriksson Baaz and Stern, 2018, 2013, 2010). Second, using research methodologies that help ensure purposeful inclusion of diverse, yet reliable and valid perspectives while *acknowledging uncertainty* in the research findings and conclusions is a key strategy. Undoubtedly, other strategies will be obvious to other researchers. Still, these priorities alleviate the main threats while also addressing bias in the empirical material and enriching research on wartime sexual violence.

Sustaining complexity

Wartime sexual violence has already been shaped by policy and advocacy as mainly a brutalization of women through widespread reporting of extreme cases (Boesten and Henry, 2018; Eriksson Baaz and Stern, 2018, 2013, 2010). My research could easily fit into an inevitable swing of the pendulum, away from images of lawless men who rape unreservedly and toward representations of heroic rebel leaders who protect women and girls from rape.

Sustaining complexity is essential, but the question is how to do it. I have found three key opportunities. First, my study is a comparative study of actors, capable of revealing 'granular' variation in a common outcome. If I focused on a single case study, it would be easy to miss the fluctuations in disciplinary practices, or in stigmatization. But the differences between the ANC-MK, the NRA and Palipehutu-FNL (and within each case) facilitate a sweeping insight on the wider phenomena. The design has helped me to dig deeper into why prohibitions seemed to hold sway at the frontlines, for instance, but not in camps (the ANC-MK) or during demobilization while awaiting reintegration (Palipehutu-FNL), in contrast to the NRA's rural strongholds where they conducted training.

Second, I visit each field site multiple times, over several years. This increases the likelihood of hearing other stories. Indeed, in one example participants revealed an instance of 'transactional' sex that occurred just after the war (NRA) carried out by one of my interlocutors who had in fact upheld the code against rape during the war. This provided clues to complicate my findings.

Lastly, the informed consent procedure explicitly assures participants of anonymity and confidentiality. I take care to make sure that I will protect the identities of my sources and that it is impossible to trace particular insights back to any single individual. At the same time, I triangulate my data in order not to hide difficult truths that should be told. I purposely try to gain access to a range of participants, including senior and junior commanders and foot-soldiers, from different time periods, who have diverse social and political agendas. These strategies help to make my findings more complex.

Acknowledging uncertainty

In addition to clearly communicating the scope and conditions of any social science inquiry, it is important to fearlessly accept uncertainty. The narrow number of cases in my design jettison potential claims that I am testing a new theory or provide generalizable results for the population of armed groups. Still, I need to acknowledge uncertainty more systematically and genuinely in my research conclusions. There are three ways I envisage doing so in future work (and which I wish I had in previous work).

First, my conclusions should reflect upon alternative explanations more explicitly. Previous research on wartime sexual violence has not yet systematically explained the 'non-cases', but there may be insights from that scholarship or its additional observations that can provide alternative explanations for the prevention that I find exhibited by

Palipehutu-FNL, the ANC-MK and the NRA. How would the 'weapon of war' thesis explain the willingness to punish perpetrators? Are my findings complementary or contradictory with previous explanations?

Second, the research findings and conclusions I present must not be overextended. They are based on a particular question, detailed definitions and specifications, and on a limited number of cases. I cannot say anything about extreme sexual violence during genocide or ethnic cleansing, which is usually ordered. I may have found some evidence about prevention, but I cannot say much about perpetration.

Finally, my research should be considered in relation to a wide array of narratives, scholarship, media reporting and NGO survivor advocacy. I do not seek consensus about my findings within this wide spectrum of perspectives, but I hope that my work is critiqued. And, I choose to participate in inclusive arenas that involve survivors of other forms of sexual violence as well as researchers from other perspectives.

Conclusions

The ethical risks this research poses are multifaceted. First, although some armed groups work to prevent sexual violence, they may commit other harms. My research in this area opens up possibilities for expunging their culpability for other human rights violence committed in the course of war. Second, the lessons of how these actors stigmatize sexual predation is useful empirically and theoretically. But survivors of unreported incidents may feel uneasy with my research. There is a risk that a story of prevention could silence survivors of other forms of abuse. There are numerous types of sexual coercion that can take place in peacetime and war. Sex with soldiers because of their power is not always consensual. Finally, the armed groups I study have been exemplars in protection—but their messages to their fighters may undermine female sexual autonomy. The risk that I may validate ideals of 'male protectors' and 'female victims' warrants attention.

Yet, lifting the burden is not an inevitable outcome of research and fieldwork on cases of prevention of wartime sexual violence. It is worth becoming aware of potential dangers and, importantly, mitigating the ethical risks in the research design, during field research and in reporting the results. Of critical importance are strategies that lift up the complexity of the prevention of wartime sexual violence and the uncertainty of research findings and conclusions.

Note

1 'Wartime sexual violence', 'sexual and gender-based violence during conflict' and 'conflict-related sexual violence' are terms used *incorrectly* but inter-changeably within the literature in the social sciences and in the media.

References

African National Congress (ANC) (1996) 'African National Congress Statement to the Truth and Reconciliation Commission', August, https://eur02.safelinks.protection.outlook.com/?url=http%3A%2F%2Fwww.justice.gov.za%2Ftrc%2Fhrvtrans%2Fsubmit%2Fanctruth.htm&data=02%7C01%7C%7Cd8c3690b1e347527a1f08d6dc8de742%7Cd47b090e3f5a4ca084d09f89d269f175%7C0%7C0%7C636938899364558342&sdata=00vw8ImSwE%2BCrQkb9i9Z%2BhQtMskdGH2nhZLe0ypVkKQ%3D&reserved=0.

Boesten, J. and Henry, M. (2018) 'Between fatigue and silence: the challenges of conducting research on sexual violence in conflict', *Social Politics: International Studies in Gender, State and Society*, 25(4): 568–88.

Checkel, J.T. (2017) 'Socialisation and violence: introduction and framework', *Journal of Peace Research*, 54(5): 592–605.

Cohen, D.K. (2013) 'Explaining rape during civil war: cross-national evidence (1980–2009)', *American Political Science Review*, 107(03): 461–77.

Cohen, D.K. (2017) 'The ties that bind: how armed groups use violence to socialise fighters', *Journal of Peace Research*, 54(5): 701–14.

Cohen, D.K. and Nordås, R. (2014) 'Sexual violence in armed conflict: introducing the SVAC dataset, 1989–2009', *Journal of Peace Research*, 51(3): 418–28.

Dolan, C. (2016) 'Has patriarchy been stealing the feminists' clothes? Conflict-related sexual violence and UN Security Council Resolutions', *IDS Bulletin*, 45(1): 80–4.

Eriksson Baaz, M. and Stern, M. (2010) *The Complexity of Violence: A Critical Analysis of Sexual Violence in the Democratic Republic of Congo (DRC)*, Stockholm: The Swedish International Development Cooperation Agency (Sida).

Eriksson Baaz, M. and Stern, M. (2013) *Sexual Violence as a Weapon of War? Perceptions, Prescriptions, Problems in the Congo and Beyond*, London: Zed Books.

Eriksson Baaz, M. and Stern, M. (2018) 'Curious erasures: the sexual in wartime sexual violence', *International Feminist Journal of Politics*, 20(3): 295–314.

Eriksson Baaz, M., Gray, H. and Stern, M. (2018) 'What can we/do we want to know? Reflections from researching SGBV in military settings', *Social Politics: International Studies in Gender, State and Society*, 25(4): 521–44.

Gutiérrez Saní, F. and Wood, E.J. (2014) 'Ideology in civil war: instrumental adoption and beyond', *Journal of Peace Research*, 51(2): 213–26.

Hoover Green, A. (2016) 'The commander's dilemma: creating and controlling armed group violence', *Journal of Peace Research*, 53(5): 619–32.

Hoover Green, A. (2017) 'Armed group institutions and combatant socialisation: evidence from El Salvador.', *Journal of Peace Research*, 54(5): 687–700.

Hoover Green, A. (2018) *The Commander's Dilemma: Violence and Restraint in War*, Ithaca, NY: Cornell University.

Hultman, L., and Muvumba Sellström, A. (2018) 'WPS and protection of civilians', in S.E. Davies and J. True (eds), *Oxford Handbook of Women, Peace, and Security*, Oxford: Oxford University Press.

International Committee of the Red Cross (ICRC) (2018) *The Roots of Restraint in War*, written by F. Terry and B. McQuinn, Geneva: ICRC.

Kirby, P. (2012) 'How is rape a weapon of war? Feminist international relations, modes of critical explanation and the study of wartime sexual violence', *European Journal of International Relations*, 19(4): 797–821.

Lieby, M. (2009) 'Wartime sexual violence in Guatemala and Peru', *International Studies Quarterly*, 53: 445–68.

Meger, S. (2016) 'The fetishisation of sexual violence in international security', *International Studies Quarterly*, 60(1): 149–59.

Muvumba Sellström, A. (2015a) 'Impunity for conflict-related sexual violence: insights from Burundi's Former Fighters', in S. Cheldelin and M. Mutisi (eds), *Deconstructing Women, Peace and Security: A Critical Review of Approaches to Gender and Empowerment*, Cape Town: Human Sciences Research Council.

Muvumba Sellström, A. (2015b) *Stronger than Justice: Armed Group Impunity for Sexual Violence*, Uppsala: Department of Peace and Conflict Research, Uppsala University.

South African Press Association (SAPA) (1996) 'MK commander alleges sexual abuse in ANC exile camps', SAPA, Umtata, 18 June.

South African Press Association (SAPA) (1997) 'ANC women cadres were sexually abused, Modise admits', SAPA, Cape Town, 12 May.

Sivakumaran, S. (2007) 'Sexual violence against men in armed conflict', *The European Journal of International Law*, 18(2): 253–76.

Uppsala Conflict Data Programme (2019) UCDP Conflict Definitions, www.pcr.uu.se/research/ucdp/definitions/.

Wood, E.J. (2006) 'Variation in sexual violence during war', *Politics and Society*, 34(3): 307–42.

Wood, E.J. (2009) 'Armed groups and sexual violence: when is wartime rape rare?', *Politics and Society*, 37(1): 131–61.

Wood, E.J. (2014) 'Conflict-related sexual violence and the policy implications of recent research', *International Review of the Red Cross*, 96(894): 457–78.

Wood, E.J. (2018) 'Rape as a practice of war: toward a typology of political violence', *Politics and Society*, 46(4): 513–37.

17

Unexpected Grey Areas, Innuendo and Webs of Complicity: Experiences of Researching Sexual Exploitation in UN Peacekeeping Missions

Henri Myrttinen[1]

Researching sexual exploitation and abuse (SEA) and sexual and gender-based violence (SGBV) in conflict-affected situations and in relation to peacekeeping operations (PKOs) is a delicate undertaking. It is fraught with a range of challenges and sensitivities, from the ethical to the practical, the political to the legal. It is also a field that is problematically seductive in many ways (Henry, 2013a), one that seemingly allows for easy categorizations and for the researcher to side with the right side of history. Certainly, some issues are quite straightforward: cases of sexual abuse and violence, at times horrific, are unequivocally illegal and criminal. As discussed in this chapter, however, the issue of what constitutes exploitation and how to react to it is far less clear-cut. What is also evident is that efforts to end SEA/SGBV in UN or UN-mandated PKOs have been unsuccessful in spite of decades of knowledge of the issue and numerous action plans (Dahrendorf, 2006; Martin, 2005). The reasons for why this is so, however, are less evident. The academic and policy fields are also divided and highly politicized: while there is broad consensus on the need to end SEA/SGBV, and most academics and policymakers are working in the same direction, there are major political fights. Issues such as which categories of victims/survivors should be recognized, what the best way to address prostitution/commercial sex work would be, or how to deal with consensual sex are all highly, and acrimoniously, contested.

I will focus here less on the issue of SEA/SGBV and the responses (or lack thereof), and more on some of the murkiness and dilemmas, gaps, methodological issues and ethical challenges that I encountered in conducting research on these issues. I focus, in particular, on sexual exploitation rather than SGBV or sexual abuse, as it is here that I felt the greatest challenges lie. After a brief digression to my experiences starting out on researching SEA/SGBV in Timor-Leste, I will examine some of the grey areas related to the theoretically black-and-white issue of SEA in PKOs. This is followed by a discussion of methodological challenges of conducting research on these issues, especially on dealing with unverifiable data and the risks of collusion with interlocutors. While there are detailed guides on some, in particular more technical aspects of researching SEA/SGBV (see for example World Health Organisation, 2005), other dilemmas require personal judgement calls and choices between different unsatisfactory options. I end with a discussion of what this could mean for research methods.

This chapter draws on my experiences of researching SEA/SGBV in conjunction with PKOs, which started with a comparative study on gendered impacts of peacekeeping in Cambodia and Timor-Leste (Koyama and Myrttinen, 2007). Later research on the issue in Timor-Leste was published in Myrttinen (2016). The LSE Women, Peace and Security Centre generously provided funding for research on peacekeeper abuses in Central African Republic (CAR) in 2016. Further insights came from a collaborative project on analyzing Finnish peacekeeper masculinities (Mäki-Rahkola and Myrttinen, 2014) as well as from observations while working on other issues in areas with PKOs in the Democratic Republic of the Congo (DRC), Haiti and Kosovo. Additionally, insights have come from engagement with academic and policy debates around these issues for several years.

Assumptions clash with reality: fieldwork in Timor-Leste, 2004

In 2004, I embarked on my first field research project on SEA/SGBV, examining the impact of the UN missions in Timor-Leste. In retrospect, I can see how I was seduced by the issue in some of the problematic ways Marsha Henry (2013a) outlines. Upon setting out, I held somewhat naïve assumptions about how straightforward the research and how clear-cut the issues were—but I was soon disabused of those notions as I started navigating a messy reality.

The first group interview of the research project was an awkward one. Sitting in plastic chairs outside a bar in Dili on a workaday afternoon, I interviewed a group of male Australian contractors about their relations with commercial sex workers in Timor-Leste.[2] The men were all working on projects associated with, and funded by, the UN's mission at the time. The respondents, in cut-off jeans shorts and singlets, cradling Victoria Bitter beer stubbies, were all middle aged, white, and performing a 'hard man' working-class masculinity. Their accounts were crudely misogynist and racist, as befitted their particular performance of Australian 'manliness'—perhaps in part pointedly so, as they viewed me as what in today's parlance would be called a 'liberal snowflake'. A senior anthropologist once commented to me that successful ethnographic work requires having empathy with your interviewees. My empathy was in decidedly short supply. Nonetheless, regardless of my personal feelings, I needed to engage seriously with their views as well and not merely dismiss them, as they also formed part and parcel of the issue I was grappling with. Though I had deliberately broadened my scope to look beyond military peacekeepers, had I let myself be guided too much by preconceived ideas of who, in terms of gender and class, would be SEA perpetrators, thus missing others?

My second interview for the project was no less awkward, even if there was more empathy from my side. The middle-aged Thai masseuse I was interviewing was wistfully reminiscing about the 'good old days' of the previous UN mission. This had been far larger with more uniformed peacekeepers and civilian staff, and my interlocutor was reeling off lists of the nationalities of the men who had sought her services in the decidedly 'dual-use' massage parlour/brothel that she was working in—and which was about to close due to a lack of customers. How did her narrative fit into the simplistic notions of agency-less sex workers that had informed my prior thinking? How could I do justice to her views, while simultaneously not glossing over her personal exploitation and broader systems of repression? While the first interview reaffirmed, perhaps too much, my assumptions of what kind of men would be perpetrators, the second one troubled my preconceived ideas about victimhood.

Both sets of interviews also raised questions around consensual sex versus exploitation, and of whose sexual lives a UN mission could and should regulate. Much of the rest of the research time in Dili was spent trying to parse rumour and urban legend from fact, trying to gain access to gatekeepers, and negotiating my own positionality vis-à-vis those who were at least rhetorically committed to ending SEA, but were clearly not doing an effective job at it. These dilemmas had not disappeared when I reengaged with the issue as a research topic in later years, though by now I was much warier about how I was approaching it, and where I stood in relation to my interlocutors.

Zero tolerance and definitional grey zones

One of the fundamental dilemmas I quickly encountered in the vignettes was that of how the research focus—and, by extension, the policy—should be delineated. Different forms of SEA and SGBV were and are conflated and seeming clarity has led to grey areas. While rape and sex with minors by UN staff were and are clearly criminal and led to a blanket 'zero-tolerance' approach, did this cover all forms of sexual activity between locals and internationals? Did it cover contractors? What was the situation of national staff? What about sexual relations between UN staff? As I will discuss later for CAR, responses to cases at the extreme end of the SEA spectrum have at least seemed to have focused on less clear-cut cases of co-habitation—while there is a sense that the more extreme cases went unpunished.

In theory, there are no grey areas when it comes to SEA/SGBV in UN missions. The UN has a zero-tolerance policy on SEA since 2003, set out a strategy to eliminate SEA in PKOs in 2005, and individual missions have separately announced policies (al-Hussein, 2005; UN, 2017). In practice, however, things look very different, and across the board the efforts have not succeeded in eliminating SEA in PKOs (Westendorf, 2019). In part, this is due to lax implementation, but paradoxically it is also the seeming clarity of the zero-tolerance approach itself that creates problems and grey areas in practice. The conflation of very different forms of SEA under one concept is problematic and does not allow for a better understanding of different dynamics underpinning different forms of SEA (Henry, 2013b; Westendorf and Searle, 2017). The comprehensive and unequivocal nature of the policy and lack of clear implementing guidelines have led to it being ignored by staff in managerial positions in PKOs (Westendorf, 2019). The definition also 'suggests that no adults in conflict-affected communities have the capacity to consent in the context of unequal power dynamics, which is infantilising and disempowering' (Westendorf, 2017: 10).

The cases of SEA/ SGBV in CAR and the responses to them highlight the problems arising from the current strategies to tackle them. The UN's MINUSCA mission (Mission multidimensionnelle intégrée des Nations unies pour la stabilisation en Centrafrique) came into being in 2014, and the majority of its peacekeepers-to-be were already on the ground as part of the African Union's MISCA (Mission internationale de soutien à la Centrafrique sous conduite africaine). Simultaneously, there was a French military mission (Operation Sangaris, 2013–16) on the ground, as well as a European Union mission, EUFOR RCA (European Union Force in the Central African Republic). As related to me in interviews in Bangui, a number of the MISCA peacekeepers were already co-habitating with local 'girlfriends' before being 'rehatted' as UN peacekeepers. According to my interlocutors, these were, at least in part, consensual relationships between adults, albeit ones in which the peacekeepers were expected to provide economically, to some degree, for their CAR partners.[3] However, some of these 'co-habitation' arrangements were exploitative and abusive, including allegedly ones with under-age girls (Kleinfeld, 2018).

The allegations of SEA/SGBV that initially came into public knowledge were, however, far more serious than the issue of co-habitation with local adult women. French Sanagris forces as well as MISCA troops from Chad and Equatorial Guinea were accused of coercing children to perform sexual acts in exchange for food, and some children were raped (Deschamps et al, 2015). Further accusations followed, including by around 100 girls who claimed to have been abused, and allegations that a French military commander had abused four girls and forced them to have sex with a dog, after which one of the girls died (Aids Free World, 2015; Dearden, 2016). Later accusations have also implicated EUFOR RCA forces and MINUSCA soldiers from various countries (Kleinfeld, 2018; MINUSCA, 2018; OHCHR, 2016; Reuters, 2017). The French abuses and the actions taken by the UN, in particular by the UN Office of the High Commissioner for Human Rights (OHCHR) against the Swedish whistle-blower aiding the investigations rather than against the abusers, have been at the spotlight of international media attention (Aids Free World, 2015).

The grey areas created by a conflation of different forms of SEA, the paradoxes caused by an unenforced but theoretically categorical zero-tolerance policy and local frustrations over responses shape the field the researcher enters and needs to navigate. By the time I was conducting interviews in Bangui in late 2016, the MINUSCA mission was trying to take measures against SEA and SGBV, even if many of the initial accusations were against EUFOR RCA, Sangaris and MISCA troops rather than MINUSCA.[4] SEA/SGBV were what outsiders such as myself were interested in, to the chagrin of mission staff tired of answering the same questions. The focus on the SEA cases was also exasperating for those who were trying to address the many other conflict-related abuses occurring in the country, which did not gain anywhere close to the same level of international interest.

Due to the confidential nature of ongoing investigations and the internal nature of the SEA/SGBV prevention work, many outsiders saw the main focus of this work chiefly as being on ending the practice of co-habitation. The critiques of the work done by national SEA/SGBV investigators coming in from the troop-contributing countries, their focus on primarily debunking allegations, and the practice of repatriating suspected perpetrators contributed to a sense among non-UN interviewees that the UN had its priorities wrong.[5] As Westendorf (2017: 10) argues, 'raping children with dogs, as French Sangaris soldiers allegedly did in the Central African Republic, is a world away from consensual transactional sex between adults even in the context of unequal power dynamics, and is different again to direct or indirect involvement in sex trafficking and forced prostitution'. The impression that less serious issues such as consensual co-habitation were being cracked down upon while egregious cases of SGBV/SEA were being dealt with leniently was further reinforced when no criminal charges were brought against the French soldiers (The Guardian, 2017).[6]

The focus on ending co-habitation by military peacekeepers also raised questions around the particular position that men in uniform take in the imaginary of who perpetrates SEA/SGBV. A military peacekeeper having a relationship with a local civilian would be seen as out of bounds. However, this censure would not necessarily pertain to all civilian peacekeepers, even if the socio-economic disparity between, say, a UN political advisor with a P-4 salary and an unemployed local artist would be greater than between a regional military peacekeeper and a local civilian. This raises questions around what criteria are used to judge, officially or by means of social censure, and which relationships between internationals and locals are deemed to be legitimate or illegitimate. Should all relationships be considered unequal and therefore illegitimate? Or only the ones for certain groups, such as military peacekeepers? The application of zero tolerance rules is in any case easier in the case of peacekeeping forces (PKF) than civilians. The extension of non-fraternization rules to international civilians would already be tricky, but likely unworkable for local civilian staff or locally hired international staff, who might be in a pre-existing relationship with local civilians.

Navigating these grey areas required that I needed to redefine the scope of my research for myself—did I want to use a similar blanket approach as the UN, or did I want to differentiate? As I chose the latter, I also needed to then embark on the difficult and ongoing task of trying to position myself clearly.

Innuendo, drunken rumours and urban legends

One of the key methodological challenges I faced in SEA/SGBV research was the lack of verifiable facts and difficulty of triangulating or double-checking allegations. Often, cases are not reported or documented in any way, especially if they are not even viewed as being problematic in the first place by the institutions in charge of investigations. Power differentials, shame and stigma as well as fear of retribution militate against reporting, as do the rumours and knowledge of aggressive questioning of the veracity of victims'/survivors' and witnesses' testimonies by investigative teams. If and when there was a documentation of cases, this tended to be inaccessible to me as it was in the hands of internal enquiry and disciplinary bodies, be it of the mission itself or of the personnel-contributing countries.

While hard information was difficult or even impossible to come by, rumour, innuendo and urban legends tended to abound, both among international staff and the 'peace-kept' community (cf. Fluri, 2011). Sensationalist stories of sexual escapades make the rounds nationally and internationally, usually linked to particular military PKF or UN Police (UNPOL) contingents—often with racialized undertones (cf. Bliesemann de Guevara and Kühn, 2015). For example, I heard both in Haiti and in Timor-Leste the story of a Jordanian peacekeeper who allegedly had to be medically evacuated with a goat after anally penetrating the animal and not being able to get his penis out, with the urban legend picking up various degrees of detail and embellishment depending on the storyteller. Stories of dozens or even hundreds of peacekeeper babies also did the rounds in several of the locations I conducted fieldwork in, as did stories of child sexual abuse, with little hard evidence to go by. None of this means that these were not real phenomena, but the degree of their veracity had become difficult to establish.

What was also noticeable was how these rumours and urban legends tended for the most part to only refer to uniformed male personnel and acts against the local population—rumours of possible cases involving other perpetrators, in particular civilian peacekeepers, were not doing the rounds. This reflects the dominant ways in which SEA/SGBV in PKOs tends to be imagined, but as pressing and important as it is to address the abuses by uniformed peacekeepers, there is also a risk of other abuses and abusers escaping attention. This pertains especially to abuse, exploitation and harassment within a mission, among international personnel more broadly, or between national and international staff, or the invisibilized sexual harassment and abuse that may occur between domestic workers and their mission-affiliated employers (Jennings, 2014). While anecdotes of SEA by uniformed personnel do the rounds at staff parties and in bars and cafés frequented by 'the internationals', sexually predatory, abusive or harassing behaviour by, for example, senior civilian staff is seldom openly discussed, even if the problematic reputations of key personnel are often more or less open secrets. Regardless of the degree of prominence of the narratives, however, neither the sensational cases nor the more invisibilized forms of SEA have been properly addressed.

Furthermore, the rumours and urban legends are also doing other work, such as establishing racialized and/or national hierarchies of peacekeeper masculinities. A common 'explanation' offered off the record for peacekeeper SEA/SGBV is that "this is what you get when you get troops from *those* kinds of countries", that is less prosperous Global South troop contributing countries, obscuring the numerous cases committed by personnel from Global North countries. These lines of differentiation also run between members of different contingents,[7] where one's own national peacekeeper performances are cast in a positive light, indeed in part defined through their comparison to other countries' peacekeepers (Higate and Henry, 2009; Mäki-Rahkola and Myrttinen, 2014).

A further ethically complicating factor with the rumours was that I often heard them in a private conversation, at times in a bar setting and under the influence of alcohol, off the record. Following up on the leads I gained this way often led to the accusations being neither confirmed nor denied on the record, with the insinuation that there probably was some truth to them, but no way to establish this.

Complicity and critique

Conducting the research also raised issues around neutrality and potential complicity with those I was researching, in particular those persons seeking to address these issues within the system and whose trust I had gained. While I see it as my task to critique their work, which often remains very much imperfect in spite of their best efforts due to factors beyond their control, I feared at times that my critique could be seen as a breach of that trust or undermining of their efforts (see also Kostić, in this volume).

While I did not censor myself consciously, my empathy for the predicament as well as a broad aligning of our politics and a wish to support their work may well have subconsciously affected my analysis and outputs. I also had at times the sense that I was being pushed to take sides between different individuals, institutions or parts of institutions, all of whom were working towards broadly the same goal but through different approaches. I was for a large part only privy to the information that my informants-cum-gatekeepers shared with me, especially on internal processes of the UN missions, so I found myself repeatedly asking myself why certain information was being shared with me and other insights were not and to what degree I was being pulled into one camp. Assumptions about my politics likely also affected the kinds of answers I received from those not directly working on SEA/SGBV but whose mandate included taking steps to prevent it occurring, such as force commanders. These tended to be exceedingly careful in crafting their answers to me.

While I am very much an advocate for more comprehensive, nuanced and complex understandings of SEA/SGBV, I am also aware of the risk that this may contribute to a stalling of prevention efforts or a dilution of the message of its unacceptability, in a political environment where there is already a push to pursue the issue (Westendorf, 2019). A further challenge is how to remain truthful to voices that nuance the conversation, such as those of the sex worker in the second vignette, without becoming an apologist for sexual exploitation, and keep the focus on patriarchal structures of exploitation, while also problematizing simplistic understandings of the issue (Jennings, 2019). Conversely, I also need to craft my critiques in ways that remain true to my convictions but do not dehumanize informants such as the men of the first vignette.

Conclusion

Reflecting on what has and what has not changed in terms of SEA/SGBV in the 15 years since my first research, the outcome is decidedly mixed. Research and reporting on SEA/SGBV in PKOs has proliferated, but much of this has focused on that perpetrated by military personnel against civilians or their use of sex workers.[8] While this deserves all of the attention it has received—*and* hopefully sooner rather than later effective counter-measures—problematic and illegal behaviour by non-military staff has received far less attention, and even less so that of contractors and others associated with PKOs. Also, what is only slowly being increasingly discussed in the wake of #MeToo and #AidToo, but still hardly researched, is the often pervasive sexism, sexual harassment and SEA within missions and among staff, in particular the abuse of power by more senior staff.

The UN system has still not been able to address even the most unequivocal part of SEA/SGBV prevention, that is acts that are clearly and unambiguously abusive and criminal and perpetrated by soldiers who are far easier to control and discipline than civilian staff. On the other hand, SEA/SGBV has at least been rhetorically cast as being unacceptable and it would be unlikely that souvenir shops in PKO-hosting countries would now sell t-shirts with slogans such as "Stay Safe—Sleep With A Peacekeeper", which were somewhat popular in Dili in 2004. While there are serious efforts to counter SEA/SGBV in missions, the 'train and punish' approach does not seem to work, and mission-specific training is still often lacking (Dahrendorf, 2006; Westendorf, 2017). The UN system as a whole seems still too often to be more preoccupied with trying to protect its own reputation and quashing or downplaying allegations of SEA/SGBV rather than seriously addressing them.

In terms of my own research methodologies, the area proved far more complicated than I had naïvely assumed when I first started researching it, with multiple conundrums rather than the moral clarity I had expected as a young, eager researcher. A more open and honest discussion of the messiness of it all was needed, if only with myself; of the difficulty of drawing clear lines in a grey zone of SEA; of how I and others preconceive victims and perpetrators; of how salacious, spectacular urban legends abound and real, everyday abusive practices are invisibilized; of the pull of certain informants' narratives over others; of the political nature of it all. Awareness, reflection and self-critique do not make these conundrums disappear, but do help in developing better research methodologies and lenses of analysis.

For myself, this involved questioning on a continuous basis my own biases, starting with the framing of the issue of what violence, abuse and exploitation were. Next, I needed to be more aware of my own simplistic assumptions as to what perpetrators and presumed victims were like and what they thought—and learning to listen better. I needed to be conscious of the risk of succumbing to ethnographic seduction as well as to its opposite: was I subconsciously predisposed to giving more credence to charismatic, earnest, likeable interlocutors who were at least claiming to make a change rather than to those whose gender and racial politics I did not share and who struck me as unsympathetic, such as the Australian contractors? Lastly, I needed to—and continue to—put more effort into triangulating data and thinking through what work different narratives that I am told are doing.

Notes

1. I would like to thank the editors as well as Megan Daigle, Marsha Henry and Sarah Martin for their immensely helpful comments on earlier drafts.
2. The terminological debate around whether to use 'prostitution' or 'sex work' is an acrimonious one. I have chosen to use sex work as it comprises a broader range of activities than 'prostitution'.
3. Interviews, Bangui, November 2016
4. There have, however, also been accusations levelled against MINUSCA.
5. Interviews Bangui, November 2016. For critiques of the investigations, see for example Code Blue (2017) and Kleinfeld (2018).
6. Given the confidential nature of the proceedings, it is difficult to know for outsiders if they were let off the hook or genuinely innocent of the crimes.
7. For example, a Brazilian military officer used the argument to implicitly cast Brazilian and Global North peacekeepers as being superior to African peacekeepers with reference to the CAR abuse—although the abuses we were discussing were acts attributed to French soldiers (Personal communication, 2015).
8. For academic studies on SEA in different PKOs, see for example Fluri (2011), Henry (2013b), Higate (2007), Higate and Henry (2004), Jennings (2010, 2014, 2019), Jennings and Nikolić-Ristanović (2009) and Oldenburg (2015).

References

AIDS Free World (2015) *The UN's Dirty Secret: The Untold Story of Anders Kompass and Peacekeeper Sex Abuse in the Central African Republic*, New York: AIDS Free World, www.codebluecampaign.com/carstatement/.

Al-Hussein, Z.R. (2005) *A Comprehensive Strategy to Eliminate Future Sexual Exploitation and Abuse in United Nations Peacekeeping Operations (A/59/710)*, New York: United Nations.

Bliesemann de Guevara, B. and Kühn, F.P. (2015) 'On Afghan footbaths and sacred cows in Kosovo: urban legends of intervention', *Peacebuilding*, 3(1): 17–35.

Code Blue (2017) 'Leaked files reveal hidden scope of UN sex abuse', Code Blue Press Release, 13 September, www.codebluecampaign.com/press-releases/2017/9/13.

Dahrendorf, N. (2006) *Sexual Exploitation and Abuse: Lessons Learned Study, Addressing Sexual Exploitation and Abuse in MONUC*, New York: UNDPKO, www.peacewomen.org/sites/default/files/dpko_addressingsexualviolenceinmonuc_2006_0.pdf.

Dearden, L. (2016) 'French troops accused of "forcing girls into bestiality" in CAR as rape claims mount against UN peacekeepers', *The Independent*, 31 March, www.independent.co.uk/news/world/africa/french-troops-accused-of-forcing-girls-to-have-sex-with-dog-in-car-as-rape-claims-against-un-a6961711.html.

Deschamps, M., Jallow, H.B. and Sooka Y. (2015) *Taking Action on Sexual Exploitation and Abuse by Peacekeepers: Report of an Independent Review on Sexual Exploitation and Abuse by International Peacekeeping Forces in the Central African Republic*, New York: UN External Independent Panel, https://digitallibrary.un.org/record/840749/files/A_71_99-EN.pdf.

Fluri, J. (2011) 'Armored peacocks and proxy bodies: gender geopolitics in aid/development spaces of Afghanistan', *Gender, Place and Culture: A Journal of Feminist Geography*, 18(4): 519–36.

Henry, M. (2013a) 'Ten reasons not to write your Master's Dissertation on sexual violence in war', *The Disorder of Things* blog, 4 June, https://thedisorderofthings.com/2013/06/04/ten-reasons-not-to-write-your-masters-dissertation-on-sexual-violence-in-war/.

Henry, M. (2013b) 'Sexual exploitation and abuse in UN peacekeeping missions: problematising current responses', in S. Madhok, A. Phillips, and K. Wilson (eds), *Gender, Agency, and Coercion*, Houndmills: Palgrave Macmillan, pp 122–42.

Higate, P. (2007) 'Peacekeepers, masculinities, and sexual exploitation', *Men and Masculinities*, 10(1): 99–119.

Higate, P. and Henry, M. (2004) 'Engendering (in)security in peace support operations', *Security Dialogue*, 35(4): 481–98.

Higate, P. and Henry M. (2009) *Insecure Spaces—Peacekeeping, Power and Performance in Haiti, Kosovo and Liberia*, London: Zed Books.

Jennings, K. (2010) 'Unintended consequences of intimacy: political economies of peacekeeping and sex tourism', *International Peacekeeping*, 17(2): 229–43.

Jennings, K. (2014) 'Service, sex, and security: gendered peacekeeping economies in Liberia and the Democratic Republic of the Congo', *Security Dialogue*, 45(4):1–18.

Jennings, K. (2019) 'WPS and peacekeeping economies', in S. Davies and J. True (eds), *The Oxford Handbook of Women, Peace, and Security*. Oxford: Oxford University Press, pp 237–47.

Jennings, K. and Nikolić-Ristanović V. (2009) *UN Peacekeeping Economies and Local Sex Industries: Connections and Implications*, MICROCON Research Working Paper No.17, https://papers.ssrn.com/sol3/papers.cfm?abstract_id=1488842.

Kleinfeld, P. (2018) '"I have no power to complain"—victims of sexual abuse by UN peacekeepers find little support or justice', Central African Republic Special Report, IRIN News, 25 July, www.irinnews.org/special-report/2018/07/25/central-african-republic-peacekeeper-sexual-abuse-investigation.

Koyama, S. and Myrttinen, H. (2007) 'Unintended consequences of UN peacekeeping operations from a gender perspective—the cases of Cambodia and Timor-Leste,' in C. Aoi, C. De Coning and R. Thakur (eds), *Unintended Consequences of Peacekeeping Operations*, Tokyo: United Nations University, pp 23–43.

Mäki-Rahkola, A. and Myrttinen, H. (2014) 'Reliable professionals, sensitive dads and tough fighters—a critical look at performances and discourses of Finnish peacekeeper masculinities', *International Feminist Journal of Politics,* 16(3): 470–89.

Martin, S. (2005) *Must Boys be Boys? Ending Sexual Exploitation and Abuse in UN Peacekeeping Missions,* Washington, DC: Refugees International, www.pseataskforce.org/uploads/tools/mustboysbeboysendingseainunpeacekeepingmissions_refugeesinternational_english.pdf.

MINUSCA (2018) 'MINUSCA has been informed of an allegation of sexual abuse, by a member of the military battalion from the Democratic Republic of the Congo', MINUSCA Press Release, 19 February, https://minusca.unmissions.org/en/minusca-has-been-informed-allegation-sexual-abuse-member-military-battalion-democratic-republic.

Myrttinen, H. (2016) 'The camp, the street, the hotel, and the brothel—the gendered, racialised spaces of a city in crisis. Dili, 2006–2008', in A. Björkdahl and S. Buckley-Zistel (eds), *Spatializing Peace and Conflict—Mapping the Production of Places, Sites and Scales of Violence,* London: Palgrave Macmillan, pp 98–117.

OHCHR (2016) 'More allegations of sexual abuse of children by foreign soldiers in the Central African Republic,' *OHCHR News,* 29 January, Geneva: United Nations Office of the High Commissioner for Human Rights, www.ohchr.org/en/NewsEvents/Pages/DisplayNews.aspx?NewsID=16995.

Oldenburg, S. (2015) 'The politics of love and intimacy in Goma, Eastern DR Congo: perspectives on the market of intervention as contact zone', *Journal of Intervention and Statebuilding,* 9(3): 316–33.

Reuters (2017) 'Congo troops may be sent home from Central African Republic: U.N.', *Reuters Intel,* 7 June, www.reuters.com/article/us-centralafrica-violence/congo-troops-may-be-sent-home-from-central-african-republic-u-n-idUSKBN18Y2AJ.

Guardian (2017) 'No charges sought over abuse claims against French troops in CAR', *The Guardian*, 5 January, www.theguardian.com/world/2017/jan/05/no-charges-sought-over-abuse-claims-against-french-troops-in-car.

United Nations (2017) *Glossary on Sexual Exploitation and Abuse* (2nd edn), New York: United Nations.

Westendorf, J.-K. (2017) 'WPS, CRSV and sexual exploitation and abuse in peace operations: making sense of the missing links', *LSE Women, Peace and Security Working Paper Series*, 9/2017, London: London School of Economics and Political Science Centre for Women Peace and Security.

Westendorf, J.-K. (2019) 'WPS and SEA in peacekeeping operations', in S. Davies and J. True (eds), *The Oxford Handbook of Women, Peace, and Security*, Oxford: Oxford University Press, pp 222–36.

Westendorf, J.-K. and Searle, L. (2017) 'Sexual exploitation and abuse in peace operations: trends, policy responses and future directions', *International Affairs*, 93(2): 365–87.

World Health Organisation (2005) *Researching Violence against Women: Practical Guidelines for Researchers and Activists*, Geneva: World Health Organization, www.who.int/iris/handle/10665/42966.

18

Sexual Exploitation, Rape and Abuse as a Narrative and a Strategy

Ingunn Bjørkhaug

When I arrived at Nakivale Refugee Settlement, Uganda, in August 2013, I came with a mattress, a blanket, a bucket and some items needed for my seven-week stay in the settlement. My colleague and I each rented rooms in a small hostel run by a Congolese refugee family, and I looked forward to an ethnographic approach to our fieldwork. I had many expectations for the real-life perspectives I would learn from interviewing and observing the refugees there but was unprepared for the dilemmas my presence in the settlement would engender. The research aim was to learn how interactions between the refugees and the community that received them shaped the livelihoods of both. However, during fieldwork, I often found myself in a context in which the refugees perceived me as part of an international community with authority to bring forward their cases. Less than a day after our arrival, rumour in Nakivale spread like wildfire: "Norway is back to select more refugees for resettlement". I had not anticipated how my qualitative interviews could create the refugees' expectations for resettlement to a third country (or help their current situation in the settlement) or how they consequently would openly share vulnerable stories of sexual violence without my probing.

The fieldwork challenges described in this chapter have methodological implications for how to analzse collected data (discussed in Bjørkhaug, 2017). Here I argue that, in settings like in Nakivale where sexual exploitation may easily become the dominating subject even when this is not our study's focus or aim, we have to be prepared to read and interpret how actors employ such stories to navigate in a competitive terrain, reconstruct the meaning of their public stories in the wider context and thus understand the power politics of narrative(s) across different groups. This chapter's contribution is that it discusses how researchers can implement fieldwork, as well as self-care, in a complex context by addressing three dilemmas: (1) how the research is situated in a wider context we cannot necessarily influence, (2) how participants can be strategic in their responses to the researcher and, therefore, potentially influence data collection, and (3) the researcher's role in the field when we listen to others' distress and find ourselves struggling to provide a response we are not prepared to give. Although we may not be trained social workers, can we provide some comfort when people confide their stories of rape and violence?

Research among refugees entails a number of ethical challenges widely discussed in the literature, including the subjects of power and consent, confidentiality and trust, risks to researchers and payments to respondents, as well as potential harm to study participants (for example Head, 2009; Kabranian-Melkonian, 2015; Krause, 2017; Pittaway et al, 2010; Sieber, 2008, 2009). Less has been written about the actual experience of conducting sensitive research (Dickson-Swift et al, 2007; Palmer, 2014; Ullman, 2014). This chapter therefore contributes to the debate on dilemmas that arise during fieldwork among people living in dire circumstances. It does not provide a set of 'correct' answers on how to resolve these dilemmas; instead, it encourages rethinking and discussing some fieldwork challenges in an environment where human suffering is endemic.

Dilemma 1: when research is situated in a socio-political context we cannot change

Uganda is hailed as one of the world's most hospitable refugee destinations, with 1.4 million refugees and asylum seekers, approximately 100,000 of whom reside in Nakivale Refugee Settlement (UN Development Programme, 2017; UNHCR, 2018). Located in the Isingiro District of southwest Uganda, Nakivale was established in 1959 as a sanctuary for Tutsi refugees fleeing the Hutu-initiated 'social revolution' in Rwanda. Later, it became a place where refugees from Burundi, the Democratic Republic of the Congo (DRC), Ethiopia, Eritrea, Rwanda, Somalia and Sudan live side by side. The settlement represents a unique setting in which refugees from different nations live under the protection of the government of Uganda, as implemented by the Ugandan Office of the Prime Minister (OPM) and the UN Refugee Agency (UNHCR). Nakivale is one of the largest and oldest refugee camps still operating in Africa. Its resources have become critically overstretched as the refugees increased in numbers. Nakivale has a landscape of refugees and Ugandan villages next to one another. In the middle of the settlement, Base Camp (Zone 2)—one of Nakivale's three administrative zones—holds the highest density of refugees from different nationalities in its urban setting; it encompasses small shops, pharmacies and even a guesthouse for outsiders. Most refugees live among their own, but close to other, nationalities.

Our fieldwork objective was to investigate the economic conditions of displacement and how interactions between refugees and receiving community shape livelihood opportunities in Nakivale. The fieldwork used both a qualitative and quantitative approach. I conducted qualitative interviews (from which the exchanges described in this chapter are taken); my colleague was responsible for quantitative data collection. Our research team's visibility—including 20 fieldworkers from Mbrarara University of Science and Technology—reinforced the impression we were a Norwegian delegation. The fact that Norway had recently resettled a quota of refugees from Nakivale made it almost impossible for many refugees to hope for anything other than that we had returned for the same purpose.

Resettlement—the transfer of refugees from an asylum country to another state that agreed to grant them permanent settlement—is often discussed in Nakivale. A male respondent from Burundi reflected on life in the settlement, telling me, "The eyes of the international community are not on us." The only aim for refugees is resettlement to a Western country, he said, and, "Not a day goes by without [the refugees] discussing resettlement"—except for the Rwandese, who were not eligible for resettlement because of Rwanda's relatively stable political situation. He explained that some people register in refugee camps in Tanzania, Uganda, Kenya and Rwanda to increase their chances of selection for resettlement. The UNHCR resettlement office recognized this challenge and referred to it as 'resettlement shopping'. This strategy could backfire once the refugees were accepted, but they still took the risk: when the UNHCR accepts people for resettlement, it checks the extent to which those persons have registered elsewhere, and rejects them if they are found to be registered in another country.

To be eligible for resettlement, refugees must (1) be recognized as refugees by UNHCR, (2) be unable to return voluntarily to their country of origin or integrate into their asylum country, and (3) fit one of seven resettlement categories: at-risk women and girls, legal or physical protection needs, survivors of torture or violence, medical needs, lack of foreseeable alternative durable solutions, family reunification, and at-risk children and adolescents (UNHCR, 2011). The UNHCR can initially select eligible refugees through a series of interviews, but its authority is limited to presenting resettlement candidates; the receiving country conducts the final interview and makes the ultimate decision. Annual quotas are small; to most refugees, selection is unachievable. Just to be selected for the initial UNHCR interview is challenging. Nevertheless, refugees hope for a new future in a world where all other durable situations seem elusive (McQuaid, 2017).

According to the online Oxford Living Dictionaries (2019), context is 'the circumstances that form the setting for an event, statement or idea, and in which it can be fully understood'. The context in which our study took place—the prospect of resettlement—undoubtedly influenced the research. Refugees, constantly striving to tell their stories to the agents responsible for resettlement, often expressed feelings of hopelessness regarding life in Nakivale: "I have given up on knocking on the doors of UNHCR and OPM. They only tell me to wait, and nothing happens. The line outside the OPM office is too long, and what meets me is, 'Wait'. My hope is God, the prayers and resettlement. Life in Nakivale is no life" (Congolese refugee, Nakivale).

The most desired destination for refugees living in uncertainty was a new beginning in Europe or the US. It was not easy to be seen or heard in an environment where virtually everyone is potentially eligible for resettlement: it was a race to win a future elsewhere, a competition among all refugees to tell their stories to an authority that could process their cases. Since the fact of suffering was insufficient in an environment where suffering is endemic, the general perception was that, to be selected, one had to propose an extra need for protection. My respondents perceived sexual discrimination and exploitation as the *utmost suffering* that could expedite the process.

A quota of refugees had been resettled to Norway in March of the same year that our fieldwork took place. Contrary to regular practice, the Norwegian Directorate of Immigration had conducted in-camp interviews before granting the final selection of refugees access to Norway (Government of Norway, 2013). The resemblance of their interviews to how we conducted our fieldwork was salient. Our research team was frequently in contact with OPM and UNHCR for either an interview or a polite visit. I was obliged to meet regularly with the camp commandant, who granted us final access to carry out the fieldwork. I walked around the settlement and asked for interviews, which enabled many refugees to share their stories with me—stories many had longed to share with an audience. The ambiguity of my role in Nakivale was reasonable; even if the refugees accepted that I did not represent the Norwegian government, it made no distinct difference in their perception of my ability to help them, since they perceived me as someone with authority to at least present their case to relevant authorities in Norway. I represented a glimmer of hope to be heard and to achieve social mobility (Bjørkhaug, 2017).

Dempsey (2017) argues that one should find ways to upset the structural inequalities between the role of the researcher and the constituted power relations in research. She suggests empowering participants to generate their own inquiries. From my own experience, however, it seems overambitious to try to influence the actual context. Instead of looking for (and subsequently failing) at ways to illuminate the power differences, I rather suggest we seek to understand and communicate how systemic factors, which we as researchers cannot change, shape unequal power relations and our research data. A Western researcher in a refugee setting will always inevitably create a degree of structural inequality and unequal power relations, and we must be transparent about the challenges and limitations arising from this in all aspects of the research. If not, we risk creating misleading results, which can eventually lead to poor policies in an environment where seeking to 'do no harm' is a key principle. Thus, we need to be aware of and transparent about the effects our research has on the population we study.

A relevant question is to consider whether the fieldwork should take place at all, if the respondents misunderstand the purpose of the research:

> Refugees may mistrust the motives and independence of researchers as well as the information provided to them about the research, and may therefore be very wary about how we will use any information they provide. Alternatively, some participants may have unrealistic expectations of the benefits of the research, believing that researchers may have the power to influence legal or resettlement processes. (Mackenzie et al, 2007: 303)

In order to address this question, I turn now to discussing how stories unfolded in the course of the fieldwork, suggesting that we should not underestimate the agency that they involve.

Dilemma 2: when participating in research interviews is a strategy

The first step towards resettlement is to argue to a UNHCR protection officer who decides the case for a special protection need that Nakivale does not offer. While in an environment where suffering is endemic one strategy among the refugees can be to exceed the stories of the others, presenting such narratives can also be a way to negotiate their lives in Nakivale (Bjørkhaug, 2017). A number of refugees discussed the power of the narratives they presented to the authorities, like in this example:

> The culture of the refugees is influenced by telling the good story. In Kampala, there are people called 'the caseworkers'. These are urban refugees who offer to write stories to the new-coming refugees for the price of $100. The problem is that there is little variation in the stories; some are almost the same with new names. The caseworkers hang outside the OPM office, waiting for the new arrivals of refugees. They are chased away when they are discovered, but find their way back again. (Female refugee, Nakivale)

Describing the phenomenon of refugee stories, a male respondent said: "In Nakivale, there are refugees who are richer than the nationals. They make business through driving, digging and engagement in various businesses. However, a refugee will always tell you that he is poor." What arises from these two examples is that telling one's story is one way to exercise agency. The narratives shared with the researcher during fieldwork thus capture both, the power- and inequality-laden context of the narrative and the individual story deliberately told to an audience (Moen, 2006):

> We need medicines, we need soap. If I find work, I can work. I have never talked with the commandant about our problems; I do not even know who he is. If they do not help us in peace, what can they help us with? We have told about our challenges with a lawyer at the UNHCR. He is a protection officer. ... Today I went to the protection office at 14:00 hours. She [a protection officer] did not open the door. We do not know why. They promise and promise, but we do not know why. For three months, we

have been looking for the lawyer I spoke with three months ago. (Male refugee, Nakivale)

In their management of aid to refugees, implementing agencies face the phenomenon of strategizing to maximize benefits (Kibreab, 2004; Sandvik, 2013; Schmidt, 2007). One desk officer at the UNHCR protection office, which was responsible for the initial interview in the resettlement process, reported how similar stories would circulate in the refugees' resettlement interviews. The UNHCR tried to validate the stories through seven different interviews and available documentation, which is out of scope for a qualitative researcher. Malkki (1996: 51) emphasizes how 'the success of the fieldwork hinged not so much on determination to ferret out "the facts" as to a willingness to leave some stones unturned, to listen to what my informants deemed important and to demonstrate my trustworthiness by not prying where I was not wanted'. During my fieldwork, however, the practical implications of the refugees' expectations of me as someone who could influence the resettlement process was that refugees would approach me actively to share their stories, and this required adequate response.

A young man and his friend came to me one evening with information he did not want to share publicly. He described life back in Burundi as one of discrimination and conflict between political parties. It was not easy to find a job; regulations made life difficult if you were not a member of the ruling party. He was a victim of political persecution but felt he needed to defend his position as a refugee. A durable solution for the Burundian population in Nakivale was a problem because Burundi was not a prioritized nation for resettlement, he explained. He had to apply for resettlement as an individual case. His parents were from the DRC and Burundi. He said his father had been killed when the young man was 14 years old. His mother fled to the DRC, where her parents lived, and he and his younger brother fled to Tanzania. At the age of 20, he returned to Burundi to find everything they once had was gone. He went to his mother in the DRC, but a Mai-Mai group attacked the family. They killed his mother after forcing him to have sex with her. The soldiers also raped him. He feared the stigma of being a male survivor and thus felt he should be prioritized for resettlement. Discussing his brothers and sisters living elsewhere in Africa, the young man said, "How can I assist them? I am a refugee in Uganda. Protection today is difficult. I have a ration card, but few activities; I have no land and no skills to add to my livelihood. I asked the camp commandant for a transfer to a third country, but the response was that there was no country for me" (Male refugee, Nakivale).

He asked me to bring his case forward to the protection office. My response was to tell him how sorry I was for his loss and to explain carefully that I was unable to influence his access to resettlement. As tempting as it was at times, a promise to try to expedite the process was not (and should not be) my responsibility as a researcher. It is human to empathize in the face of distress and search for opportunities to help; however, I decided to maintain professional distance as researchers in the field and leave social work to the implementing agencies.

The young man's story was not unique. At times when someone approached me to tell yet another story about sexual violence, trauma and their utmost need for protection, I thought, "Here we go again". At some point, I wondered if I needed to change the research design or if I could include the interviews in my analysis. The Burundi man's story exemplifies how a narrative can be a strategic representation of self rather than documentation of reality—but not necessarily (for example Eastmond, 2007; Sandelowski, 1991). Fujii (2010) questions the extent to which we can trust narratives generated in a politically sensitive context. She argues that, instead, we should seek to understand the metadata as indicators of what people are willing to say about past violence, what they have reason to embellish or minimize and what they prefer to keep to themselves (Fujii, 2010: 231). I decided to frame the stories as a dimension of collective identity in exile, as Malkki (1996) describes. I continued to listen to individual stories in their social context without questioning the stories themselves. The interviews provided me with an analytical tool to understand how desperate it felt be to be stuck in a protracted refugee setting without a life of predictability and social security, which also reflected the refugees' livelihood opportunities. It was nevertheless challenging to respond adequately to the stories because they all mirrored suffering and desperation, which at times led to the hopeless feeling of not being able to make a difference for the refugees.

Dilemma 3: how to respond to pain and suffering

The balance between an emotional presence that generates trust and the professional distance that implies self-care can be tricky. The majority of refugees had been subject to immense physical, psychological and emotional suffering, and I do not question the high prevalence of refugees who were victims of sexual exploitation. Life in Nakivale was difficult, regardless of the degree of vulnerability to which each had been exposed. What was interesting in this setting is that, contrary to the literature's description of sexual violence as a sensitive subject in research (Krause, 2017), both women and men in Nakivale shared stories of sexual violence without hesitation or probing. Sexual violence—especially men raped by men—is socio-culturally taboo (for example McQuaid, 2017). A female Congolese refugee described the general taboo in the following words:

> If you tell your husband that you have been raped, he will live separately with you in the house. He will not tell anyone but he will distance himself from you. You feel sick inside your heart. The husband will further question if the child is his and traumatize the child. If you want to talk with someone about your rape, you can tell your best friend. (Female refugee, Nakivale)

However, in Nakivale, the choice between *breaking a taboo* and *not speaking at all* was ambiguous because refugees perceived stories of suffering as narratives that could lead to a better future elsewhere. They could benefit from breaking the taboo, especially when everyone else did so. The final question in this chapter is then: can we as researchers listen to horrific stories without responding to them?

A woman in a female focus group started the discussion, saying,

> The problem is not only that we are raped. The water is not safe, the food is too little and the children have no schooling and the men no work. We are indeed suffering here in Nakivale. Nothing has changed. The hospital, the OPM, the UNHCR. We thank them for the place to sleep, but they do not want to hear about our problems. (Female refugee, Nakivale)

Another Congolese refugee woman added, "We wash for the Somalis; we prostitute ourselves. ... If you are lucky, you only have to sleep with one man. A woman went to wash for a Somali man. He claimed that he did not have any change and asked her to come back again. When she did, he raped her instead" (Female refugee, Nakivale).

The Somali population in Base Camp were the top tier of economic and social status, and other refugees would find their way to them for income-generating activities (Bøås, 2015). Stories of Somalis raping Congolese women recurred during the focus group discussion, often in the context of insecurity in a place where the women had initially sought protection: "We are coming from the DRC. We do not know if our father lives or not. In Goma, we did not cultivate. Here we have to dig and fetch water. Now we have to look after us. I used to wash for the Somali. They offered me one dollar to sleep with me. My friend was raped" (Female refugee, Nakivale) .

I listened and shared my sympathy but fell short of words. Another Congolese woman in the focus group described feeling hopeless when reporting sexual violence to an authority:

> I feared it in the DRC and now I fear the rape again. It makes me feel traumatized. I go to the police and the doctor. They give me a letter, a document that I can bring to the protection officer. The protection office at the UNHCR tells you, 'You Congolese women—there is nothing I can do for you'. The protection office is tired of the problems of DRC. You go there but receive no counselling, no visit and no follow up. When you go and meet the protection officer, you feel trauma. (Female refugee, Nakivale)

Many refugees living in Nakivale shared her hopelessness. As a researcher, I saw the challenges: everyone wanted an authority to hear their story, but the protection offices were overloaded with cases. Not everyone could be transferred to Europe or the US, no matter how desperate their situation. I felt for both the refugees and the people in the UNHCR office.

On one of my last days in the field, a man from the DRC approached me. He said:

> We wait and wait and wait and wait. Now when I meet you, I am very happy. I want you to tell my story when you are back in Norway. We can die any day with the life we are living. The same insecurity we ran away from in Congo we now face in Nakivale. The children sleep in a bad place. ... We eat at noon and, if possible, we eat at night. ... My wife is in a bad situation, and I look for soya to feed the kids. (Male refugee, Nakivale)

My response felt bleak as I answered that I had no authority to process his case and once again repeated that I was sorry for his pain. For seven weeks, I listened to stories of people in utmost need and was careful not to make promises I could not fulfil. I felt heartless at times but argued with myself that it was better than breaking a promise.

Vanderstaay (2005) discusses the challenge of being in the fieldwork without becoming part of it. He concludes: 'Fieldwork is not a justification for turning one's back on the suffering of human beings. Yet, fieldwork is not social work, and ... well-meaning efforts to help can easily go awry' (Vanderstaay, 2005: 371). It can be tempting to say something comforting, such as, "I will do my best to help you", but such promises are not rooted in the reality of what we can influence. They create false hope for change. We have a responsibility to be compassionate with the respondents, and there will always be unexpected situations where researchers must navigate using discretion. However, as a guiding rule, we should aim to leave social work to the humanitarian agencies and focus on our task as researchers—to provide sound information to the public and to policymakers as one way to influence the refugees' situation, even if we make few (or no) changes in the short term.

Conclusions

As a researcher, I will always be an outsider in a refugee setting. The structural inequalities between me and my interviewees are not shaped necessarily by the fieldwork's design but by its context. A range of structural factors, including how refugees can perceive me as someone who can bring their narratives to authorities who can process their cases and, at best, influence resettlement, affect the unequal power relations. We must never stop relating to these uncomfortable dilemmas but continuously discuss them among ourselves. Conversely, we should not perceive refugees as passive victims who must be rescued from the researcher's impact. Refugees are people with agency (even within constrained choices), and presenting their narratives is one way to negotiate their lives in Nakivale. For many refugees, my presence in their setting represented a glimpse of hope for change; it also was a way to share their narrative of pain with an audience. Our responsibilities as researchers are to be stern in our responses about our limitations to help them and to resist the temptation to act as social workers. The latter is the responsibility of the implementing agencies. Our responsibility is to be the voice of the weak.

References

Bjørkhaug, I. (2017) 'The tales of loss and sorrow: addressing methodological challenges in refugee research in Uganda', *Forum for Development Studies*, 44(3): 453–71.

Bøås, M. (2015) *The Politics of Conflict Economies: Miners, Merchants and Warriors in the African Borderland*, London: Routledge.

Dempsey, K.E. (2017) 'Negotiated positionalities and ethical considerations of fieldwork on migration: interviewing the interviewer', *ACME—An International Journal for Critical Geographies*, 17(1): 88–108.

Dickson-Swift, V., James, E.L., Kippen, S. and Liamputtong, P. (2007) 'Doing sensitive research: what challenges do qualitative researchers face? *Qualitative Research*, 7(3): 327–53.

Eastmond, M. (2007) 'Narratives in forced migration research', *Journal of Refugee Studies*, 20(2): 248–64.

Fujii, L.A. (2010) 'Shades of truth and lies: interpreting testimonies of war and violence', *Journal of Peace Research*, 47(2): 231–41.

Government of Norway (2013) 'Norway's first mission to interview Congolese in Uganda's Nakivale settlements', www.resettlement.eu/news/norway%E2%80%99s-first-mission-interview-congolese-ugandas-nakivale-settlements.

Head, E. (2009) 'The ethics and implications of paying participants in qualitative research', *International Journal of Social Research Methodology*, 12(4): 335–44.

Kabranian-Melkonian, S. (2015) 'Ethical concerns with refugee research', *Journal of Human Behavior in the Social Environment*, 25(7): 714–22.

Kibreab, G. (2004) 'Pulling the wool over the eyes of the strangers: refugee deceit and trickery in institutionalized settings', *Journal of Refugee Studies*, 17(1): 1–26.

Krause, U. (2017) *Researching Forced Migration: Critical Reflection on Research Ethics During Fieldwork,* Oxford: Refugee Research Centre.

Mackenzie, C., McDowell, C. and Pittaway, E. (2007) 'Beyond "do no harm": the challenge of constructing ethical relationships in refugee research', *Journal of Refugee Studies*, 20(2): 229–319.

Malkki, L.H. (1996) 'Speechless emissaries: refugees, humanitarianism, and dehistoricization', *Cultural Anthropology*, 11(3): 377–404.

McQuaid, K. (2017) '"There is violence across, in all arenas": listening to stories of violence amongst sexual minority refugees in Uganda', *The International Journal of Human Rights*, online first, DOI: 10.1080/13642987.2017.1347342.

Moen, T. (2006) 'Reflections on the narrative research approach', *International Journal of Qualitative Methods,* 5(4): 56–69.

Oxford Living Dictionaries (2019) 'Context', online: https://en.oxforddictionaries.com/definition/context.

Palmer, J. (2014) 'Ethics in fieldwork: reflections on the unexpected', *The Qualitative Report,* 19(28): 1–13.

Pittaway, E., Bartolomei, L. and Hugman, R. (2010) ' "Stop stealing our stories": the ethics of research with vulnerable groups', *Journal of Human Rights Practice*, 2(2): 229–51.

Sandelowski, M. (1991) 'Telling stories: narrative approaches in qualitative research', *IMAGE: Journal of Nursing Scholarship*, 23(3): 161–4.

Sandvik, K.B. (2013) 'Rights-based humanitarianism as emancipation or stratification? Rumours and procedures of verification in urban refugee management in Kampala, Uganda', in B. Derman, A. Hellum and K. Bergtora Sandvik (eds), *Worlds of Human Rights. The Ambiguities of Rights Claiming in Africa*, Leiden: Brill, pp 257–76.

Schmidt, A. (2007) ' "I know what you are doing": reflexivity and methods in refugee studies', *Refugee Survey Quarterly*, 26(3): 82–99.

Sieber, J.E. (2008) 'Refugee research: strangers in a strange land (editorial)', *Journal of Empirical Research on Human Research Ethics*, 4(3): 1–2.

Sieber, J.E. (2009) 'Evidence-based ethical problem solving (EBEPS)', *Perspectives of Psychological Research*, 4(1): 26–27.

Ullman, S.E. (2014) 'Reflections on researching rape resistance', *Violence against Women*, 20(3): 343–50.

UN Development Programme (2017) *Summary of Study: Uganda's Contribution to Refugee Protection and Management*, Kampala: UNDP, https://data2.unhcr.org/en/documents/download/64687.

UNHCR (2011) *Resettlement Handbook*, Geneva: UNHCR, www.unhcr.org/46f7c0ee2.pdf.

UNHCR (2018) *Figures at a Glance*, Geneva: UNHCR, www.unhcr.org/figures-at-a-glance.html.

Vanderstaay, S.L. (2005) 'One hundred dollars and a dead man: ethical decision making in ethnographic fieldwork', *Journal of Contemporary Ethnography*, 42(4): 371–409.

19

Ten Things to Consider Before, During and After Fieldwork in a Violent or Closed Context

Berit Bliesemann de Guevara and Morten Bøås

If there is one general lesson we can learn from the chapters in this book, it is certainly this one: there is neither a recipe for 'good' or 'successful' fieldwork, nor can we prepare for all eventualities of what might happen when conducting intervention-related fieldwork in violent or illiberal contexts. While all types of research, fieldwork-based or not, confront us with questions of ethics or risk in one way or another, violent and closed contexts throw them into much sharper relief. This is because the potential negative consequences of researchers' mistakes may be particularly severe. Putting forward guidelines is therefore not only impossible given some of the unsolvable dilemmas discussed, but it would also be irresponsible to give the impression that if the researcher only followed a 'ten commandments of fieldwork'-type list, they would be properly prepared for hassle- and risk-free, ethical data collection/generation and able to leave their field with a good conscience to write up their outputs 'at home'.

Research reality in violent and closed contexts is complicated and fieldwork often involves confusion, failures and mistakes. What the contributions to this book suggest instead of a recipe, is that there are several tough questions we should ask ourselves before, during and after fieldwork. Their consideration will help to navigate our research as ethically, sensibly and safely as possible in view of the manifold dilemmas along the way. Yet, the answers to these questions will not be uniform. In this conclusion, we summarize ten areas of concern we think stand out as major take-aways from our contributors' honest insights and thoughtful reflections and which researchers ought to consider when planning fieldwork-based research.

Before going to the field…

Fieldwork must start long before the researcher actually goes to 'the field'—not least because most researchers will have little time to wander the world for an extended period, familiarize themselves with different localities and learn from local communities, before finally settling on research puzzle and fieldwork location. These days, due to changes in how universities work and research is financed, fieldwork is often much more business-like and about getting the work done, which means the researcher should be prepared.

1. Do I really need to do fieldwork?

A first question to ask is: Do I really need to do fieldwork to address my research puzzle? This question may seem counterintuitive in a guidebook about fieldwork, but as Lai (in this volume) has cautioned us, a fieldwork industry has emerged around certain geographical areas and topics of intervention research. This industry is not only driven by an increase in fieldwork-based research but also of study trips for students at Northern universities, which are as much a consequence of an increased awareness of the necessity to better train academics for field research as it is a consequence of market competition over fee-paying students (Mitchell, 2013; Bliesemann de Guevara and Poopuu, 2020). Over-research has severe consequences for both those individuals and groups who are over-researched and fatigued by the armies of (aspiring) academics who ascend upon them and for those who remain overlooked, silenced and forgotten. What is more, over-research changes the very field we set out to study—research is an intervention (Lai, in this volume).

It is thus crucial to ask whether a specific research question can be answered with the data that is already available—in other literature, databases, on the Internet—and whether there is any value in going to the field other than accumulating the authority of 'having been there', evidenced by the direct quotes fieldwork interviews equip the researcher with. This also involves the question of whether the particular topic area a researcher has chosen to study actually needs yet another research project, or whether there are other, acutely understudied areas and topics that would make a much greater contribution to knowledge, while at the same time practically tackling the problem of research fatigue.

2. Which type of fieldwork is feasible, and where is the field?

If fieldwork is indispensable, questions about what type of research is needed and feasible, and where the field is, need to be pondered. This concerns, first, the fit between the thematic field of interest, the research questions, and the nature of the planned fieldwork. As Casey McNeill's contribution (in this volume) illustrates, the field can be in several locations, not all of which are in the Global South, and the research puzzle will help to think this through.

Secondly, regarding fieldwork in violent and illiberal contexts there is the factor of one's personal propensity to go to certain areas that demands serious consideration. Simply put, not everybody can or should go on every kind of fieldwork. Fear is not a good travel companion and, while it may arise and can caution us against inconsiderate moves when in the field, it should certainly not be a factor from the very beginning. There are all sorts of reasons why people may shy away from a dangerous field site, family obligations being just one of them, and there is no shame in redirecting the research to things that can be done elsewhere or to redesign the study as a desk study. Fieldwork is not a competition in heroism.

A final set of questions concerns the resources at one's disposal, which, together with institutional constraints at the home institution (for example presence times due to teaching), co-determine how long the fieldwork can be, what type of methods can be used (for example, is there money to transport participants), whether the researcher can hire an interpreter or research assistant, whether some form of renumeration can be paid to participants for giving their time, and so on. More often than not, research questions need to be shrunk to what is possible resource-wise.

3. Juggling the institutional and vocational approaches to fieldwork ethics and risk

For those who are not independent self-funded researchers, there will be institutional approaches to fieldwork ethics and risk that simply must be dealt with. Simply ignoring official travel advice or institutional requirements is certainly a bad idea, as insurance policies, legal support when things go wrong, and the permission to use data may be at stake. Ethics and risk assessment procedures should thus be treated seriously, but there is also an imperative to argue our case, if we have a good one. The chances of getting fieldwork approved by an ethics board is higher if researchers can document some previous experience in these types of contexts and/or dispose of a good network or hosts on the ground in the planned fieldwork location.

However, as several authors in this book show, the institutional approach has a number of limits and, as much as we encourage everybody to take these requirements seriously, they must be supported by a strong vocational approach to fieldwork ethics and risk (see all the chapters to Part II in this volume). Things change quickly on the ground in volatile and tense environments and, at times, decisions must be taken quickly and wisely. Strong collaboration between Northern and Southern researchers may prove useful in this regard, and this becomes so much easier if one treats colleagues in the location of the fieldwork as partners and not simply as fixers and data gatherers (see especially Bøås, Sangaré and Bleck, and Verweijen, in this volume).

While in the field…

Once the first three questions have been answered, the researcher is ready to embark on the actual fieldwork, where the likelihood of losing control and the need for researcher flexibility grows exponentially. Here are five things that seem crucial to consider regarding this on-the-ground phase.

4. *Questions of research access*

Questions of access relate to both physical and social access. Physical access is about the location of the research, which may be out of reach due to acute violence (like in the Sahel or Darfur) or because of state control (like in Myanmar or Tajikistan). Verweijen, and Sangaré and Bleck have addressed strategies to directly research highly insecure places using context-sensitive security assessments and preparing well, but sometimes the situation may be so bad that the place is simply out of reach. A strategy adopted by one of the editors in the Sahel, where the hinterlands and peripheral areas are largely unsafe, is to interview people who live in those areas when they travel to more secure places. Such a strategy is dependent upon substantive background knowledge about the conflict, these places and the people who dwell there, to avoid the research being biased, for those who can afford to travel will most likely be people from certain socio-economic strata.

The researchers interviewed by Kušić (in this volume) worked with Myanmar nationals to circumvent travel restrictions for foreigners and carry out workshops with populations in conflict regions of Kachin and Rakhine—-a strategy that worked to a certain extent but similarly depends on deep additional context knowledge to meaningfully make sense of the data.

Another or complimentary strategy is to seek official permission to go to such places as part of an official visit (Heathershaw and Mullojonov, in this volume) or accompany peacekeepers or some other type of intervention force (Peter, in this volume). Such embedded research may allow for better research than none at all but, as Mateja Peter (in this volume) discusses, also comes with several ethical and knowledge caveats attached, main problems being the distance of peacekeepers from actual people or the threat that a controlling state poses to informants. Who is embedded, how, and with what research question in mind certainly plays a central role to determine whether such embedded research is able to achieve any meaningful research or whether its main purpose is merely to be able to say that one 'has been there' (see point 1).

Social access to informants or interviewees can be as tricky as physical access. Establishing as many contacts as possible before leaving for fieldwork is useful. Usually there are other researchers, journalists, diplomats and so on who can be help in this regard, and local research assistants and fixers often also have useful contacts or ideas. There is also reason to be cautious with previous contacts, however, as using other colleagues' access and informants may end up replicating the same conversations with the same people: information can be circular within established networks of contacts and informants (Käihkö, 2019). Kostić (in this volume) also reminds us that not every social access is equal and that in some cases deeper insights may be dependent on some form of shared background between researcher and researched (here: intervention elite), which again comes with caveats. Physical and social access will have a huge influence on the outcomes of the research and need to be reflected upon thoroughly when analyzing the data.

5. Researcher, activist, social worker, friend? How different roles affect fieldwork

We are not machines but humans and, as humans, we crave for respect and friendship and are affected by what we see around us and by the stories we hear in violent or closed contexts. It would be sad if this were different, as this could mean that we do fieldwork for our own careers only. Caring is a good thing, but how we care, and how we show that we care, also has wider implications.

As researchers our first and foremost role is to document, analyze and enable understanding. We are neither journalists nor NGO workers or social activists, and we are certainly not criminal investigators. At the same time, the push for research impact in many countries as well as our own political convictions and agendas may prompt us to see ourselves as more than just researchers. Jesse Driscoll's scenario (in this volume) cautions us against using research as political activism in highly state-controlled contexts, pointing to the potential costs we may cause for others. Wanting to help is also a common urge, especially when working with marginalized or vulnerable groups, but Ingunn Bjørkhaug cautions us against promising things we cannot keep, and both Bjørkhaug and Jennings (in this volume) discuss what responsible empathy can look like short of acting as a social worker.

Friendship in fieldwork is possible, but will more often than not involve highly uneven relationships (see Bøås, Clausen, and Kostic, in this volume) and there is good reason to remind ourselves what our main role is. This also means that we as researchers and academics have a responsibility to avoid sensationalism and victimization of our complex subjects who have agency—both in what we ask our participants about and how we represent them in our research outputs (Jennings, Bjørkhaug, and Muvumba Sellström, in this volume).

6. Negotiating positionality and identity in the field

How we deal with the different possible roles discussed earlier is also significant for how we negotiate our positionality and identity in the field. We represent, misrepresent and misunderstand others, and we are represented, misrepresented and misunderstood in the field. This may be due partly to how we present ourselves and how well we are able to read the local context. But identities can also shift from micro-context to micro-context, as Clausen (in this volume) unpacks.

We are outsiders who do not belong here, and this also applies to the 'hybrid researchers' who originate from the context they study (for example, Kostić, in this volume) or national researchers who study communities in their own country (for example, Sangaré, in this volume). The differences between the Northern researcher and their interlocutors tend to increase when research does not take place with expats, representatives of an intervention or local elites, but with ordinary people. Particularly in areas of large-scale international intervention, people will often think of researchers as part of the intervention, no matter whether this is factually correct, and this will affect the research (see Bjørkhaug, Clausen, and Kostic, in this volume).

Our hunch is that in order not to multiply misunderstandings, it will be best to be honest about who we are. Taking advantage of a local misrepresentation of who we are in order to gain access to something or somebody is not only ethically questionable, but may also come back to us in unpredictable and unwanted ways, leaving us in a nest of lies and compromises with our real identity that in the end may bring danger both to the researcher and those around them (for example, local assistants and interpreters).

7. *Questions of money and other power differentials*

We live in a highly uneven world, and money matters. Most often it is the researcher(s) from the Global North who bring funding opportunities, control the research process and spend a considerable amount of the project resources. Unless we work with well-off intervention or other elites, this obviously has an impact on research relationships in the field, which we need to be aware of. In most fieldwork situations discussed in this book, equality between Northern researchers and Southern research assistants and participants did not exist.

Several contributions caution us to establish concrete contracts upfront when money is involved (for example, Kušić, Bøås, and Jennings, in this volume). Clearly discussing obligations, tasks, deadlines, and payments amounts and schedules with all parties may help avoid mistrust and establish good working relationships. Starting a relationship in such a business-like manner may seem difficult, but as Kušić's contribution (in this volume) shows, leaving these things hanging can create uneven expectations that may undermine the collaboration. Issues such as the possible co-production of research in the form of joint articles, reports or op-eds can be treated in a similar contractual manner and should also involve the question of whether they are potentially harmful (see Heathershaw and Mullojonov, in this volume). In any case, researchers need to consider carefully the power they may represent to others in terms of access to money, publications, jobs or just as an access point to the outside world, as this perception of power may make people take risks they would otherwise avoid (Bøås, in this volume).

8. *Managing emotions, confusions and failures while in the field*

In many people's experiences, fieldwork is an emotional rollercoaster. The confusion discussed in the contributions to Part I of this book is a main source for emotions such as anxiety and the feeling that one is utterly inadequate and failing to do this work. Interview partners may belittle or patronize us, and some researchers experience sexual harassment or worse (cf. Bliesemann de Guevara and Poopuu, 2020). Work with vulnerable or marginalized participants may give rise to strong emotions of sadness and helplessness, when our urge to do something meets with the reality of not being in a position to help (Bjørkhaug, in this volume). While there will be people around for most of the day in the field, loneliness is not uncommon as we are rarely able to replicate the social relationship we left 'at home' in the field, for reasons beyond our control (Bøås, in this volume). It is also quite common to experience moments of anger when we are let down or confronted with views and actions we are strongly opposed to (cf. Myrttinen, in this volume). And during fieldwork in violent or closed contexts, being scared of physical or other harm to us or those we interact with is also common.

Controlling our emotions in the research situation should be the rule. Crying in front of those we work with or losing our temper with assistants or participants happens, but is usually counterproductive and does not help anyone. While every individual is different, researchers should consider preparing for the emotions that fieldwork may involve. This may include measures such as having a network of trusted colleagues or friends to talk to, either in the field or online, to create a safe space to vent emotions, or to exchange with others in similar research situations to explore what empathy in the field may look like (cf. Jennings, in this volume).

When back from the field...

Our ethical and risk-assessment obligations do not cease when back from the field. Field and home are linked through what we leave behind, what we do (or do not) return to participants and partners, and what we create in our writings.

9. Writing up our research

Anton Blok, the Dutch social anthropologist who famously studied the Sicilian mafia (Blok, 1975), once told one of the editors that after writing his seminal book he never dared going back for reasons of personal safety. The decision to disclose particular types of information had permanently closed his access to the field. Roland Kostić (in this volume) ponders what it means to keep the doors to key informants among intervention elites open, and realizes that this comes at a cost in terms of what he omits from his writings, including knowledge about unethical and criminal behaviour, and how he straddles the fine line between policy expert and critical academic. Yet, writing is about more than the question of whether what we write closes the door for future research with the same participants. For us editors, there is an ethical imperative to write with empathy about the people we encounter in our research—even those our fieldwork has made us dislike (cf. also Myrttinen, in this volume). We believe that our task is to bring understanding, not to be judgmental, a task we rather leave to political activists.

Another, perhaps less negotiable, imperative is to keep in mind our obligation to protect our informants. This is our holy grail that should overrule other considerations. This means that there may be times when there is a piece of information of huge interest (not least because it may boost our academic careers or citation count) that simply should not be published, as it could severely damage an informant, a research assistant or the wider community in which our research takes place (cf. Heathershaw and Mullojonov, Driscoll, and Kostić, in this volume). Any participant should be offered anonymity, and any persons or communities our research may impact should be considered regarding the consequences of our writing, no matter what we think about them.

This leads to a last challenge of the writing process. Writing is a powerful tool that contributes to shaping how readers see the world. Kathleen Jennings (in this volume) reminds us that we need to strike the balance between representing suffering and agency when working with marginalized or vulnerable groups, while Angela Muvumba Sellström (in this volume) cautions us not to let nuance out of sight when writing up our research findings, even or especially when we write from the margins of our field.

10. *The long-term consequences of fieldwork, and the question of giving something back*

Ethical fieldwork does not only ask after the risks involved for outside researchers while physically in the field, but also the potential long-term consequences of the way they conduct their fieldwork—for themselves, other researchers, assistants and partners, participants and informants, and wider communities. What we write about and how can affect our future access to the field and put people into danger after the fieldwork, as the previous section has started to discuss, and there are further potential consequences. Some researchers' actions may have negative consequences for what research is possible for subsequent generations of researchers. The propensity of a majority of researchers to never feed their research results back to those who shared their insights may mean that some groups and individuals start to refuse research participation or limit it to little insightful general information (Lai, in this volume).

There may also be physical risks that research can put participants in even after the fieldwork is completed—for example, when conflict dynamics change the authority structures of a geographical area or when association with a Western researcher is read as espionage by state security agencies (Sangaré and Bleck, and Heathershaw and Mullojonov, in this volume). The disclosure of revealing information about an authoritarian regime may not contribute much to the cause of political activism against a repressive regime, but actually set into motion a process that leads to repressive measures against the researcher and their national collaborators (Driscoll, in this volume). None of these wider consequences of fieldwork should be taken lightly. Ethical research requires an awareness of the immediate but also wider or long-term effects our actions have.

Conclusions

Fieldwork can be very difficult and, in most fieldwork-based research, there will come times when frustration, confusion and other emotions bite hard. In that regard, fieldwork is a rollercoaster—but is that not also what life is? We learn from fieldwork, it enhances our understanding of the world and how it works, and of how for many people it does not work very well. And we also learn a lot about ourselves during fieldwork, and some of these lessons are very valuable. If nothing else, at least we often learn that we should take ourselves much less seriously. And we also come to realize our limitations about a whole lot of things.

However, we also believe that researchers on fieldwork can in fact do something very useful. The world is not a fair place and our various relationships with participants and colleagues in the field are marked by this. However, this does not mean that we cannot make these relationships work, if we acknowledge our different positions and how these can jointly be used for mutual benefits. Such benefits will not make us equal, nor will they necessarily be equally divided. But it will make working with research partners and participants in the places where we conduct our fieldwork less extractive and more equitable and fair.

References

Bliesemann de Guevara, B., and Poopuu, B. (2020) 'Preparing for fieldwork interviews', in R. Mac Ginty, B. Vogel and R. Brett (eds), *Companion to Conducting Field Research in Peace and Conflict Studies*, London: Palgrave.

Blok, A. (1975) *The Mafia of a Sicilian Village, 1860–1960: A Study of Violent Peasant Entrepreneurs*, New York: Harper Torchbooks.

Käihkö, I. (2019) 'On brokers, commodification of information and Liberian former combatants', *Civil Wars*, 21(2), 179–99.

Mitchell, A. (2013) 'Escaping the "field trap": exploitation and the global politics of educational fieldwork in "conflict zones"', *Third World Quarterly* 34(7): 1247–64.

Index

Note: Page numbers in *italics* indicate figures.

A

abuse of office, 32–4
academic researchers
  strategic relationship with state security forces, 143–54
  analysis, 148–53
access, 274–5
  to local population, 117–19
  to policy elites, 26–31
  to research participants, 217, 233–5
  travel restrictions, 188–90, 200
active conflict environments, 113–24
  research quality, 119–20
  safety and research ethics, 114–19
  weak state capacity and ongoing conflict, 120–3
  see also open conflict
activists
  Bosnia and Herzegovina (BiH), 171, 172, 174–7
  game of chicken, 144, 147–8, 149, 150, 153, 154
  Myanmar, 202
  Tajikistan, 101
  Yemen, 164
advocacy, 117
'African barbarism', 133
AFRICOM (US African Command), 37–47
  interpretivist interview research, 38–41
  limitations of interview research, 41–6
agency, 221, 222, 262
Akiner, Shirin, 104–5
ambushes, 135–6
ANC (African National Congress), 236, 238
Andijan events, 152
anonymity, 104
anti-corruption campaign, 32–3
Anzac Memoirs (Thomson), 57

armed forces personnel, 128–9, 132, 133–4
armed groups, 121, 122, 129, 130, 135
  wartime sexual violence, 229–39
    ethical risks of research, 235–9
    research set-up, 231–5
art, 202, 203–4
Australian war veterans, 57–8

B

barbarian syndrome, 132–4
Belmokhtar, Mokhtar, 69
bias, 86, 102–3, 133, 135
Boesten, J., 218–19
Bosnia and Herzegovina (BiH)
  policy elites, 23–35
    access to, 26–31
    knowledge production, 31–4
  research as intervention, 171–81
    over-research, 175–7
    peripheral regions, 177–80
Brandt, Marieke, 164
bunkerization, 200–1
bureaucracy, 15
bureaucratization of research, 78
Burundi, 231, 233–4, 235

C

Carpenter, C., 97
children, 247, 248
Clark, J.A., 105
closeness and distance, 12–14, 157
collaboration, 82–3, 96, 103, 106–8, 115, 277
  Raising Silent Voices: Harnessing Local Conflict Knowledge for Communities' Protection from Violence in Myanmar, 199–210
    experiential and local knowledge, 202–3
    research design, 203–4

283

research implementation, 205–7
research outputs, 207–9
see also co-production of knowledge;
research relationships
commander's dilemma, 232
compensation, 224–5
see also payment
complexity, 237–8
complicity, 250–1
confidentiality, 104, 194–5
Congolese armed forces (FARDC), 128, 132, 133–4, 135
consent, 53–4, 84, 96, 105–6, 118, 193–4
context, 260
context knowledge, 114–15
control, 29, 52, 57–8, 163, 165, 204
and confusion, 5–8, 21
Coordination of Movements for Azawad (CMA), 121
co-production of knowledge, 107, 208
see also collaboration
corruption, 32–4
crisis bargaining, 144
critical empathy, 222–3

D

Darfur, 187–90
embedded research, 190–6
Dauphinee, Elizabeth, 185
Dayton Peace Agreement, 23
Democratic Republic of the Congo (DRC)
security expertise, 127–39
ambushes, 135–6
FARDC (Congolese armed forces), 133–4
humanitarian organizations, 136, 137
MILOBS (UN military observers), 128–30, 131
MONUSCO blue helmets, 132–3
risk assessments, 131–2
sex workers, 215, 216–18, 219–20
compensation, 224–5
gatekeepers, 223–4
interviews, 220–3
security, 225
Dempsey, K.E., 261
Designing Social Inquiry (King, Keohane and Verba), 3
digital media, 28–9
displaced persons, 44, 45, 120, 194–5
see also refugees
distance and closeness, 12–14, 157
Dodik, Milorad, 23, 24
drawing, 203–4
duty of care, 77, 81–2, 83

E

Egypt, 76
elections, 150
elites, 6
Bosnia and Herzegovina (BiH), 23–35
access to elites, 26–31
knowledge production, 31–4
US Africa Command (AFRICOM), 37–8
interpretivist interview research, 38–41
embassy aid programs, 150
embedded research, 186–7, 275
Darfur, 187–90
ethical challenges, 190–6
emotions, 277–8
empathy, 245
critical, 222–3
Eriksson Baaz, M., 225–6
ethical obligations, 218–20
ethical reflection, 94–5
ethical risks, 235–9
ethics
active / open conflict environments, 114–19, 185
embedded research, 190–6
over-research, 176
post-conflict environments (PCEs), 93–109
procedural v. practical ethics, 97–109
writing up research, 279
ethics advisors, 86
ethics clearance procedures, 80
ethics review committees, 80, 105
see also Research Ethics Committees (RECs)
ethics self-assessment, 83, 86–7
ethnographic sensibility, 47
European Commission, 83–5, 86–7
experiential knowledge, 202–3
experts, 164
see also security expertise

F

failure, 5, 8
FARDC (Congolese armed forces), 128, 132, 133–4, 135
Farrimond, H., 97
female sexual autonomy, 236–7
fieldwork, 2, 3–4
control, confusion and failure, 5–8, 21
distance and closeness, 12–14, 157
security and risk, 8–12, 73
things to consider
after, 278–80
before, 272–4

during, 274–8
vulnerable and marginalized
   participants, 14–17, 213
fieldwork industry, 272
flexians, 27, 31
flex-nets, 26
France, 82
French Sanagris forces, 247, 248
friendship, 64, 65, 66, 275–6
Fujii, L.A., 98, 104, 264
Fulani people, 118
funding, 150, 203
funding bodies, 83, 103

G

game of chicken, 144–8
   game payoffs, *149*
   mixed strategy equilibrium, 151–3
   pure strategy equilibrium, 149–51
gatekeepers, 223–4
Gatumba massacre, 235
gender, 160–3
   see also sexual and gender-based
      violence (SGBV); women's sexual
      autonomy
General Data Protection Regulation
   (GDPR), 87
global political analysis, 41–2
Gray, H., 225–6
Gulf Cooperation Council, 159

H

Haiti, 220, 223–4, 249
harm minimization, 223
Hart, Gillian, 41–2
Henry, M., 218–19
Hoover Green, A., 232
humanitarian organizations, 136, 137

I

ICG (International Crisis Group)
   Balkans, 30
identity, 12, 160–3, 166–8, 276–7
   see also multiple identities
impact, 103
impact model, 41–2
impartiality, 102, 103
informality, 52–8
informed consent, 53–4, 84,
   105–6, 193–4
insider/outsider distinction, 167–8
Internal Review Boards (IRBs), 95,
   97–8, 108–9, 115
internally displaced population
   (IDP), 194–5
International Criminal Court (ICC), 188

International Criminal Investigative
   Training Assistance Programme
   (ICITAP), 32
international intervention, 177–9
   post-conflict environments
      (PCEs), 173–5
international intervention elites, 6
   Bosnia and Herzegovina (BiH), 23–35
      access to elites, 26–31
      knowledge production, 31–4
   US Africa Command
      (AFRICOM), 37–8
   interpretivist interview
      research, 38–41
International Relations, 42
interpretive research, 199–210
   experiential and local
      knowledge, 202–3
   by proxy, 199, 201
   research design, 203–4
   research implementation, 205–7
   research outputs, 207–9
intervention elites *see* international
   intervention elites
intervention research, 3, 6–7
   post-conflict environments
      (PCEs), 171–81
   over-research, 175–7
   peripheral regions, 177–80
   sex workers, 215–26
      compensation, 224–5
      ethical obligations, 218–20
      gatekeepers, 223–4
      interviews, 220–3
      security, 225
   see also military intervention research
interview guidelines, 53–4
interview research
   interpretivist methodology, 38–41
   limitations, 41–6
interviewer-expectancy effect, 86
interviews, 6–7, 24–5
   confidentiality, 194–5
   displaced persons, 44, 45, 194–5
   gender, 161–3
   identity and insider/outsider
      distinction, 166–8
   Office of the High Representative
      (OHR), Bosnia and
      Herzegovina, 24–5, 28, 29
   over-research, 171, 175–7
   positionality and power, 163–6
   refugees, 265, 266
   with researchers, 201, 203–4, 205,
      206–7, 209
   sex workers, 220–3
      compensation, 224–5
      gatekeepers, 223–4

security, 225
sexual exploitation and abuse (SEA), 245
Tajik war veterans, 49–59
  mistakes made, 50–2
  spontaneity and informality, 52–8
  see also research questions
Italy, 82
iteration, 116

J

jihadists, 62, 65, 69, 121–2
journalists, 99
judiciarization of research, 78
justice, 172–3, 180

K

knowledge
  context, 114–15
  co-production of, 107, 208 *see also* collaboration
  experiential, 202–3
  local, 99–100, 202–3
knowledge production, 31–4, 217, 218
Kyrgyzstan, 104, 152

L

legends, 249–50
Liberia, 220
  sugar babies, 215–16
LinkedIn, 28–9
local knowledge, 99–100, 202–3
local researchers / research assistants, 61–71
  benefits of working with, 204
  friendship, 64–6
  power imbalance, 106–7, 203, 205–7
  respect, 67–8
  risk, 68–71
  safety and security, 82, 115
local turn, 201
loneliness, 278

M

Mali, 64–5, 113
  access to the field, 118
  military intervention research, 42, 43, 44, 45, 46, 47
  research quality, 120
  research relationships, 65–71, 116–17
  violent extremism, 121–2
Malkki, L.H., 263
marginalised regions, 177–80
marginalized participants, 14–17
  see also displaced persons; refugees; sex workers
micro-dynamics of violence, 128–30
military intervention research, 37–47

interpretivist interview research, 38–41
limitations of interview research, 41–6
military personnel, 128–9, 132, 133–4
MILOBS, 128–30, 131
MINUSCA mission, 246–7
mixed strategy equilibrium, 151–3
MK (uMkhonto weSizwe), 236, 238
Modise, Joe, 236
money, 16, 70, 277
  see also compensation; funding; payment
MONUSCO, 132–3, 134, 216
Moore, Roderick, 31
Mostar, 31, 32
Movement of the National Liberation of Azawad (MNLA), 65
multiple identities, 27, 30, 31, 34
Myanmar, 199–210
  experiential and local knowledge, 202–3
  research design, 203–4
  research implementation, 205–7
  research outputs, 207–9

N

Nakivale Refugee Settlement, Uganda, 257–67
  refugee stories, 262–4
  researcher's role, 264–7
  socio-political context, 258–61
NATO, 30–1
networks, 26
Niger, 42, 43, 45, 46, 47
non-state armed groups *see* armed groups
Nonviolent Peaceforce (NP), 199–200
Norway, 260
NRA (National Resistance Army, Uganda), 236–7, 238

O

Office of the High Representative (OHR), Bosnia and Herzegovina, 23, 24, 27, 28, 31, 32–3
open conflict, 186–7
  Darfur, 187–90
  see also active conflict environments
Oral History Society, 53–4
OSCE (Organization for Security and Cooperation in Europe), 178
over-research, 171, 175–7, 219, 233, 272

P

Pader, Ellen, 47, 48
Palipehutu-FNL, 235, 238
payment, 206, 224
  see also compensation; money

INDEX

Peace and Conflict Studies, 94
peripheral regions, 177–80
permission, 96, 104–5
positionality, 96, 102–3, 118, 163–6, 276–7
post-conflict environments (PCEs)
  ethics, 93–109
    collaboration, 106–8
    consent, 105–6
    permission, 104–5
    positionality, 102–3
    safety, 99–102
  research as intervention, 171–81
    over-research, 175–7
    peripheral regions, 177–80
    research scope, 145
    self-censorship equilibrium, 153
post-exposure preventive treatment kit, 138
power, 15–16, 163–6
power dynamics, 130, 203, 205, 277
power imbalance, 70, 106–7
power relations, 177, 261
procedural v. practical ethics, 97–109
  collaboration, 106–8
  consent, 105–6
  permission, 104–5
  positionality, 102–3
  safety, 99–102
prostitutes *see* sex workers
pure strategy equilibrium, 149–51

R

Raising Silent Voices: Harnessing Local Conflict Knowledge for Communities' Protection from Violence in Myanmar, 199–210
  experiential and local knowledge, 202–3
  research design, 203–4
  research implementation, 205–7
  research outputs, 207–9
rape, 137, 138, 248, 263, 265–6
reflexivity, 160, 196, 222
refugee stories, 262–4
  researcher's response to, 264–7
refugees, 257–67
  socio-political context, 258–61
  see also displaced persons
Regeni, Giulio, 76, 77
research access *see* access
research as intervention *see* intervention research
research consortia, 82–3
research ethics *see* ethics
Research Ethics Committees (RECs), 95, 97–8, 108–9

research fatigue, 219
  see also over-research
research focus, 191–3
research participants
  access to, 217, 233–5
  marginalized and vulnerable groups, 14–17 *see also* displaced persons; refugees; sex workers
  power relations, 261
  risk, 105, 280
  safety, 76, 82, 104
research permits, 85, 90n13
research quality, 119–20
research questions, 116, 118
research regulation, 79–85
  side effects, 86–7
research relationships, 61–71, 116–17, 209, 275–6
  embedded research, 186–7
  friendship, 64–6
  over-research, 171, 175–7
  power imbalance, 203, 205–7
  respect, 67–8
  risk, 68–71
  see also collaboration; local researchers / research assistants; research participants
research security, 75–89
  research regulation, 79–85
  side effects, 86–7
researchers *see* academic researchers; local researchers / research assistants
resettlement, 259–60
refugee stories, 262–4
respect, 67–8
risk
  ethical, 235–9
  local researchers / research assistants, 68–71
  research participants, 105, 280
  and security, 8–12, 73
risk assessments, 101, 114–15, 121–2, 131–2
rumours, 249–50
Russia, 90n13
Rwanda, 104

S

SAFEResearch, 77–8
safety, 82, 96, 99–102, 114–19
  see also security
Sahel region, 42, 43, 45–6, 61–2, 64, 69, 114
Sana'a, 159
schools, 75
Schwartz-Shea, P., 98, 105
Scott, James C., 38–9

securitization of research, 78
security, 42, 75–89
  interviews, 225
  research regulation, 79–85
    side effects, 86–7
  and risk, 8–12, 73
  see also safety
security advice, 131
security concerns, 61–2, 63, 65, 67–8, 68–71, 160–3
security dynamics, 129–30
security expertise, 127–8, 133–4, 135, 136–7, 138–9
security forces
  academic researchers' strategic relationship with, 143–54
  analysis, 148–53
security practices, 42, 43, 45, 46
security regimes, 78–9, 88
"Self-Censorship" equilibrium, 149, 151, 153
Serma Camp, 121–2
sex workers, 215–26, 226n, 245
  interviews, 220–3
    compensation, 224–5
    ethical obligations, 218–20
    gatekeepers, 223–4
    security, 225
sexual and gender-based violence (SGBV), 243–53
  complicity and critique, 250–1
  definitional grey zones, 246–9
  methodological challenges, 249–50
  Timor-Leste, 244–6
sexual autonomy, 236–7
sexual exploitation and abuse (SEA), 220
  peacekeeping operations (PKOs), 243–53
    complicity and critique, 250–1
    definitional grey zones, 246–9
    methodological challenges, 249–50
    Timor-Leste, 244–6
sexual violence, 14–15, 16, 213, 229–39
  ethical risks of research, 235–9
  over-research, 218–19
  refugee stories, 263, 265–6
  research set-up, 231–5
  sex workers, 221
Shelling, Thomas, 144
social desirability bias, 86
socio-economic dimensions of justice, 172–3, 180
Sodiqov, Alexander, 92–3, 97, 100, 101
South Africa, 231, 236
Soviet-Afghan War veteran
  interviews, 49–59
  mistakes made, 50–2

spontaneity and informality, 52–8
state security forces
  academic researchers' strategic relationship with, 143–54
  analysis, 148–53
Stern, M., 225–6
Stringfellow, W., 98
Sudan see Darfur
sugar babies, 215–16, 219
  see also sex workers
supervisors, 83
survivors see victim-survivors
"Symbolic Confrontation" equilibrium, 149, 150, 151

T

Tajik war veteran interviews, 49–59
  mistakes made, 50–2
  spontaneity and informality, 52–8
Tajikistan, 92–3
  collaboration, 107–8
  consent, 106
  impartiality, 103
  permission, 104
  safety, 100–1
third gender, 161, 162
Thomson, Alistair, 57–8
Timor-Leste, 244–6, 249
training, 208, 210n6
transitional justice, 172–3
travel advisories, 99, 102
travel restrictions, 188–9, 200
triangulation, 40, 41
Tuaregs, 64–5

U

Uganda, 231, 234, 236
  Nakivale Refugee Settlement, 257–67
    refugee stories, 262–4
    researcher's role, 264–7
    socio-political context, 258–61
UN blue helmets, 136–7
UN military observers (MILOBS), 128–30, 131
UN peacekeeping missions
  sexual exploitation and abuse (SEA), 243–53
    complicity and critique, 250–1
    definitional grey zones, 246–9
    methodological challenges, 249–50
    Timor-Leste, 244–6
UNAMID (United Nations-African Union Hybrid Operation in Darfur), 188–9
uncertainty, 238–9
UNHCR (United Nations Refugee Agency), 259–60, 262–3

US Africa Command
  (AFRICOM), 37–47
  interpretivist interview research, 38–41
  limitations of interview research, 41–6
US Army, 187
US Department of Justice, 32
Uzbekistan, 104–5, 106, 152

V

Vanderstaay, S.L., 265–6
victimhood, 221, 222
victim-survivors, 218–19, 233, 235–6
violence
  micro-dynamics of, 128–30
  see also sexual and gender-based violence (SGBV); wartime sexual violence
violent conflict *see* open conflict
violent extremism, 113, 114, 120, 121–2
vocational ethics, 98
  see also procedural v. practical ethics
vulnerable participants, 14–17, 120
  see also displaced persons; refugees; sex workers

W

war crime trials, 172–3
war veterans *see* Tajik war veteran interviews

wartime sexual violence, 14–15, 16, 213, 229–39
  ethical risks of research, 235–9
  over-research, 218–19
  refugee stories, 263, 265–6
  research set-up, 231–5
  sex workers, 221
weak state capacity, 120–3
weak states, 145
Westendorf, J.-K., 248
Williams, Teddy, 236
women's sexual autonomy, 236–7
World Bank, 164
writing, 278–9

Y

Yanow, D., 98, 105
Yemen, 159–69
  identity and insider/outsider distinction, 166–8
  positionality and power, 163–6
  security and gender, 160–3

Z

Zenica, 174, 179, 180
zones of danger, 78